CRAFTING PEACE

(II) Dep: # months of peace post settlement (not civil war).

(A)
(B)

Indep:
(a) terms of settlement: 0—4
* (settlement institutionalization)

(III) Dep: settlement sucess: absence of violent war.
indep: military implemenation within 5 years.

(I) Dependent: 4-0 according to state power dimension

Indep: (49)
(A) Nature of conflict
  → Stakes of the conflict: identity vs. other.
* → conflict duration: # of months, start & end.
* → conflict intensity: monthly battle deaths.
(B) conflict environment.
  → dem. polity IV
* → life expectancy *
* → PKO, dichotomous. *
* → during cold war end, vs. after

[handwritten annotations:]

2 (A) what process is necessary to establish peace? which conflicts are amenable?

3 (B) what types of instit. foster enduring peace?

4 (C) How do competitors actions foster/hinder peace?

~~(D)~~ what role do institutions play in fostering peace?

Preconditions:
① ~~*Which conflicts are amenable?~~
  └ avenues of accomodation in an unwinnable war

② conflict environment.

  └→ DOMESTIC
    (A) Past experience w/democracy
    (B) level of development.
  └→ INTL
    (A) introduction of a PKO
    (B) Structure of the intl system

Dimensions of State power
① Military
② Political
③ territorial
④ economic

CRAFTING PEACE

POWER-SHARING INSTITUTIONS AND
THE NEGOTIATED SETTLEMENT OF CIVIL WARS

Caroline A. Hartzell
Matthew Hoddie

THE PENNSYLVANIA STATE UNIVERSITY PRESS
UNIVERSITY PARK, PENNSYLVANIA

LIBRARY OF CONGRESS CATALOGING-IN-PUBLICATION DATA

Hartzell, Caroline A.
Crafting peace : power-sharing institutions and the negotiated settlement of civil wars / Caroline
A. Hartzell, Matthew Hoddie.
p.   cm.
Includes bibliographical references and index.
ISBN 978-0-271-03208-5 (pbk.:alk.paper)
1. Pacific settlement of international disputes.
2. Peace-building.
3. Power (Social sciences).
4. Civil war.
I. Hoddie, Matthew, 1969– .
II. Title.

JZ6010.H37 2007
327.1'72—dc22
2007005045

Dedicated to our parents

BART AND LUZ HARTZELL
JAMES H. AND KATHY HODDIE

CONTENTS

TABLES

ACKNOWLEDGMENTS

This study would not have been possible without the encouragement and support of a great many people. Special thanks go to our professor, mentor, and friend, Donald Rothchild. In addition to helping us develop and refine our personal interests in the study of conflict and its management, Don was the catalyst to our working relationship. Because we entered and left the graduate program at the University of California, Davis, at different times, it took an introduction by Don to get us started down the road to this book.

Thanks are also due to those sources of support that made this project possible: Gettysburg College, Texas A&M University, the Fulbright Foundation, and the Colombian Government Agency of Foreign Studies (ICETEX).

We are grateful to people who read parts of the manuscript and encouraged us along the way—Fritz Gaenslen, Robert Harmel, Robert Jackman, Dave Lewis, Roy Licklider, and John T. Scott.

A number of students at Gettysburg College and Texas A&M University ably provided us with research assistance on this project over the years. We thank Liala Buoniconti, Christie Maloyed, Sibel McGee, Chris Tyler, and Andrew Watkins for their help and interest.

We also thank the anonymous reviewers of the manuscript for their perceptive suggestions. We are particularly grateful to Sandy Thatcher at Penn State Press for his support and encouragement. His reputation as an author's editor is well warranted.

On a personal note, Caroline would like to express her gratitude to her husband and daughter, David and Meghann Lewis. Dave and Meghann have been encouraging and supportive of this project over an extended period of time. Finally, "cheers" to my political science colleagues Rob Bohrer, Fritz Gaenslen, Kathy Iannello, and Bruce Larson at Gettysburg College for their sanity and sessions at the Blue Parrot.

ABBREVIATIONS AND ACRONYMS

ANC	African National Congress
ARMM	Autonomous Region for Muslim Mindanao
CCFA	Joint Commission for the Constitution of Armed Forces
CCPM	Political-Military Joint Commission
CIDCM	Center for International Development and Conflict Management
CMVF	Mixed Commission for Verification and Supervision
COPAZ	National Commission for the Consolidation of Peace
COW	Correlates of War
ECOMOG	Economic Community of West African States Monitoring Group
FMLN	Farabundo Martí Front for National Liberation
FRUD	Front for the Restoration of Unity and Democracy
ICFM	Islamic Council of Foreign Ministers
INSCR	Integrated Network for Societal Conflict Research
INSSBI	Nicaragua Institute of Social Security and Welfare
JVP	Janatha Vimukthi Peramuna (People's Liberation Front)
MFUA	Unified Movements and Fronts of Azawad
MILF	Moro Islamic Liberation Front
MNLF	Moro National Liberation Front
MPLA	Popular Movement for the Liberation of Angola
NCO	noncommissioned officer
NEP	New Economic Policy
OIC	Organization of the Islamic Conference
RENAMO	Mozambican National Resistance
RUF	Revolutionary United Front
SADF	South African Defense Forces
SANDF	South African National Defence Force
SIPRI	Stockholm International Peace Research Institute
SPCD	Southern Philippine Council for Peace and Development

SZOPAD   Special Zone of Peace and Development
UNAVEM   United Nations Angola Verification Mission
UNITA   Union for the Total Independence of Angola
URNG   Guatemalan National Revolutionary Unity

INTRODUCTION:
INSTITUTIONS AND THE NEGOTIATED
SETTLEMENT OF CIVIL WARS

→ institutionalization of
conflict drivers.

Institutions can have a powerful influence on the shape of social conflict. South Africa, a country that endured a brutal civil war throughout the 1980s between its black majority and white minority, is a particularly telling example of the capacity of institutions to foster either conflict or cooperation among collectivities with distinct interests. Institutions that fostered violent conflict appeared in South Africa early in the twentieth century. Several pieces of legislation, including the Natives Land Act (No. 27) of 1913, marked the institutionalization of racial discrimination in that country.[1] The reaction of blacks to such measures was swift and included, most prominently, the formation of the South African Native National Congress (renamed the African National Congress [ANC] in 1923). Following the initiation of the policy of apartheid in 1948, ANC leaders called on the organization to use strikes, boycotts, and other forms of civil disobedience and noncooperation to challenge the apartheid system. With no other means of securing institutional change once the South African government outlawed the ANC and the Pan-Africanist Congress in 1960, efforts to change the rules of the game turned violent and took the form of a civil war in the early 1980s.

Despite the bitterness provoked by the conflict, the divided communities of South Africa proved capable of constructing an enduring peace. During the early 1990s, adversaries began the process of crafting a mutually accept-

---

1. The Natives Land Act allocated areas to blacks and whites in which they could own freehold land. Blacks, who made up two-thirds of the country's population, were restricted to 7.5 percent of the land; whites, with one-fifth of the population, were allocated 92.5 percent (Byrnes 1997).

able settlement intended to ensure that minorities enjoyed a degree of influence at the political center and that the majority would be prohibited from using state power to threaten others. The means that the architects of the South African settlement relied upon to accomplish these goals were a series of power-sharing and power-dividing institutions. Institutions of this nature fostered an environment in which warring groups could lay down their arms and work together to fashion a peaceful future for South Africa that has now endured for more than ten years.

The tragedy associated with the civil conflict in South Africa is not an isolated incident. Today, intrastate conflicts are more common than wars between states. Twenty-five countries had ongoing civil wars as recently as 1999.[2] The human costs associated with these conflicts are staggering. One estimate places the total number of deaths directly attributable to civil wars fought since World War II at 16.2 million.[3] Another study calculates that the average number of refugees displaced by the fighting in each of these conflicts is more than one-half million.[4] The indirect costs of these wars extend well beyond the hostilities themselves. Civilians, for example, continue to bear the costs of domestic warfare long after the fighting has ended. The breakdown in the provision of government services following civil wars leaves in its wake crises ranging from the rapid spread of infectious diseases to a higher incidence of violent criminal behavior.[5]

This book, which is about the bargained resolution of civil wars, focuses on one means of bringing these conflicts to an end and building an enduring peace. The conventional wisdom is that negotiated settlements of civil wars are not only difficult to construct but are also among the forms of civil-conflict resolution least likely to produce an enduring peace.[6] As the South African case illustrates, however, civil wars can successfully be ended via negotiated settlements. Drawing on a data set of all civil wars ended through negotiations between 1945 and 1999, we seek to draw attention to the merits of this particular means of ending civil conflicts as well as to identify those features of negotiated settlements that facilitate a long-lasting peace among former adversaries.

Our central argument is that those settlements that include an array of institutions designed to address the issue of central concern to adversaries

---

2. Fearon and Laitin 2003, 75.
3. Ibid.
4. Doyle and Sambanis 2000.
5. Ghobarah et al. 2003.
6. See, for example, Wagner 1993, Licklider 1995, and Walter 2002.

emerging from civil war—the question of who will control the levers of state power—are the ones most likely to produce an enduring peace. Whatever the issues that may have given rise to armed conflict—diverging ideological preferences (as was the case in Cambodia, Laos, and Mozambique) or ethnic divisions (as seen in Bosnia and Zimbabwe)—after prolonged periods of fighting and large numbers of casualties, the core concern on which armed opponents ultimately fix their attention is the rules governing the use of power. Before they agree to lay aside their weapons permanently, adversaries seek to clarify who is to hold state power, how it is to be exercised, and to what end. In the case of negotiated settlements, this is most often accomplished by creating power-sharing and power-dividing institutions. In some cases the negotiated settlements that secure an end to the fighting are complex documents constructed with the assistance of international actors, as was the case with the 1991 Cambodian settlement. Others are simply verbal accords composed by the parties to the conflict, as was true of the 1970 Yemeni settlement. Either way, the power-sharing and power-dividing institutions contained in these agreements are the central mechanisms for establishing enduring, peaceful relations among former enemies.

This book is thus also about the role institutions play in structuring peace following civil wars. We argue that institutions perform three valuable functions that facilitate the construction of an enduring peace. First, institutions can be designed to address opponents' concerns regarding who is to exercise power and the ends to which that power is to be used following a conflict's termination. Rival groups will be more likely to commit to peace if assured that some group will not be able to seize power and use it at the expense of others. A case in point is the 1957 National Front Agreement constructed by Colombia's long-term rivals, the Conservative and Liberal parties. The two entities fought repeated civil wars during the nineteenth and twentieth centuries as each sought monopoly control of the state. Tiring of this cycle of violence, the elite of the two parties resolved to end the conflict by dividing power on the basis of a 50/50 power-sharing formula. For a period of sixteen years, the presidency rotated between the two parties every four years and seats in the congress were split evenly between the Conservatives and the Liberals. By adhering to this power-sharing arrangement, each party was placed in a position of prominence that provided the opportunity to both participate in governance and monitor the behavior of their former adversaries.

Second, the process of designing and implementing institutions as part of a negotiated civil war settlement signals the commitment of foes to building an enduring peace. Neither the design nor implementation of power-sharing and power-dividing institutions is a cost-free process; antagonists must typically abandon their interest in sole control of the state in exchange for the compromises associated with the sharing or dividing of power. The willingness of adversaries to endure these costs over time has the potential to serve as a costly indicator of their commitment to an enduring peace. Such a dynamic is apparent in the price exacted from both the government of the Philippines and the Moro National Liberation Front (MNLF) to end their civil war (1972–96). The government conceded a greater degree of political and economic autonomy for the MNLF on its home island of Mindanao than previously had been considered acceptable; simultaneously, the MNLF compromised its goals by abandoning its separatist demands and instead recognizing the legitimacy of the central state's continued participation in the governance of the island. That both the government and the rebels willingly endured these losses in the interest of peace served to enhance the credibility of their mutual commitments to the creation and maintenance of a previously elusive stability.

Third, the institutions designed as part of a civil war settlement define the means by which social conflict is to be managed in the postwar state. Domestic order is reconstructed following a civil war on the basis of these institutions. If a stable peace is to be secured, groups must have a means, other than relying on the use of force, for resolving their disagreements. By making the design of institutions a central part of the process of ending a civil war, rival groups lay the foundations necessary for building an enduring peace. An example of this can be found in Malaysia. The institutions that formed the basis of that country's settlement involved communal compromises designed to give Malays a larger stake in the economy while increasing non-Malay participation in the political system. Although these institutions eventually came under challenge and postelection race riots broke out in May 1969, a history of institutional accommodation made it possible for the country's communal leaders to act in concert to resolve the crisis. The principal response they devised was a "New Economic Policy" (NEP). The NEP, announced in 1970, sought to create conditions for national unity by reducing the socioeconomic disparities that were believed responsible for interethnic resentment within the state.

A central contribution of this book is to develop these claims regarding the role institutions play in fostering peace in order to define what we term an institutional approach to the resolution of civil wars. This approach emphasizes the need to look beyond simply stopping the killing and encourages adversaries also to participate in constructing the institutional underpin-nings of a lasting and self-enforcing peace. A durable peace is, after all, as much the product of the rules designed to govern postconflict society as it is of processes that succeed in getting factions to stop shooting at one an-other and lay down their arms. Unless new rules for managing conflict are agreed upon, groups may well (re)arm and initiate another round in the cycle of civil wars, which has been the disturbing pattern of recurring vio-lence in countries such as Angola, Indonesia, and Iraq.

Ending Civil Wars: Negotiated Agreements as a Means of Stopping the Fighting

Civil wars may end in one of four ways. First, domestic wars may conclude by the process of military victory. Whether one group of actors triumphs over the other(s) by virtue of its own efforts (e.g., Argentina's brief civil war in 1955) or whether foreign aid and/or foreign intervention prove decisive in leading one of the factions to win (e.g., Guatemala's intrastate conflict in 1954), the outcome is the same: one party claims victory and the other(s) admits defeat. Table 1 demonstrates that this is the most common way by which civil wars have been ended. Of the 108 civil wars that were fought and then experienced a cessation in the fighting for some period of time between 1945 and 1999, fifty-five (51 percent) were ended through the process of mili-tary victory.[7]

Second, civil wars may end by adversaries mutually conceding to negoti-ate a settlement. A negotiated settlement brings together representatives of the opposing groups, none of which acknowledge defeat, to discuss and agree to the terms by which they will bring armed conflict to a conclusion. One of the central characteristics of a negotiated settlement is that adversar-ies involved in this form of war-ending bargain directly address the question of how power is to be distributed and managed in the postwar state. Civil war adversaries may negotiate a settlement on their own (e.g., Colombia in 1957) or third parties may facilitate the development of such an agreement. Third-party involvement in the peace process has the potential to take var-ied forms, including military intervention intended to push for a negotiated settlement of the conflict (e.g., the United States in the Dominican Republic

---

7. Fourteen civil wars were ongoing at the end of 1999. These cases, which include, for example, a reinitiation of the war in Afghanistan in 1992 after a very brief period of peace, are not listed in table 1.

Table 1   Civil war settlement types, 1945–1999

Military victory	Negotiated settlement	Negotiated truce
Afghanistan, 1978–92	Angola, 1975–89	Azerbaijan, 1990–94
Algeria, 1962–63	Angola, 1989–91	Burma, 1968–80
Argentina, 1955–55	Angola, 1992–94	Chechnya, 1994–96
Bolivia, 1952–52	Bosnia, 1992–95	Congo/Brazzaville, 1993–94
Burma, 1948–51	Cambodia, 1978–91	Congo/Brazzaville, 1998–99
Burma, 1983–95	Chad, 1979–79	Congo/Zaire, 1998–99
Burundi, 1965–69	Chad, 1989–96	Croatia, 1991–92
Burundi, 1972–72	Colombia, 1948–57	Georgia/Abk, 1992–94
Burundi, 1988–88	Costa Rica, 1948–48	Georgia/S. Oss, 1989–92
Cambodia, 1970–75	Croatia, 1995–95	Moldova, 1991–92
Chad, 1980–88	Djibouti, 1991–94	Morocco, 1976–91
China, 1946–49	Dominican Republic, 1965–65	**Number = 11**
China, 1956–59	El Salvador, 1979–92	
China, 1967–68	Guatemala, 1963–96	
Congo/Brazzaville, 1997–97	Guinea Bissau, 1998–98	
Congo/Zaire, 1960–65	India, 1946–49	
Congo/Zaire, 1967–67	Indonesia/East Timor, 1975–99	
Congo/Zaire, 1996–97	Iraq/Kurds, 1961–70	**Peace Negotiated with**
Cuba, 1958–59	Kosovo, 1998–99	**or Imposed by Third**
Ethiopia/Ogaden, 1977–85	Laos, 1959–73	**Parties**
Ethiopia/Eritrea, 1974–91	Lebanon, 1958–58	Cyprus, 1963–64
Ethiopia/ideology, 1974–91	Lebanon, 1975–89	Cyprus, 1974–74
Greece, 1946–49	Liberia, 1989–93	Israel/Palestine, 1948–49
Guatemala, 1954–54	Liberia, 1994–96	Sri Lanka, 1983–87
Hungary, 1956–56	Malaysia, 1948–56	**Number = 4**
India, 1948–48	Mali, 1990–95	
Indonesia/Mol, 1950–50	Mozambique, 1982–92	
Indonesia/Darul I., 1953–53	Nicaragua, 1981–89	
Indonesia, 1956–60	Papua New Guinea, 1989–98	
Iran, 1978–79	Philippines/MNLF, 1972–96	
Iran, 1981–82	Rwanda, 1990–93	
Iraq/Shammar, 1959–59	Sierra Leone, 1992–96	
Iraq/Kurds, 1974–75	Sierra Leone, 1997–99	
Iraq/Kurds, Shiites, 1991–91	South Africa, 1983–94	
Jordan, 1970–70	Sudan, 1963–72	
Laos, 1975–75	Tajikistan, 1992–97	
Nicaragua, 1978–79	Yemen/YAR, 1962–70	
Nigeria/Biafra, 1967–70	Zimbabwe, 1972–79	
Nigeria/F. Islam, 1980–84	**Number = 38**	
Pakistan, 1971–71		
Pakistan, 1973–77		
Paraguay, 1947–47		
Peru, 1980–92		
Philippines/Huks, 1950–52		
Romania, 1989–89		
Rwanda, 1963–64		
Rwanda, 1994–94		
Sri Lanka, 1971–71		
Uganda/Buganda, 1966–66		
Uganda, 1978–79		
Uganda/NRA, 1980–86		
Vietnam, 1960–75		
Yemen/YAR, 1948–48		
Yemen/YPR, 1986–86		
Yemen, 1994–94		
Number = 55		

in 1965) or the offer of good offices to help facilitate such a settlement (e.g., the Quakers in the Sudan in 1972). Thirty-eight of the 108 conflicts (35 percent) that ended during the period under consideration experienced a cessation of hostilities as a result of a negotiated settlement.

Third, what we refer to as negotiated truces also have been used as a means of securing an end to violent civil conflict. Eleven civil wars since the end of World War II (10 percent of the conflicts we consider) have stopped, at least for some period of time, in this fashion. Negotiated truces differ from negotiated settlements in two ways. First, negotiated truces tend to focus on the process and modalities of ending violence in the short term. Much of the content of negotiated truces thus consists of the design of confidence-building measures and discussions of how truces are to be policed and enforced. Although some negotiated truces do include power-sharing and power-dividing institutions, these tend to focus on military and territorial issues such as the creation of safe havens and the means of protecting them. Negotiated truces, in other words, seldom address the challenging question of how power is to be exercised in the postwar state and by whom. Second, negotiated truces differ from negotiated settlements in that the former often make it a point to delay decisions regarding explicitly political issues. As a result, the peace secured by negotiated truces often resembles a type of "limbo" in which the fighting has come to an end but the ultimate state of relations among combatants and the rules of conflict regulation remain unclear, with a definitive characterization of these items postponed until some indefinite future.

The negotiated truce that secured an end to the fighting in Morocco following fifteen years of civil war illustrates the difference between negotiated settlements and truces. Civil war broke out in Morocco in 1976 after that country occupied territory formerly claimed by Spain as the overseas province of Spanish Sahara. The conflict pitted the Popular Front for the Liberation of Saguia el Hamra and Río del Oro (Polisario), a nationalist group seeking to transform the former Spanish Sahara into an independent country, against the Moroccan army. A UN-sponsored truce brought the armed violence to an end in 1991 when a peacekeeping force arrived in the area to organize a referendum on self-determination for the territory. The referendum, originally scheduled for January 1992, has been postponed a number of times during the intervening years. Despite the lack of any permanent political agreement on the status of the former Spanish Sahara, a tenuous peace remains in place as groups continue discussions regarding the holding of a referendum.

A final path by which civil wars may experience a cessation of hostilities occurs when an arrangement is negotiated by one of the sets of combatants with third parties involved in the conflict or a peace of sorts is imposed by third parties. This process is apparent in only a handful of civil wars (four of all civil wars we consider, or 4 percent). The 1987 attempt to resolve the civil war in Sri Lanka is an illustration. Sri Lanka experienced a brief two-month respite from civil war stemming from an agreement signed by Sri Lankan President J. R. Jayewardene and Indian Prime Minister Rajiv Gandhi.[8] India, which had for years lent support to minority Tamil movements seeking to carve a separate state out of the Sinhalese-dominated island, committed itself to securing the surrender of weapons held by Tamil militants and to provide military assistance for implementation of an accord that would have established a system of provincial councils on the island. Although the Tamil militant groups initially cooperated in the implementation of the peace accord the Indian and Sri Lankan governments had constructed without their consent, the agreement began to unravel as members of the minority collectivity became progressively more disenchanted with an arrangement adopted without their assent.

Why focus on negotiated means of ending civil wars? One reason is that negotiating an end to a war has the potential to be a less costly means of stopping the killing than waiting for one side to achieve military victory. The costs of a civil war may be calculated in a variety of different ways, including the loss of lives, destruction of property, and the damage done to relations with other states. Typically, however, the costs of civil wars are measured in terms of the numbers of lives lost in the conflict.[9] Based on this measure, military victory appears to be a consistently more costly means of ending civil wars than any of the variants of negotiated agreements referred to above.[10] The civil wars that ended via military victory between 1945 and 1999 produced an average of 170,706 battle deaths per conflict during this period. In contrast, the battle death average was 87,487 for wars in which

8. Sri Lanka's previous experience with civil war in 1971 saw the Janatha Vimukthi Peramuna (JVP, or People's Liberation Front), a radical left-wing organization dominated by educated youths and the unemployed, suppressed by the government following a month-long period of insurrection (*Regional Surveys* 2002).

9. Generally speaking, most civil war models focus on the number of battle deaths that take place in a conflict. The focus on battle deaths rather than other measures of civil war costs reflects the fact that better data exist for this indicator than other measures that could be used to assess costs, including the number of overall conflict-related deaths.

10. This observation should not be taken as an argument regarding causation; we simply observe that military victories tend to be correlated with higher levels of casualties than do negotiated settlements.

the fighting was brought to an end through a negotiated settlement, 35,182 for wars ended via negotiated truces, and 15,000 for wars in which third parties imposed a peace.[11]

A second reason for concentrating on negotiated settlements of civil wars is the prospect that this particular means of ending wars may produce a *enduring* more enduring peace than wars terminated via military victories. Perhaps taking their cue from the study of interstate wars, academics concerned with civil wars typically have argued that military victories are likely to produce a more enduring peace in comparison to negotiated settlements.[12] Recent studies, which take into account the current proliferation in the number of negotiated settlements to civil wars and employ methodologies appropriate to examining the question of the duration of the postwar peace, have, however, cast some doubt on that proposition. Negotiated settlements of civil wars may in fact produce just as stable a peace as military victories.[13]

One means of demonstrating this claim regarding the durability of negotiated settlements is to investigate the association between the way civil wars end and the potential for renewed conflict. Between 1945 and 1999, fifty-five civil wars ended via a military victory; among these cases, thirty-two, or 58 percent of the total, went on to experience renewed fighting. In contrast, negotiated settlements experience a lower failure rate, with peace breaking down in only thirteen of the thirty-eight cases (34 percent of the total). Five of the eleven negotiated truces (46 percent of the total) experience a breakdown of peace while two of the four settlements negotiated with or imposed by third parties (50 percent of the total) see a return to war. Cumulatively, twenty of the fifty-three civil war cases (38 percent of the total) in which the fighting was ended via a negotiated agreement of some form experience a breakdown in peaceful relations.

11. These figures are particularly interesting in light of the fact that there is a tendency to associate longer conflicts with higher levels of death and destruction. At an average duration of 32.79 months, however, wars that ended in military victory were shorter than wars that ended in negotiated settlements (89.02 months on average), conflicts that ended in negotiated truces (46.18 months on average), and wars in which peace was negotiated or imposed by third parties (an average of 15.69 months). The longer average length of wars that end in some form of negotiated agreement is not all that surprising, however, since a sense of stalemate may eventually compel combatants to end their conflict through a negotiated settlement. We discuss this in greater detail in Chapter 2.

12. The most common explanation supporting this argument is that the party that achieves a military victory is in a position to destroy the organizational identity of all other factions that participated in the civil war, thus impeding their ability to regroup and fight another war. For more regarding this line of argument, see Wagner 1993. Edward Luttwak claims that military victory as a form of settlement "can resolve political conflicts" (1999, 36).

13. See, for example, Hartzell 2004.

Although the contrasting failure rates for the different settlement types are instructive, we cannot decisively conclude that negotiated civil war settlements prove more stable than do settlements secured via military victory. One reason is that the periods of peace following the civil wars in our data set vary enormously. Greece, for example, experienced fifty years of peace following the military victory that brought an end to that country's civil war in 1949, a period of peace that was still enduring at the point at which we terminate our data set; by comparison, the peace in Kosovo, engineered by a negotiated settlement, had lasted only seven months by the end of 1999. For this reason, one needs to use a method for comparing the stability of the different settlement types that takes into account not only whether or not civil wars ended via different means experience a return to war but also the length of the time peace endures in each case. Such a method should also account for the possibility that periods of peace that were ongoing at the point in time we cut off our data set may still break down at some point in the future. Recent studies using this method, known alternately as survival, hazard, or event history analysis, have found that *both* settlement types—military victories and negotiated settlements—decrease the likelihood of a return to civil war.[14]

A final and very practical reason for focusing on negotiated settlements of civil wars is that the bargained resolution of conflict has recently become the dominant method for bringing about an end to the fighting. As table 2

Table 2   Trends in means of ending civil wars, 1945–1999

Settlement type	1940s	1950s	1960s	1970s	1980s	1990s
Military victories	5	11	8	13	8	10
	(62.5%)	(79%)	(80%)	(65%)	(62%)	(23%)
Negotiated settlements	2	3	1	6	3	23
	(25%)	(21%)	(10%)	(30%)	(23%)	(54%)
Negotiated truces	0	0	0	0	1	10
	(7.5%)	(23%)				
Peace negotiated with/ imposed by third parties	1	0	1	1	1	0
	(12.5%)	(10%)	(5%)	(7.5%)		

14. The models used to test the proposition that one settlement type produces a more enduring peace than another control for a variety of other factors that might have an influence on the longevity of peace following the end of a war. These factors include the duration and intensity of the conflict, the issue over which the armed adversaries were fighting, and the country's level of economic development. One study (Hartzell 2004) found not only that the two settlement types decreased the likelihood of war but that each had fairly comparable hazard rates, with a military settlement decreasing the risk of settlement failure by 92 percent and a negotiated settlement reducing the risk of civil war recurrence by 83 percent.

demonstrates, the majority of civil wars during the first forty-five years of the post–World War II era concluded by the process of military victory; in contrast, during the 1990s negotiated settlements became the principal means by which civil wars ended. We think it is more than mere coincidence that negotiated resolutions have become a favored method of conflict resolution since the end of the cold war. The superpowers once supported or sought to manipulate civil war adversaries for their own ends in countries such as Afghanistan, Angola, and El Salvador by providing both military aid and troops; with the end of the ideological competition between these two states they have become progressively more involved in efforts to facilitate civil war peace settlements or have stepped aside and allowed international organizations such as the United Nations to do so.

These three factors—the lower costs of ending intrastate conflicts through negotiations in comparison to military victory, the prospects for fostering an enduring peace, and the increasing prevalence of negotiation as a means of ending civil wars—form the basis for our chosen emphasis on negotiated agreements as a means of ending civil wars. This study is intended to increase and improve our knowledge concerning the substance of negotiated agreements and how the content of these agreements may facilitate a self-enforcing peace. With this knowledge in hand, the international community may be encouraged to do more to assist in ending civil wars through peaceful means as well as improve the cost-effectiveness of their efforts.

Stabilizing Peace: Institutions and the Construction of Order

Securing an end to the fighting does not, in and of itself, guarantee that a stable peace will emerge in countries that have experienced civil wars. A durable peace is characterized by more than just the absence of armed conflict. The hallmarks of a stable peace include regularized practices of conflict management and the emergence of a self-enforcing domestic order. Such practices do not, we emphasize, emerge automatically from a formal agreement on the part of adversaries to stop shooting at one another. Stable relations among formerly hostile groups are instead the product of established governing institutions that both mitigate and channel societal competition.

To consider the challenges associated with constructing a stable, postwar order in the wake of the negotiated settlement of civil wars, in this book we address three themes related to the creation of a post–civil war conflict-management system. These themes are best framed in terms of the following questions: (1) What motivates institutional choice in states emerging from civil war? (2) What role does the institution-building process play in the creation of a self-enforcing domestic order? (3) What institutional arrangements are most likely to facilitate an enduring peace among former adversaries? We offer a brief discussion of these items below in an effort to provide an outline of arguments developed more fully in later chapters.

DETERMINANTS OF INSTITUTIONAL CHOICE

A core determinant of institutional choice in societies emerging from civil war through the process of negotiation is that no party to the dispute has proved itself capable of victory on the battlefield. The inability of any actor unilaterally to dictate the institutional rules associated with the postwar state encourages a predisposition to compromise given that, under these conditions, the development of postwar state structures requires the acquiescence of all relevant actors.

Civil war adversaries' willingness to compromise, however, is very much shaped by the security concerns these groups bring to the negotiating table. These concerns, including recognition by former adversaries that despite recently killing one another "with considerable enthusiasm and success" they will have to coexist within the borders of a single state, play a central role in shaping institutional choice.[15] As a result, groups seek to design institutions that will provide them with guarantees that the coercive power of the state will not be employed to their disadvantage once they lay down their arms and lack the capacity to provide for their own safety.

It is because no single set of antagonists is capable of imposing its will, coupled with the central importance of post-war security concerns, that negotiators are predisposed to create power-sharing and power-dividing institutions. Such institutions encourage groups to "give peace a chance" by providing them with a measure of state power that they might not enjoy in the absence of such an arrangement as well as an elevated capacity to monitor the behavior of their adversaries. In this sense, collectivities can better rest assured about their security and begin to engage in more routine interactions.

15. Licklider (1993) uses these words to highlight one of the dilemmas faced by former civil war adversaries.

Power-sharing institutions may be constructed to share or divide power among groups along one of several dimensions of state power, notably military, political, territorial, or economic power. The intent of these institutions is to define how decisions will be made by collectivities within the postwar polity as well as to allocate decision-making rights among competing groups. By designing institutions that balance or distribute power among these groups, those responsible for crafting the settlement intend that groups will feel secure enough to settle into the routine of normal politics. Because these institutions also define the new rules of the political game, groups have a means for resolving future intergroup conflicts that does not require a resort to violence. These conflict-management rules thus provide a basis for reconstructing order following civil war.

THE INSTITUTION-BUILDING PROCESS

The institution-building process in a negotiated postwar environment typically consists of the negotiation, creation, and implementation of power-sharing arrangements. Each of these stages has significant costs associated with it that must be endured by those engaged in the process of compromise. We argue that the costs tied to these stages of the process make the commitment to peace credible, thus laying the foundations for a self-enforcing domestic order.

The first stage consists of the decision by the parties to begin the process of negotiation toward a settlement. Group leaders run the risk of being accused by their followers, or outside actors seeking to usurp their authority, of compromising group interests by engaging in dialogue with the enemy. This stage can be particularly costly to governments that, by agreeing to negotiate with the representatives of rebel groups, transform these individuals from "criminals" or "terrorists" into credible political actors recognized by the state.[16] Sierra Leone's President Alhaji Ahmad Tejan Kabbah endured these costs upon entering into negotiations with the rebel Revolutionary United Front (RUF) in a process that ultimately culminated in the 1999 Lomé Peace Accord.[17] Although the majority of Sierra Leone's population desperately sought an end to the country's brutal civil war, many were concerned with what they saw as the legitimization of the RUF, given its notoriety for mutilating civilian victims of the war.[18]

16. Rothchild 1997.

17. The government of President Kabbah had previously negotiated a settlement with the RUF in 1996. The settlement collapsed following the overthrow of the government by a coup d'état in 1997.

18. A number of international actors were critical of the Lomé Peace Accord. Human Rights Watch, for example, "condemned the United Nations for acting as moral guarantor of a peace

The second stage of this process, which consists of the design of institutions within the context of a peace agreement, generates two sets of costs for the leaders of the collectivities that sign on to a settlement. The first cost consists of recognizing the impossibility of achieving war objectives (including, in most instances, the desire to achieve dominance of the state) and the necessity of compromise with rivals. The second cost is the strong likelihood that the act of agreement will create divisions within parties to the settlement between those who prove more or less amenable to the bargains that have been reached. The peace accord agreed to by the government of the Philippines and the MNLF in 1996 is a case in point. As noted earlier, this agreement provided for a degree of autonomy for the Muslim-dominated island of Mindanao. Nevertheless, the leadership of the MNLF found itself harshly criticized and under scrutiny by its own membership and the elites of other Muslim groups who suggested that the arrangement provided little more than a façade of self-rule for the region.[19]

The third stage on which we focus in the process of institutional construction is the implementation of the rules agreed to as part of the negotiated peace accord. The costs associated with this stage are comparable to those associated with signing a settlement—establishing limits on access to state power and enduring potential challenges from militant interests from within and outside one's own coalition of actors—but also include having to make tough decisions about committing often scarce resources in order to implement the terms of the settlement. Foot-dragging or the failure to follow through on putting into place the institutions that have often painstakingly been agreed to can undermine a negotiated settlement by casting doubts on parties' commitment to peace. This appears to have been a factor in the case of Angola's 1991 Bicesse Accords. Incomplete processes of demobilization and disarmament on the parts of both the Union for the Total Independence of Angola (UNITA) and the MPLA were followed by a return to war less than a year and a half after the negotiation of that peace settlement.

The costs associated with these three stages of the process enhance the credibility of commitments to peace. Actors demonstrating a willingness to endure the costs associated with the process of compromise have unambiguously signaled their willingness to pay a price in the interest of fostering a previously elusive stability. Such acts, or costly signals, are important indica-

---

agreement that includes a blanket amnesty for atrocities committed in Sierra Leone's civil war" (Human Rights Watch 1999).

19. These groups included the Moro Islamic Liberation Front (MILF) and Abu Sayyaf. Neither of these groups, which continued to fight in Mindanao, signed on to the peace accord.

tions of a credible commitment during a period of state and societal transformation in which the actions of the relevant parties are under close scrutiny for signs of cooperation or defection from the postwar arrangement.

INSTITUTIONAL ARRANGEMENTS AND THE PROSPECTS FOR AN ENDURING PEACE

Neither civil wars ended through military victories nor those resolved through a process of negotiated settlement consistently facilitate a stable peace. Although at present no empirically validated explanation exists regarding why military victories are followed by an enduring peace in the case of some civil wars but not others, the institutional approach to the negotiated resolution of civil wars that we outline above provides us with an effective means of explaining why some negotiated civil war settlements prove more durable than others. We contend that the most extensively institutionalized settlements—in other words, those that call for the construction of a variety of power-sharing and power-dividing institutions across the four dimensions of state power identified above—should have the greatest potential to produce a stable peace.

What accounts for the importance of specifying a diverse array of power-sharing arrangements as part of a peace deal? Settlements that include institutions designed to cover only one or no dimensions of state power have a strong potential to leave rival parties apprehensive about how and to what ends other dimensions of state power may be used. For example, a commitment to share political power may prove insufficient to a country plagued by the problem of recurrent military coups unless it is coupled with a commitment to power-sharing within the ranks of the military. In the face of such insecurities, groups may be hesitant to commit to a lasting peace unless they feel that all avenues through which their collectivity might be threatened are addressed within the settlement.

In keeping with our earlier discussion of the importance of costly signaling and credible commitments, we also expect that agreements that produce only a small number of power-sharing and power-dividing institutions may be perceived by contending group leaders as indicating a reluctance on their rival's part to incur the costs necessary to build an enduring peace. Settlements that design institutions along several of these dimensions of state power, on the other hand, prove more reassuring to former adversaries regarding their security and the commitment of others to peace. In short, a higher number of power-sharing arrangements reflects a greater willingness to bear heavy burdens in the interest of facilitating a mutual sense of security.

Finally, a number of states in which civil war has broken out are weakly institutionalized—a problem that is likely to be even more severe in the aftermath of civil war. Designing a number of institutions that speak to the immediate concerns of groups in the postwar environment—security and the exercise of power—can help address this problem. Not all types of institutions, it should be emphasized, will be perceived by former adversaries as effectively addressing these concerns. Groups seem most likely to commit to a set of institutions in whose design they have played a role and those they perceive to be relevant to their survival in the aftermath of war. To the extent that power-sharing and power-dividing institutions are created with the active participation of former combatants, they can help provide a foundation for building an enduring peace.

Integrating Perspectives

This book is written with two audiences in mind. One audience consists of those who have an interest in civil wars and their termination. The other is composed of readers with an interest in institutions, particularly power-sharing and power-dividing institutions. We hope to communicate to these two groups that, at least in the case of the negotiated settlement of civil wars, these two sets of issues are intertwined in significant ways. Armed conflicts emerge when the institutional means of managing conflict rupture or are under challenge. These conflicts, including the means by which they are ended, play an important role in structuring institutional choice.[20] In turn, the institutions designed as part of a negotiated settlement of civil wars have an impact on the possibilities for managing future conflict through nonviolent processes.

Our conceptualization of the relationship among negotiated civil war settlements, the design of power-sharing institutions, and the prospects for an enduring peace builds on the efforts of international relations scholars to explain war as the product of a bargaining failure. According to this perspective, groups have an incentive to negotiate an efficient solution to conflict

20. The notion that war plays an important role in developing institutions is not a novel concept. This claim is consistent with the studies of Tilly 1975, North 1990, and Ikenberry 2001.

because war is inherently costly. The fact that actors are often unable to reach a resolution and instead engage in war is attributed to bargaining failure. Bargaining may fail and war occur if one or more of the following conditions holds. First, a bargaining failure may arise if parties to the conflict have private information and incentives for misrepresenting it to competing parties. Relevant types of information might include, for example, the actors' preferences regarding the nature of a bargain. Second, problems of credible commitment constitute another condition under which bargaining has the potential to fail. In order for a bargain to be considered credible, it must be in the interests of all the parties that strike the bargain to stick to its terms. Finally, groups may find arriving at a bargained alternative to war impossible if the issues over which they are experiencing conflict are somehow indivisible.[21]

The bargaining model has been applied principally to the analysis of interstate wars. Research in this area has extended to conceiving of the bargaining model as covering all phases of war, with each phase considered part of the bargaining process. These phases are aptly described by Dan Reiter: "Fighting breaks out when two sides cannot reach a bargain that both prefer to war. Each side fights to improve its chances of getting a desirable settlement of the disputed issue. The war ends when the two sides strike a bargain that both prefer to continuing the war, and the outcome is literally the bargain struck. Finally, the duration of peace following the war reflects the willingness of both sides not to break the war-ending bargain."[22] Although some scholars have focused on the difficulty particular conditions pose for successfully negotiating settlements of civil wars, to date no one has attempted to explain how the bargaining model might apply to all phases of civil war.[23] One important issue that has not been addressed, for example, is that contending groups within states often do strike bargains short of war that stick.[24] How can one account for why bargaining succeeds in some cases but fails in others? How might civil war settlements be designed to overcome a variety of the conditions that produce bargaining failure? And why do some settlements produce an enduring peace while others do not? Impor-

---

21. The concept of bargaining failures was first applied to an analysis of the outbreak of war by James Fearon (1995). For more on the bargaining model of war, see Reiter 2003 and Lake 2003.

22. Reiter 2003, 29.

23. Barbara Walter (1997, 1999, 2002) has written about the implications of credible commitments, and Monica Duffy Toft (2003) has analyzed the question of issue indivisibility.

24. A case in point is the "velvet revolution" that produced the peaceful breakup of Czechoslovakia into the Czech Republic and Slovakia.

tant answers to all of these questions can be found, we argue, by focusing on domestic institutions.

In our view, civil wars break out following a challenge to or collapse of the rules for managing conflict within a state. In the absence of such functioning rules, groups find reaching a bargain short of war difficult. The conditions that can produce bargaining failure come to the fore when conflict-management institutions are absent or deficient.[25] Negotiating a civil war settlement requires addressing these conditions. The best means of accomplishing this task is to negotiate a settlement that includes a number of power-sharing and power-dividing institutions. Institutions of this nature can be designed to address the credible commitment problem by giving each group at least some of what it wants—access to state power—as well as some of what it must have—a means of checking its rivals' power in order to provide security for the group. By providing incentives for participation in the settlement as well as minimizing the consequences to a group of another's defection, power-sharing and power-dividing institutions enhance the credibility of the bargain at hand. In addition, by agreeing to construct a number of these types of institutions, rival groups' leaders are, in effect, sending costly signals. The willingness (or lack thereof) to send such costly signals communicates information to groups regarding the relevant actors' preferences. This can help overcome the problem of private information with incentives to misrepresent.[26] Finally, by devising these new institutions, formerly warring groups ensure that they will have a means for managing future conflicts, thereby providing an opportunity for new and more peaceful modes of interaction to emerge.

By emphasizing the role of institutions in fostering an enduring peace following civil war, this book brings together disparate categories of scholarship centering on civil war resolution, power sharing in divided societies, and armed conflict. Through this synthesis of different perspectives we provide a unique understanding of the prospects for civil war resolution and point to mechanisms of conflict management whose capacity for shaping an enduring peace typically have been left unexplored.

25. Bargains, or conflict resolution short of war, succeed when legitimate and functioning institutions communicate information, make commitments credible, and so forth.

26. Issue indivisibility does not strike us as being as serious a source of bargaining failure as the other two conditions we outline above. The fact that former adversaries often construct a diversity of power-sharing and power-dividing institutions seems to indicate that groups are capable of making trade-offs among issues of interest to the different groups.

Plan of the Book

Building on the idea that institutions are a mechanism by which civil wars can be ended and an enduring peace facilitated, in Chapter 1 we discuss in detail four sets of institutions that are intended to share or divide power among rival groups. These institutions are constructed along the military, political, territorial, and economic dimensions of state power. We argue that these institutions, both individually and collectively, help secure peace based on their substantive and symbolic importance.

Chapters 2, 3, and 4 are structured to reflect the three phases of the settlement negotiation process—the decision to begin negotiations, the construction of institutions, and the implementation of those arrangements. In Chapter 2 we develop a statistical test intended to identify factors that affect the likelihood that opponents negotiating an end to a civil war will agree to create power-sharing and power-dividing institutions. The results suggest that, in particular, conditions that shape the perceptions of combatants as well as the international environment surrounding the state emerging from civil war play an important role in influencing the likelihood that negotiators will adopt power-sharing and power-dividing institutions.

In Chapter 3 we seek to verify that a relationship exists between the adoption of power-sharing and power-dividing institutions following civil war and the duration of peace. We find that the most consistent predictor of postwar stability is the aggregate number of power-sharing and power-dividing institutions specified in a settlement. More specifically, our results suggest that negotiated agreements requiring former adversaries to share or divide authority across as many dimensions of state power as possible have the greatest potential to foster an enduring peace.

In Chapter 4 we examine the impact that the implementation of institutions agreed to as part of a negotiated settlement has on the duration of the peace. Given its significance to post–civil war security, we focus on the implementation of military power-sharing and power-dividing institutions following a conflict. The results indicate that states in which former combatants faithfully implemented military power-sharing provisions were more likely to experience a stable peace in comparison to those countries in which parties to the settlement failed to carry out the specified arrangements.

In Chapter 5 we illustrate key concepts and supplement the statistical tests of earlier chapters by providing two case studies that focus on attempts at civil war resolution in Angola and the Philippines. Angola has experienced several efforts to negotiate a resolution to its civil war—agreements that included, variously, either no or only a nominal number of types of power-sharing or power-dividing institutions and, as a consequence, proved to be short lived. We contrast the Angolan case with the instance of the Philippines, in which all four types of power-sharing or power-dividing mechanisms were specified in the agreement and a stable peace has endured among former enemies.

In the Conclusion we review the book's central findings concerning the role of institutions in the reconstruction of domestic order following civil war. We conclude with an emphasis on the policy implications that might be drawn from our studies for those individuals involved in the challenging process of facilitating the resolution of civil wars.

1

AFTER THE FIGHTING STOPS:
SECURITY CONCERNS, INSTITUTIONS, AND THE
POST–CIVIL WAR ENVIRONMENT

Institutions play a critical role in civil war settlements. As Harvey Waterman observes, "civil wars [often] end in a deal and that . . . deal is about political institutions."[1] Institutions, defined as rules regarding the manner in which competition among actors should take place, prohibit particular behaviors and require others. It is because institutions serve to reduce uncertainty regarding the regulation of human behavior that they can help facilitate peaceful social interactions. By clarifying the means by which social conflict is to be managed in the future, institutions enable groups to contemplate relying on methods other than violence to secure their goals.

When armed opponents negotiate an end to a civil conflict, institutions structured to share and/or divide power among the groups in question are likely to play a central role in the design of the settlement. Power-sharing and power-dividing institutions, which define how decisions are to be made within a divided society and the distribution of decision-making rights within a state, have been a central element of recent peace settlements negotiated in Afghanistan, the Democratic Republic of the Congo, and the Sudan. Among the thirty-eight fully negotiated civil war settlements examined in this book, for example, only Angola's 1989 Gbadolite Accord neglected to specify some form of power-sharing or power-dividing institution. As we argue in this chapter, the principal reason adversaries design such institutions is to address the security concerns they confront in the postwar environment. By creating power-sharing and power-dividing insti-

---

1. Waterman 1993, 292.

tutions, settlement architects seek to ensure that state power—particularly forms of power that can be used to threaten others—will not be concentrated in the hands of any single group.

The institutions designed as part of the 1992 Chapultepec Agreement to end El Salvador's civil war illustrate this point. Having fought for more than a decade (1979–92) to rid the country of coercive and exclusionary institutions, the Farabundo Martí Front for National Liberation (FMLN), representing the interests of peasants, workers, and students, pressed hard for institutional reforms that would ensure that the country's economic and political elites would no longer be able to use the power of the state to repress these groups. The FMLN also sought to ensure that once its members surrendered their weapons the state would comply with its commitments, particularly a guarantee of protection for the unarmed insurgents.

These goals were secured through the design of a variety of power-sharing and power-dividing institutions specified in a series of accords. Central among these was an agreement to reform the state's security forces by incorporating some FMLN members into a new civilian police force, eliminating some elements of the security forces, reducing the overall size of the armed forces, and purging the military officer corps. Joined to the military power-sharing measures were agreements to legalize the FMLN as a political party and provide it with representation on the new Supreme Electoral Tribunal, a body designed to supervise voter registration and elections. By making it difficult for any group to use the powers of the Salvadoran state to attack and repress others, these institutional reforms provided former adversaries with a stable foundation on which to build an enduring and self-enforcing peace.

In this chapter we further develop our claim concerning the central importance of power-sharing and power-dividing institutions following the negotiated resolution of civil war. We begin by examining the kinds of security concerns facing civil war antagonists in a post–civil war environment. This is followed by a discussion of the influence of those security concerns on the process of institutional choice and the crafting of power-sharing and power-dividing institutions. In the third section we offer a detailed description of the four sets of power-sharing and power-dividing institutions groups may construct as part of a negotiated settlement. Our discussion of these institutions centers on the individual and cumulative effects they have on the management of conflict in post–civil war societies. In the fourth and final section we consider how our understanding of power-sharing and power-dividing institutions contrasts with previous conceptualizations that have appeared in studies of conflict management.

Security Concerns in the Post–Civil War Environment

Adversaries seeking a negotiated resolution to civil conflict come to the bargaining table centrally concerned about how best they can provide for their communities' safety. The very fact that war has emerged unambiguously proves that previously established means of providing for collectivities' security are inadequate. New means of ensuring that all groups are safe and that the fundamental interests of all citizens are protected must be found.

The principal actor responsible for providing for the security of people within territorially defined boundaries typically has been the modern state.[2] While a government's capacity to provide this security may have weakened or failed with the onset of civil war, state actors are once again expected to shoulder this responsibility once the violence has ended. Instead of groups continuing to rely on self-help measures to provide for their security, the state must reassert its authority vis-à-vis society, using its monopoly on the legitimate use of force to check some groups, if necessary, in order to provide for the safety of all. The state, in other words, generally is understood to be the actor responsible for enforcing social order.

The predicament associated with this emphasis on state control is its potential to generate apprehension among former combatants. As they look ahead to the postwar period, adversaries are necessarily concerned that reconstituted state power may be used to harm their interests and very survival. For groups emerging from war, the transition from relying on their defenses to entrusting the state with the responsibility of providing for their safety can be harrowing in the absence of any guarantees regarding the uses of state power. Parties to the conflict fear that once some group comes to power within the country, it may use different dimensions of state influence in such a way as to threaten the interests of others.[3]

The dimensions of power about which rival groups tend to be most concerned are those associated with the political, military, territorial, and eco-

2. That fact that states sometimes act in ways that are not in keeping with this responsibility has been amply documented. See, for example, Gurr 1993.

3. For more on the concept of the security dilemma and other security-related concerns domestic actors face in a civil war context, see Posen 1993, Spear 1996, Hartzell 1999, and Snyder and Jervis 1999.

nomic bases of state strength. As we explain below, these dimensions of state power factor into the security concerns of antagonists in a much more direct fashion than other components of state power such as legitimacy and reputation. This proves to be the case because each of these four dimensions of power can be used or manipulated to pose an immediate threat to the safety of collectivities. In addition, because these components of state power are in some sense fungible, meaning that control of them can shift among different groups, they are subject to being used to augment the power, particularly the coercive power, of any one collectivity.

Focusing on the first of these dimensions, the state's control of political power, rival groups are concerned about the possibility that politics will become a zero-sum competition in which one group seizes control of the state and uses its position of influence against others. Collectivities fear that if they are not represented in the central government, their foes will be in a position to make policy choices inimical to their interests. Previous experiences with just such an outcome led Colombia's Conservative and Liberal parties to devise the 50/50 power-sharing measures for the presidency and for congress that were at the center of that country's 1957 National Front Agreement.

Adversaries' fears regarding the state's military or coercive power are straightforward in nature. Parties to a conflict are concerned with the challenge of ensuring that the opposition does not gain control of the state's security forces and use this power to threaten others. Once a collectivity's army surrenders its weapons and disbands, what would prevent a rival from using the national army and/or police force to attack? If nothing else, what would prevent an opponent who controls the state's security forces from using them to regulate or manipulate the behavior of its rivals in the postwar state? Such concerns on the part of El Salvador's FMLN played a key role in that group's pressing for reforms of the country's security apparatus as part of the negotiated civil war settlement it participated in constructing.

Turning to the third dimension, territory, in the case of some civil conflicts the state's ability to control groups' access to land has become a significant source of power. In some cases, groups consider a piece of territory to be a defining attribute of their identity, one they deem vital to their continued existence as a group.[4] In other instances, collectivities understand the resources connected to a piece of territory to be central to their security. In yet other cases, groups believe that territory under their control is necessary

4. Toft 2003.

in order to provide for the physical protection of the group. Acting on that belief, the Nicaraguan rebels known as the "contras" bargained for the creation of "development zones" that they would be allowed to settle and patrol with their own forces as a condition for ending their involvement in civil war (1981–89). Whatever the motivation, groups attached to some piece of territory worry that state power may be used to sever their links to that land, thus causing the group irreparable harm.

Finally, groups have concerns related to control of the state's economic resources. Once some party is in authority, what would prevent it from denying groups access to economic resources they may need in order to survive? Adversaries also fear that the group controlling the state's economic resources may use those assets to build up its power base at the expense of other groups. The possibility exists that state-controlled resources might be used, for example, to finance future episodes of armed conflict. Concerns of this nature were at the center of settlements negotiated to end civil wars in countries ranging from Iraq (1970) and Sierra Leone (1999) to the Sudan (1972).

In short, groups seeking a resolution to civil war are trapped on the horns of a dilemma. On the one hand, adversaries recognize that a functioning state is necessary in order to provide for the future safety of all citizens. A state must be strong enough to enforce whatever rules are decided upon for managing social conflict if domestic order is to reemerge. On the other hand, reconstituting state power has the potential to generate further security concerns. Fearing that the state's powers may be abrogated by some party that will use them to secure its survival and well-being at the expense of other groups, opponents may find negotiating an end to a civil war impossible.

How can adversaries overcome this dilemma? We argue that this can best be accomplished by reconstituting state authority through the creation of government institutions that balance power among contending groups or at least prevent any one party from accumulating sufficient power to exercise central authority on its own. By adopting institutions that seek to share, divide, or balance power among competing groups, settlement architects can foster a security that would be elusive if power were concentrated in the hands of a single entity.

We acknowledge that creating such mechanisms is not an easily accomplished task. Reordering state institutions may generate strong opposition on the part of those who might lose power in the redefined state. This difficulty is reflected in the lower number of negotiated civil war settlements, as compared to interstate peace agreements, reached in the post–World War II period. Yet, in the absence of any victor emerging from a civil war, no clear alternative to designing power-sharing and power-dividing institutions exists as part of an effort to secure a peaceful end to the fighting and to construct an enduring stability. Having failed to secure the right by winning the war to structure institutions as they see fit, rival groups are likely to see little alternative to jointly designing institutions that address each others' concerns by providing for the sharing of power.

Negotiated Civil War Settlements and Institutional Choice

Countries emerging from civil wars are faced with the issue of institutional choice in a context with which few other countries must contend. That civil war has erupted indicates that the institutions previously in place—institutions that may well have been weak, discriminatory, and/or repressive—are no longer able to manage societal conflict successfully. The rejection of and armed challenge to those institutions by some set of actors poses dilemmas for the postwar society. Foremost among these problems is deciding what form the new rules regulating relations between the state and society are to take. Should the (failed) institutions of the past be resurrected? Should untested institutions be adopted? Who is to decide what form these new institutions should take?[5]

Given the central role institutions play in regulating conflict, the foregoing questions are ones of immediate importance to groups emerging from civil war. This is particularly true of civil wars in which an effort is being made by opponents to end the conflict through negotiations. In cases of intrastate conflict in which no single party has emerged as a victor, the institutions or rules of competition that will govern groups in the future are likely to be the subject of significant bargaining.

Recognizing that civil war adversaries face very real security concerns gives us some insight into the process of institutional choice on the part of actors seeking to negotiate an end to a civil war. Entrusted with securing not just the political and economic survival of the groups they represent but also, in many cases, their physical safety, the representatives of contending groups are likely to favor certain institutions and oppose others. Although

5. In addition, problems of this nature are likely to be exacerbated if, during the course of the conflict, competing norms and institutions regulating the behavior of each of the belligerent groups have emerged.

groups presumably would each like to control the state, thereby providing an additional measure of security for themselves, adversaries' fears regarding control of the state by rivals prompt them to design institutions for sharing, dividing, or balancing power among competing groups.

Power-sharing and power-dividing institutions minimize the security threats belligerents face when ending a civil war by allocating rights and limiting the exercise of power. By setting limits on the exercise of power, as well as bringing into rough parity contending groups' access to power, such institutions reduce the stakes of uneven gains. Power-sharing and power-dividing institutions thus help minimize the incentives former adversaries may have to challenge the newly constructed domestic order. They do so, at least in part, by helping opponents to sidestep the dilemma, identified by Adam Przeworski, in which if "increasing returns to power are [not] institutionally mitigated, losers must fight the first time they lose, for waiting makes it less likely that they will ever succeed."[6]

Institutions designed to balance or divide power among former adversaries can also help foster stability by making these actors' commitment to peace more credible. In order for antagonists to believe that the commitments their opponents make as part of a negotiated settlement are credible, each group must believe that the other will not find it in its future interest to renege on the commitment. Power-sharing and power-dividing institutions can help induce actors to stick to the deals they have made by convincing them that they will not be better off and, indeed, may be made worse off should they fail to do so. By providing former foes with enough power to effectively block or check efforts by some faction to win control of the apparatus of the state, power-balancing institutions can convince would-be challengers that such attempts would likely be made in vain and would result only in the squandering of resources.

Power-sharing and power-dividing institutions may also help enhance the credibility of former belligerents' commitment to peace to the extent that they compartmentalize or divide decision-making powers. Leaders will find breaking their promises very difficult if they are institutionally bound to obtain other actors' assent in order to change policies or make new decisions. By reducing the risk of arbitrary behavior by some set of actors, power-sharing and power-dividing institutions help enhance the negotiated settlement's credibility as a whole.

Finally, the process of negotiating, designing, and implementing power-

6. Przeworski 1991, 36.

sharing and power-dividing institutions provides civil war adversaries with an opportunity to signal to one another their level of commitment to building an enduring peace. By agreeing to establish these kinds of institutions, the parties to a settlement indicate their willingness to accommodate the concerns and interests of their adversaries. The conciliatory nature of these institutions sends an important message to groups in the postwar society regarding former foes' interest in peace as well as their inclination to adopt new norms and rules for regulating group interaction.[7]

Power-Sharing and Power-Dividing Institutions

Civil war rivals can design institutions to share and divide power in the four areas where control of state power poses major threats to their security. Institutions thus exist for sharing and dividing political power, military power, territory, and economic resources controlled by the state. These four dimensions of state power tend to be the focus of negotiations regarding institutional choice for two reasons. First, each of the rival groups can use any one or some combination of these components of state power to bolster its coercive capacity. Second, contending groups are likely to focus on these issues when bargaining to attain security guarantees because they are, generally speaking, divisible—they lend themselves to the creation of power-sharing or power-dividing institutions. These four components of state power can be divided in ways that a state's reputation, for example, cannot. This divisibility enables adversaries to construct rules that make it a challenge for any one group to use these elements of state power to enhance its coercive capacity at the expense of other groups.

Using a four-part typology, we categorize different forms of these institutions based on whether the intent of the rules is to share or divide power along a political, military, territorial, or economic dimension. We discuss these four forms of power-sharing and power-dividing institutions in detail below.

POLITICAL POWER-SHARING AND POWER-DIVIDING INSTITUTIONS

Scholars long have focused attention on different types of political institutions that might be used to manage conflict within divided societies. One of

7. Recent research suggesting that explicit acts that signal reconciliation among adversaries following civil and international conflicts tend to promote subsequent stable bilateral relations lends support to our perspective regarding the conciliatory effects of agreements to create power-sharing and power-dividing institutions. See Brecke and Long 2003.

the central debates to emerge from the literature on the use of political institutions to manage conflict is between the advocates of majoritarian and proportional strategies.

Advocates of majoritarianism suggest that political power should be monopolized by the faction or group capable of gaining the support of a majority (or at least a plurality) of citizens. Political institutions may be structured to encourage the bringing together of a diverse coalition of actors in an effort to secure a majority, but those groups left out of such an arrangement are effectively shut out of opportunities to participate in the governance of the state.[8]

In contrast, a proportional strategy calls for groups to share political power on the basis of some demographic (e.g., ethnicity) or political (e.g., party affiliation) principle. Collectivities are guaranteed a degree of representation within governing institutions by virtue of their group affiliation. A failure to achieve or maintain dominant status does not relegate a group to political irrelevance; minorities have a permanent voice within the structures of the state.

Of these two sets of rules—majoritarianism and proportionalism—we argue that only proportional systems provide adversaries with sufficient guarantees regarding their access to political power to diminish the appeal of continued warfare or ongoing reliance on self-help mechanisms such as armed militias. Political institutions associated with majoritarianism largely fail to assuage concerns about becoming permanently marginalized. Timothy Sisk highlights this point in his discussion of the meaning of majoritarian elections within polarized states:

> In many divided societies, electoral competition is a contest for ownership of the state. Minorities, particularly, equate democracy not with freedom or participation but with the structured dominance of adversarial majority groups. Permanent minorities . . . have feared the consequences of electoral competition, especially when the expected consequence of majority victory is discrimination against them. For minority groups, losing an election is a mat-

8. See Horowitz (1985, 1990b) for a discussion of majoritarian-oriented institutions that might serve as incentives for cooperation among political adversaries. The opportunities to evaluate the value of such an approach through cross-national statistical analysis are limited, as few countries have employed the mechanisms Horowitz advocates (Sisk 1996, 44). This is particularly the case in the context of post–civil war states.

ter not simply of losing office but of losing the means for protecting the survival of the group.[9]

Faced with these concerns about majority rule, collectivities—and particularly minorities—will seek a negotiated settlement that provides them with some guarantee of access to political power and/or some measure of insulation from power exercised at the center. Proportional strategies can be crucial to providing such a guarantee.

The institutions central to a proportional strategy for distributing political power are electoral proportional representation, administrative proportional representation, and proportional representation in the executive branch of a national government. Electoral proportional representation lowers the minimum level of voter support a candidate or party must achieve to gain political office, thus decreasing the intensity of political competition. Although the mechanics by which votes are translated into seats under electoral proportional representation systems differ, these rules share the aim of minimizing the disparity between a party's share of national votes and the number of parliamentary seats it occupies. A case in point is Mozambique's 1992 General Peace Agreement. The settlement, negotiated to end a decade-long civil war, provides for an electoral system based on the principle of proportional representation for election to the assembly. In addition, the agreement also calls for the establishment, in consultation with the country's political parties, of a minimum percentage of nationwide votes of not less than 5 percent or more than 20 percent for a party to obtain a seat in the assembly.

Administrative proportional representation expands the opportunities for political participation by increasing groups' access to policy-making influence. Rules of this nature seek to allocate decision- and policy-making power to collectivities by appointing a predetermined number of their representatives to positions on courts, commissions, the civil or foreign services, and other corresponding offices. The Salvadoran Peace Accords, for example, initiated the creation of a National Commission for the Consolidation of Peace (COPAZ), which would be responsible for overseeing implementation of the political agreements reached by the parties. The accords called for COPAZ to be composed of two representatives of the government of El Salvador, including a member of the armed forces, two representatives

9. Sisk 1996, 31.

of the FMLN, and one representative of each of the parties or coalitions represented in the legislative assembly.

Finally, proportional representation may also take place in the executive branch of the national government. In this instance, groups are ensured a voice in the innermost circles of political power via the appointment of representatives to ministerial, subministerial, and cabinet positions. The November 1994 Lusaka Protocol negotiated to end the civil war in Angola placed considerable emphasis on this form of proportional representation, allocating the ministerial posts of geology and mines, trade, health, hotel business, and tourism to UNITA. UNITA members were also guaranteed positions as deputy ministers of agriculture, defense, finance, home affairs, mass communication, public works, and social reintegration.

MILITARY POWER-SHARING AND POWER-DIVIDING INSTITUTIONS

Prior to negotiating a settlement to end a civil war, a warring group's army provides the greatest level of security for that group as well as its most obvious source of leverage vis-à-vis its adversaries. Rivals thus will be reluctant to give up their armed forces without some guarantee that their security will be provided for and that they will have other means of protecting their interests. A number of scholars have focused on how concerns relating to military control pose challenges for both the negotiation and longevity of civil war settlements.[10] Highlighting the dangers groups face as they demobilize, analysts have stressed the importance of confidence-building measures meant to reassure adversaries that, once they disarm, an enemy will not be able to take advantage of the settlement and achieve the victory that had previously proved elusive on the battlefield. These confidence-building measures range from the introduction of peacekeeping troops between opposing forces to guarantees by third-party actors that those groups violating the cease-fire will be punished.

Although third-party assistance may lend greater credibility to the peace process, such assistance does not mitigate adversaries' security concerns in isolation. Antagonists are well aware that these measures, which entail relying on outsiders, are beyond their control and may fail. Such measures are likely to generate concerns about whether the number of peacekeeping troops will be sufficient to the task at hand (e.g., Angola's failed 1991 Bicesse Accords) or whether the third-party guarantors' commitments are really

10. See, for example, Hampson 1990, Stedman 1996, and Walter 2002.

credible (e.g., the collapsed 1979 Transitional Government of National Unity settlement in Chad). Most significant, such measures fail to address the question of who will control the coercive powers of the state once central authority has been reconstructed and third-party forces leave the field.

If adversaries' concerns are to be mitigated, the state's coercive forces must somehow be neutralized or balanced. Parties to the conflict must believe that a rival group will not be able to direct the security forces of the state to threaten their interests. In most cases, this guarantee will involve integrating the antagonists' armed forces into the state's security forces. This can be done either on the basis of some proportional formula representative of the size of the armed factions or, perhaps more reassuring to the weaker party to the conflict, on the basis of a strict balance in troop numbers among the contending parties.

Negotiated resolutions to the conflicts in both the Philippines and El Salvador provide examples of bargains that required the integration of the state and rebel security forces. The 1996 Philippine Peace Agreement called for the integration of some 7,500 members of the Mindanao National Liberation Force's military wing into the national army and security forces. The accords ending the Salvadoran civil war abolished a number of the Salvadoran government's public security forces and founded a new national civilian police force for which a quota of 20 percent each was established for former national police officers and FMLN guerrilla troops.

Negotiated settlements may also seek to neutralize or balance the state's coercive forces by mandating the appointment of members of the subordinate group(s) to key leadership positions including general, commander, director, or defense minister in the state's security forces. This ensures that these individuals are in a position to monitor the movement of troops and to warn of policy decisions that might harm or threaten the interests of the subordinate group. Notable examples of this type of military power sharing include the commissioning of Southern Sudan Liberation Movement leader and Anya-Nya Commander-in-Chief Major-General Joseph Lagu as major-general in the unified Sudanese army as part of the country's negotiated settlement in 1972 and Violeta Barrios de Chamorro's retention of Sandinista General Humberto Ortega as head of Nicaragua's armed forces in 1990.

Finally, in rare cases, and although it may seem contrary to the notion of centralizing state power, striking a balance among antagonists may involve allowing opposing sides to remain armed or retain their own security forces. Some analysts have questioned the logic of such provisions, contending that the presence of competing armed groups complicates the task of rebuilding peacetime security forces and seemingly constitutes a threat to the stability of civil war settlements.[11] Although the first part of that statement may well be true, especially from a logistical point of view, the second proposition has yet to be empirically verified. Three of the fully negotiated agreements among the thirty-eight we consider in this study have included a provision of this nature. The settlement negotiated in 1970 that ended the Yemeni civil war between Republicans and Royalists allowed each side to retain its arms.[12] The Managua Protocol on Disarmament, signed by the government of Violeta Chamorro and the contras of Nicaragua, authorized the contras to create a security force that would provide for "internal order" within the development zones that the Nicaraguan government committed itself to create for the contras. Finally, the 1995 Dayton Accords negotiated to end the civil war in Bosnia called for the two entities within Bosnia and Herzegovina, the Bosniak-Croat Federation and the Republika Srpska, to maintain their own separate armies. Each of these settlements has proved stable to date.[13]

TERRITORIAL POWER-SHARING AND POWER-DIVIDING INSTITUTIONS

The principal means of allocating territorial power among groups is through territorial autonomy. By creating forms of decentralized government that are territorially based (e.g., federalism and regional autonomy), autonomy effectively divides political influence among levels of government. This type of institution provides groups at the subnational level with some degree of power and autonomy vis-à-vis the central government. Territorial autonomy is an institution that provides a means through which compromise can be reached among adversarial groups by allowing each collectivity a regional base from which it may protect its own interests.[14]

There are three distinct ways in which territory-based institutions reassure groups in a divided society that state power will not be seized by one group and used to threaten the security of others. First, territorial autonomy can restrict authority at the political center by shifting decision-making power to subunits of the state. If a collectivity considers issues such as education, language, social services, and access to governmental civil service to

11. See, for example, Ball and Halevy 1996 and Callahan 1997.
12. Wenner 1993.
13. The 1970 Yemeni settlement was eventually superseded by an agreement on the parts of Northern Yemen and Southern Yemen to unite.
14. Heintze 1997.

be essential to its survival, then it should find its ability to exercise regional control over these issues reassuring. By increasing the influence of policy-makers at the subnational level, groups should also gain a sense that they possess a means of protecting themselves from the exercise of arbitrary central authority. This is particularly likely to be the case when the powers of the subunits extend to their own judiciaries and police forces, as these often supplement groups' feelings of autonomous capacity.

Second, and related to the above, territorial autonomy can be used to balance power among groups. Measures that ensure that territorially based groups are included in the institutions of the federal government, for example, provide these sets of actors with policy-making influence at the political center and a means of blocking other collectivities from capturing the state. These territorial devices lessen the perceived threat of centralized control by any single group by ensuring that no individual "winner" can control an entire region precisely because a single region no longer exists. In this way, "federalism operates like an electoral reform, like proportional representation," argues Donald Horowitz, setting "one arena off from another, making and remaking legislative majorities and minorities by adjusting the territories in which their votes are to be counted."[15]

Third, territorial autonomy can be used to help reduce the stakes of competition among adversarial groups in a divided society. One way this is accomplished is by reducing disparities among collectivities by enabling a minority to rise within its own state bureaucracies and educational systems. By making material resources and opportunities available at the subunit level that did not previously exist, territorial autonomy may also diffuse some of the economic power previously controlled by the political center.

A final point worth noting is that territorial autonomy is a relatively flexible institution that can be designed to fit the parameters of the particular conflict at hand. For example, this is reflected in the federal structures associated with the negotiated settlements of civil wars in both Malaysia and South Africa. Malaysia's federal system was designed for a multiethnic country in which, with the exception of the northeast coast states of Kelantan and Trengganu, ethnic groups are not concentrated in self-contained areas. The nature of the Malaysian states' relationship to the federal government thus varies on the basis of their ethnic composition, socioeconomic structure, and history of rule by sultans. For example, the two states on the island of Borneo have a distinct status that allows them to control immigration

15. Horowitz 1990a, 124.

from the peninsula and permits greater cultural and economic autonomy than any peninsular states. The peninsular states with reigning sultans, on the other hand, have greater political influence in the Conference of Rulers than the states lacking traditional rulers.[16]

Federal institutions in South Africa were crafted to accommodate the competing interests of the majority African National Congress whose representatives favored putting into place a system of centralized government (which it hoped to use to promote a strong national policy) and the minority National Party that opposed a strong central government in hands other than its own. The resulting compromise established a strong central government that grants the provinces "exclusive" or "concurrent" powers with respect to planning, development, and services, and to the "specific socioeconomic and cultural needs" and "general well-being" of the inhabitants.

ECONOMIC POWER-SHARING AND POWER-DIVIDING INSTITUTIONS

The economic dimension of power sharing focuses on control of economic resources in the postwar state. Groups that fear for their safety as they negotiate an end to civil war have an immediate concern of an economic nature: ensuring that control of resources does not provide any one group with the means to exclude or threaten rivals. In a related manner, as they consider ending a conflict in which warfare has become the primary system of resource allocation, antagonists may become concerned about one group seizing control of economic assets that provide the source of financing for armed conflict. During the course of the Angolan civil war, for example, the oil-producing enclave of Cabinda (controlled by the Popular Movement for the Liberation of Angola [MPLA]) and the diamond-producing areas of the country (controlled by UNITA) were hotly contested by the rival forces. As the two sides tried to implement a negotiated solution to the conflict, UNITA's reluctance to cede the diamond mines it had used to finance its war efforts was seen as a hindrance to a long-term resolution to the conflict.

Faced with security fears regarding the control and use of economic resources, settlement architects are likely to attempt to design rules for the distribution of wealth and income that will, if not achieve a balance among groups, at least prevent any one group from dominating economic resources. Because market competition is likely to favor disproportionately those groups already enjoying economic privilege, collectivities concerned

16. Milne 1967.

about the control of economic resources by rival parties are unlikely to trust market mechanisms to distribute resources. Rather, groups will seek to have the state displace or place limits on market competition, directing the flow of resources through economic public policies and/or administrative allocations to assist economically disadvantaged groups.[17]

Settlements seeking to secure this type of distribution of material resources and economic opportunities tend to rely on the use of preferential policies. These are "laws, regulations, administrative rules, court orders, and other public interventions to provide certain public and private goods, such as admission into schools and colleges, jobs, promotions, business loans, and rights to buy and sell land on the basis of membership in a particular . . . group."[18] Although most settlements are not likely to specify in such detail the policies to be used to achieve the goal of distributing economic resources among rival groups, rules structuring distributive policy can range from general statements of a pattern for distributing resources to more detailed formulae.

The 1970 Yemeni settlement, for example, called for a Supreme Constitutional Court of *ulama* to ensure that taxes and economic measures were based on Islamic concepts of social justice. The 1996 Philippines peace accord calls for the state to provide the Special Zone of Peace and Development in the southern Philippines with resources to foster development within the region, including basic services such as water and socialized housing and entrepreneurial development support in the form of livelihood assistance and credit facilities. The Managua Protocol on Disarmament, one of the accords designed to bring to an end the Nicaraguan civil war, called for a number of measures meant to benefit the contras, including monthly pensions to be provided to the widows and orphans of contra fighters by the Nicaragua Institute of Social Security and Welfare (INSSBI) as well as unspecified government aid for each demobilized contra.

THE CUMULATIVE EFFECTS OF POWER-SHARING AND POWER-DIVIDING INSTITUTIONS

Negotiated civil war settlements may contain power-sharing and power-dividing institutions that reflect none, one, or several of the dimensions of

17. Esman 1994.
18. Weiner 1983, 35. Weiner's discussion of preferential policies focuses on using ethnic criteria as the basis for distributing resources. Preferential policies can also be directed toward groups based on a variety of different reasons for cohesion other than ethnicity, provided that the boundaries associated with each form of group identity are explicitly identified.

state power described above. Although a set of institutional assurances from any one of these four dimensions is likely to help mitigate the security concerns of former foes, multiple sets of power-sharing institutions should prove even more reassuring. This is likely to be the case for two reasons.

First, including multiple aspects of power sharing in an agreement should have a cumulative effect on the actors' sense of security, with the different dimensions having the potential to become mutually reinforcing. For example, mandates for political power sharing are more likely to be bolstered and durable if the military is beyond the control of any single faction that might be tempted to use the threat of a coup to alter the balance of power that exists in the political dimension or to check efforts at cooperation. Likewise, economic power sharing may enhance previously disadvantaged groups' prospects for accumulating the resources necessary to become genuinely competitive in future electoral competitions.

Once again, the accords negotiated to end El Salvador's civil war illustrate this principle of complementarity among power-sharing institutions. One of the FMLN's main goals was institutional change that would assure the group, as well as other opposition parties, that they could safely participate in civilian political life. In addition to seeking the types of electoral reforms that were mentioned at the outset of this chapter, a key element of the accords for the rebel army was a reform of the state security forces that would erode the alliance between the military and the landed oligarchy on which political power had rested. Once power-sharing and power-dividing institutions were devised that ensured the military would no longer operate at the will of the economic elite, the FMLN proved ready to sign the peace accords.

A second reason that the inclusion of multiple dimensions of power sharing in a negotiated civil war settlement proves beneficial to the prospects of long-term peace is that it serves as a source of protection against the failure to implement any single power-sharing provision of the settlement. Signatories to an agreement are likely to recognize that some provisions of a peace agreement may not be implemented in the often challenging and divisive transition from war to peace. By specifying multiple power-sharing dimensions in the settlement, the failure of any one power-sharing aspect may not necessarily result in groups becoming permanently marginalized or unable to provide for their own security.

The peace settlement signed by the government of the Philippines and the MNLF in 1996 demonstrates the protection against implementation failure offered by including multiple power-sharing provisions. Although the peace accord provides an initial level of security for the MNLF through the creation of a Special Zone of Peace and Development (SZOPAD) to consist of fourteen provinces and nine cities in southern Mindanao, the settlement also calls for a plebiscite to be held three years after the creation of the SZOPAD in order to determine the establishment of a new autonomous government and the specific area of autonomy. Perhaps because the call to hold a plebiscite introduced an element of uncertainty, the MNLF was not content to rely on territorial autonomy alone as a guarantee of its security. Thus, the settlement also calls for some 7,500 members of the MNLF's military wing to be integrated into the national army and security forces and resources meant to foster development in the region provided to SZOPAD by the state.

Putting Power-Sharing and Power-Dividing Institutions into Perspective

How does our understanding of power sharing compare with the manner in which this concept is typically treated in academic or policy-making circles? Two distinct differences emerge between our treatment of these institutions and the ways in which others have approached this subject. These differences center on the intended use and possible forms of power-sharing and power-dividing institutions.

PURPOSE OF POWER-SHARING AND POWER-DIVIDING INSTITUTIONS

A number of divided societies adopted power-sharing and power-dividing mechanisms as a means of managing conflict years before the practice was ever discussed in academic literature.[19] Power-sharing institutions first came to the attention of the scholarly community as part of the consociational model introduced by Arend Lijphart in his path-breaking work *The Politics of Accommodation: Pluralism and Democracy in the Netherlands* (1968) and expanded upon in *Democracy in Plural Societies* (1977). In these books Lijphart argued that pluralistic societies that followed power-sharing rules and practices would be able to achieve and maintain stable democratic government. Similarly, Eric Nordlinger (1972) sought to establish that power shar-

19. To cite two examples, Arend Lijphart (1996) refers to both Canada (between 1840 and 1867) and the Netherlands (between 1917 and 1967) as having put power-sharing institutions into practice.

ing could be used to regulate conflict in democracies with deeply divided societies.

While both Lijphart and Nordlinger identify institutions that might prove capable of managing conflict in divided societies, neither scholar considered the value of using these mechanisms for stabilizing peace within states emerging from civil war. Both instead focus on how these institutions can be used to secure and maintain democratic governments. Yet many of the power-sharing institutions Lijphart and Nordlinger advocate have clear applications to the post–civil war environment. In the context of negotiated civil war settlements, armed adversaries have failed on the battlefield to win the right to unilaterally design new rules and institutions for the postconflict society. Of necessity, they must agree to share state power with their former enemies. Based on this logic we extend these classic works concerning power sharing to the post–civil war environment. Rather than considering how power-sharing institutions might assist in securing democracy within diverse societies, we explore the question of how these institutions might best be designed to stabilize the transition to enduring peace following the bargained resolution of civil wars.

While the approach we adopt has only recently begun to be used in academic studies, it is interesting to note that policy-makers increasingly appear to view power-sharing and power-dividing institutions as constituting a potentially viable means of securing peace. The post–cold war period, in particular, has witnessed a number of states, with the support of the international community, negotiate settlements that call for the construction of a variety of power-sharing institutions. A case in point is the Agreement on Provisional Arrangements in Afghanistan Pending the Reestablishment of Permanent Government Institutions signed on December 5, 2001, by delegates to a UN conference on the future of Afghanistan. Both the mediators and opposing groups that served as the architects of this agreement agreed to establish a variety of institutions for sharing and dividing state power in the belief that this would foster a sense of security in the post–civil war environment that would make a return to war less likely.

FORMS OF POWER-SHARING INSTITUTIONS

Those few scholars who have sought to extend the power-sharing concept have tended to offer a narrow view of which institutions to consider under that categorization. Following Lijphart's lead, these works have focused pri-

marily on the distribution of political power across competing groups.[20]
These institutions are commonly defined as including grand coalition governments that represent all major linguistic and religious groups; cultural
autonomy for these collectivities; proportionality of political representation
and civil service appointments; and a minority veto with regard to vital
minority rights and autonomy.[21]

Although we agree with others that the political arena is important, we
emphasize that it is not the only sphere in which competing groups may
agree to share power in the post–civil war environment. In this context,
other dimensions along which state power is exercised may have equal or
greater significance to parties seeking to protect themselves and their interests. For this reason, we expand our understanding of power sharing to
demonstrate its capacity to address security concerns across four possible
dimensions—the political, territorial, military, and economic sources of
state power. While the existing power-sharing literature has at times tacitly
acknowledged these other dimensions of power, for example, by referring
to practices such as the proportional allocation of military positions and
governmental spending within diverse societies, we believe making these
distinctions explicit is important in light of the multidimensional nature of
the security concerns parties have in the wake of civil wars.

Finally, and in contrast to most other works that have focused on the
value of power-sharing institutions as a means of conflict management, we
make clear that many of the institutions on which we focus attempt to stabilize peace by dividing, rather than sharing, power among former adversaries.
Power-sharing institutions may help promote successful conflict management by bringing together antagonistic groups, fostering increased contact
among them, and perhaps even encouraging them to build coalitions. But
successful conflict management can also, we contend, be achieved through
institutions that help separate or buffer groups from one another. Forms of
territorial autonomy, for example, can be very reassuring to groups that seek
an extra measure of distance and thus protection from those with whom
they have so recently been fighting.

Institutions and Outcomes

The principal outcome with which we are concerned in this book is securing
an enduring peace following civil war. We believe that countries that have

---

20. See, for example, Sisk 1996; Walter 1997, 2002; and Dubey 2002.
21. Lijphart 1977, 1996.

experienced civil violence have within their power the ability to build a stable peace and that the formerly warring parties must play a central role in
this process. Because the postwar environment is so chaotic and threatening,
one of the first tasks in which rival groups must engage is designing institutions capable of regulating behavior among groups. Although there is likely
to be a need to design all kinds of institutions in societies where previous
institutions have come under challenge or been destroyed, concerned as
they are with providing for their security in the postwar environment, former foes are likely to place a priority on structuring institutions that will
help them achieve this goal. The institutions best able to do this, we have
argued, are ones that share and divide power among contending groups,
ensuring that no single group controls the levers of state power.

Power-sharing and power-dividing institutions can be constructed along
the military, political, territorial, and economic dimensions of state power.
Negotiated settlements that include power-sharing or power-dividing institutions grounded in several or all of these dimensions can be referred to as
highly "institutionalized" settlements. These highly institutionalized settlements, we argue, are the ones most likely to help produce a durable peace.
That multiple aspects of power sharing can reinforce one another should
prove reassuring to parties to the settlement. In addition, multiple power-
sharing institutions help insulate against the collapse of the settlement. Failure by some party to follow through on one arrangement to share or divide
power is less likely to be critical if rival groups know their interests are
protected by power-sharing and power-dividing arrangements in some of
the other dimensions in which power may be exercised. Highly institutionalized settlements thus help promote a stable peace by giving parties to the
agreement some leeway for "accidents" or even testing the settlement's
terms without leading to the collapse of peace.

By agreeing to construct highly institutionalized settlements, rival groups
may also be providing yet another signal of their commitment to the peace
process. Devising and constructing institutions to manage conflict is not a
cost-free process.[22] The time, effort, and resources adversaries invest in creating power-sharing institutions are assets they are not able to direct elsewhere—including to a continuation of the conflict. Groups that commit
themselves to creating a variety of power-sharing and power-dividing institutions communicate their intentions to abide by peace in a more costly
fashion than do parties that agree to construct only one or two types of

---

22. For more on the costs of constructing institutions, see Genicot and Skaperdas 2002.

power-sharing institutions. Because more highly institutionalized settlements impose the highest costs in their construction and implementation, groups that are part of such settlements should find their rivals' commitment to peace more credible.

Civil war settlements that incorporate power-sharing institutions (particularly highly institutionalized settlements) have a great deal to recommend them as a means for ending armed conflict and subsequently stabilizing peace. Nevertheless, it must be remembered that these institutions are most likely to be agreed to under a particular set of very challenging conditions. States that have experienced civil war, whose institutions have been challenged and/or have collapsed, where no single group has emerged from the conflict victorious or in a position to dominate society, and where, as a result, groups have serious security concerns are the ones most likely to adopt power-sharing and power-dividing institutions. None of these are very auspicious conditions for building a durable peace. Add to these difficulties the costs of war and an often hostile regional or international environment, and conceiving of any alternative set of institutions likely to succeed in initiating the transition to peace becomes difficult. Power-sharing and power-dividing institutions are valuable in conveying that conflict can be managed in ways other than at gunpoint because they enhance predictability, foster a sense of security, and communicate a credible commitment on the part of groups to accommodate the concerns of others.

If highly institutionalized settlements are most likely to help produce a durable peace, why don't all parties who negotiate an end to civil war agree to create institutions to share or divide power along a number of the four dimensions we describe in this chapter? Are there factors—perceptual or environmental—that encourage some groups to create more institutionalized settlements than others? Are any of these types of factors subject to influence by the international community? In an effort to answer these questions, we examine, in Chapter 2, a number of factors with the potential to shape the likelihood that parties will adopt power-sharing institutions in the context of the negotiated settlement of civil wars.

2

CREATING POWER-SHARING AND
POWER-DIVIDING INSTITUTIONS

That power-sharing and power-dividing institutions have the potential to encourage an enduring peace in states emerging from civil war provides no guarantee that adversaries will mutually agree to their construction at the end of hostilities. This is apparent in the analysis of the thirty-eight fully negotiated civil war settlements that were reached between 1945 and 1999. While only Angola's 1989 Gbadolite Accord failed to include any provisions for power-sharing or power-dividing institutions, just three of these settlements (approximately 8 percent) included the requirement that adversaries share or divide influence across all four dimensions—military, political, territorial, and economic—of state power.

Why did negotiations between the government and rebels in Angola's civil war, resulting in the Gbadolite Accord, not yield a single power-sharing or power-dividing provision while the parties to the conflict in South Africa opted to design an extensive array of power-sharing mechanisms? This is certainly an important question if, as we argue throughout this book, those settlements including as extensive an array of power-sharing and power-dividing institutions as possible are most likely to secure a lasting peace. We address this issue in this chapter by identifying those conditions with the potential to encourage parties to a conflict to develop power-sharing or power-dividing mechanisms and thus enhance the potential for a self-enforcing peace in a postwar state.

Theoretical Perspective

Our central theoretical expectation is that successfully negotiating a power-sharing settlement to end civil war depends on two sets of conditions. The first category of factors relates to the nature of the conflict and how it affects adversaries' perceptions of the value of a negotiated settlement. Here our main concern is accounting for those aspects of a conflict that might encourage adversaries to view a negotiated settlement, based on the principles of sharing or dividing state power, as a desirable outcome. We suggest that those civil wars in which adversaries can readily identify mutual avenues of accommodation while simultaneously perceiving themselves as locked in an unwinnable war should be among the conflicts most amenable to reaching a negotiated accord.

To a large extent, this aspect of our argument builds upon I. William Zartman's view that particular conditions heighten the potential for an ongoing conflict to be resolved through peaceful means.[1] Specifically, Zartman advances the claim that negotiations to end conflict have the greatest potential to prove fruitful when combatants recognize that they are trapped in a mutually hurting stalemate in which "the countervailing power of each side, though insufficient to make the other side lose, prevents it from winning."[2] Rather than continuing to prosecute a war that is both costly and futile, adversaries are expected to instead become increasingly amenable to efforts toward mutual accommodation advanced at the bargaining table. We extend Zartman's insight by considering a range of factors that define the conflict—including the stakes, duration, and intensity of the war—to account for the effect they are likely to have on shaping adversaries' interest in establishing mechanisms for sharing or dividing state power.

The second set of conditions we view as important are those associated with the conflict environment in which bargaining to reach a negotiated settlement is carried out. Put simply, successfully negotiating a settlement to share and divide power should be inherently more complex and challenging under some conditions as compared to others. This will prove true even if parties considering a settlement have a mutual interest in establishing a power-sharing and power-dividing arrangement. Our interest is then to identify those specific factors having the potential to either facilitate or stymie the bargained creation of these arrangements among disputants.

1. Zartman 1989, 1993.
2. Zartman 1993, 24.

We consider conditions originating from both the domestic and international environments that might affect bargaining success. In terms of domestic factors, the influences for which we account are states' previous experience with democracy and level of development. The influences originating outside the state that could shape the negotiating environment we consider are the introduction of a peacekeeping operation and the structure of the international system.

In summary, we expect that the prospect of power-sharing and power-dividing arrangements emerging at the end of civil war is contingent on both how the nature of the conflict affects the settlement's perceived value on the part of those involved in the fighting as well as the degree to which the conflict environment facilitates negotiations' success. Our theory holds that the most permissive environment for creating power-sharing and power-dividing measures will be one in which combatants mutually recognize that sharing or dividing power is in their best interest *and* that these actors confront domestic and international environments conducive to productive negotiations. We expect that in those instances in which these conditions hold, settlement architects will agree to create an array of power-sharing and power-dividing institutions.

Explaining the Development of Power-Sharing and Power-Dividing Institutions at War's End

To evaluate the strength of our theoretical claims, we develop a series of statistical tests designed to predict the likelihood that civil wars resolved between 1945 and 1999 would result in a negotiated settlement specifying the different types of power-sharing and power-dividing institutions. Our expectation is that those factors reflecting both the nature of the conflict and the wartime environment play a central role in shaping the prospects that such an arrangement will develop in an effort to end civil war. To initiate our discussion of these tests we identify the variables we use and how they reflect the concepts that inform our theoretical perspective.

DEPENDENT VARIABLE: POWER-SHARING AND POWER-DIVIDING PROVISIONS SPECIFIED AT WAR'S END

Our dependent variable takes the form of the total number of different dimensions of state power that combatants agree to share or divide at the conclusion of hostilities. A high score for the dependent variable is a "4," which reflects an agreement that specifies sharing or dividing state power across political, military, territorial, and economic dimensions. Failure to specify a particular dimension results in a one-unit reduction in the value of the dependent variable; those settlements that fail to specify any power-sharing and power-dividing mechanism are assigned a score of "0." Table 3 identifies the particular types of power-sharing and power-dividing measures included in each of the civil wars that have ended in the post–World War II era. Readers interested in the specific criteria we use for coding civil war settlements will find the coding rules outlined in the Appendix.

 It is important to emphasize that we code only those wars ended via negotiated settlement or truce as including provisions for power-sharing and power-dividing institutions. This coding decision is based on the assumption that the winning side of a conflict has no inducement to share power with those it has defeated; rather, the victor will seek to create those institutions that best allow it to promote its interests, regardless of the costs imposed on others.[3] Even if rare instances exist in which an especially magnanimous party did include provisions for sharing or dividing power following a military victory, the absence of input by defeated groups regarding the particulars associated with these institutions makes it unlikely the latter would ultimately deem these mechanisms a satisfactory means of addressing their interests, thus limiting their desired effect.[4]

Do the architects of negotiated agreements consider any one of the four types of power-sharing or power-dividing measures to be more important or desirable than others in providing for the security of competing groups? One might expect actors emerging from the violence of civil war to be particularly sensitive to issues related to the use of coercive force, followed by attention to the distribution of political power in the reconstructed state, questions regarding territorial control, and, finally, the design of institutions for the distribution of resources. This, at least, is the description numerous

3. This does not necessarily mean, of course, that members of the losing coalition will be permanently excluded from power. For example, as Stephen John Stedman observes of the U.S. Civil War, the only action the victorious North took against Southern secessionist leaders following the end of the war was "the temporary forfeiture of rights of voting and office holding" (1993, 184).

4. A similar logic forms the basis of the decision to code the four instances of peace imposed by third-party actors as cases in which power-sharing and power-dividing institutions are absent. Because these agreements were forced on civil war combatants, there is little reason to expect that the relevant parties would view any new institutional arrangements as sufficient for addressing their postwar security concerns.

Table 3 Power-sharing and power-dividing institutions specified in agreements to end civil wars

Case	Means settled	Political power sharing	Military power sharing	Economic power sharing	Territorial power sharing
Afghanistan (1978–92)	Military				
Algeria (1962–63)	Military				
Angola (1975–89)	Neg. sett				
Angola (1989–91)	Neg. sett	√	√		
Angola (1992–94)	Neg. sett	√	√		√
Argentina (1955–55)	Military				
Azerbaijan (1990–94)	Neg. truce		√		√
Bolivia (1952–52)	Military				
Bosnia (1992–95)	Neg. sett	√	√		√
Burma (1948–51)	Military				
Burma (1968–80)	Neg. truce				
Burma (1983–95)	Military				
Burundi (1965–69)	Military				
Burundi (1972–72)	Military				
Burundi (1988–88)	Military				
Cambodia (1970–75)	Military				
Cambodia (1978–91)	Neg. sett	√	√		
Chad (1979–79)	Neg. sett	√			
Chad (1980–88)	Military				
Chad (1989–96)	Neg. sett	√	√		
Chechnya (1994–96)	Neg. truce	√	√	√	√
China (1946–49)	Military				
China (1956–59)	Military				
China (1967–68)	Military				
Colombia (1948–57)	Neg. sett	√		√	
Congo/Brazza (1993–94)	Neg. truce				
Congo/Brazza (1997–97)	Military				
Congo/Brazza (1998–99)	Neg. truce		√		
Congo/Zaire (1960–65)	Military				
Congo/Zaire (1967–67)	Military				
Congo/Zaire (1996–97)	Military				
Congo/Zaire (1998–99)	Neg. truce		√		
Costa Rica (1948–48)	Neg. sett	√		√	
Croatia (1991–92)	Neg. truce	√			
Croatia (1995–95)	Neg. sett	√			
Cuba (1958–59)	Military				
Cyprus (1963–64)	Imposed				
Cyprus (1974–74)	Imposed				
Djibouti (1991–94)	Neg. sett	√	√		
Dominican Rep. (1965–65)	Neg. sett		√		
El Salvador (1979–92)	Neg. sett	√	√	√	
Ethiopia/Eritrea (1974–91)	Military				
Ethiopia/ideology (1974–91)	Military				

(continued)

Table 3 Continued

Case	Means settled	Political power sharing	Military power sharing	Economic power sharing	Territorial power sharing
Ethiopia/Ogaden (1977–85)	Military				
Georgia/Abk (1992–94)	Neg. truce	✓			✓
Georgia/SO (1989–92)	Neg. truce		✓		✓
Greece (1946–49)	Military				
Guatemala (1954–54)	Military				
Guatemala (1963–96)	Neg. sett			✓	✓
Guinea Bissau (1998–98)	Neg. sett	✓	✓		
Hungary (1956–56)	Military				
India (1946–49)	Neg. sett	✓			✓
India (1948–48)	Military				
Indonesia (1956–60)	Military				
Indonesia (ET: 1975–99)	Neg. sett				✓
Indonesia/Darul I (1953–53)	Military				
Indonesia/Moluc (1950–50)	Military				
Iran (1981–82)	Military				
Iran/rev (1978–79)	Military				
Iraq/Kurd, Shiite (1991–91)	Military				
Iraq/Kurds (1961–70)	Neg. sett	✓		✓	✓
Iraq/Kurds (1974–75)	Military				
Iraq/Shammar (1959–59)	Military				
Israel/Palestine (1948–49)	Imposed				
Jordan (1970–70)	Military				
Kosovo (1998–99)	Neg. sett	✓	✓		✓
Laos (1959–73)	Neg. sett	✓			
Laos/Pathet Lao (1975–75)	Military				
Lebanon (1958–58)	Neg. sett	✓		✓	
Lebanon (1975–89)	Neg. sett	✓	✓		
Liberia (1989–93)	Neg. sett	✓			
Liberia (1994–96)	Neg. sett	✓			
Malaysia (1948–56)	Neg. sett			✓	✓
Mali (1990–95)	Neg. sett	✓	✓	✓	✓
Moldova (1991–92)	Neg. truce	✓		✓	✓
Morocco (1976–91)	Neg. truce				✓
Mozambique (1982–92)	Neg. sett	✓	✓		✓
Nicaragua (1978–79)	Military				
Nicaragua (1981–89)	Neg. sett	✓	✓	✓	✓
Nigeria/Biafra (1967–70)	Military				
Nigeria/Fund Isl (1980–84)	Military				
Pakistan (1971–71)	Military				
Pakistan/Baluch (1973–77)	Military				
Papua N. Guinea (1989–98)	Neg. sett				✓
Paraguay (1947–47)	Military				
Peru (1980–92)	Military				
Philippines (1972–96)	Neg. sett	✓	✓	✓	✓

Case	Means settled	Political power sharing	Military power sharing	Economic power sharing	Territorial power sharing
Philippines/Huks (1950–52)	Military				
Romania (1989–89)	Military				
Rwanda (1963–64)	Military				
Rwanda (1990–93)	Neg. sett	✓	✓	✓	
Rwanda (1994–94)	Military				
Sierra Leone (1992–96)	Neg. sett	✓	✓	✓	
Sierra Leone (1997–99)	Neg. sett	✓	✓	✓	
South Africa (1983–94)	Neg. sett	✓	✓	✓	✓
Sri Lanka (1971–71)	Military				
Sri Lanka (1983–87)	Imposed				
Sudan (1963–72)	Neg. sett		✓	✓	✓
Tajikistan (1992–97)	Neg. sett	✓	✓		
Uganda (1978–79)	Military				
Uganda/Buganda (1966–66)	Military				
Uganda/NRA (1980–86)	Military				
Vietnam (1960–75)	Military				
Yemen (1994–94)	Military				
Yemen/YAR (1948–48)	Military				
Yemen/YAR (1962–70)	Neg. sett	✓	✓	✓	✓
Yemen/YPR (1986–86)	Military				
Zimbabwe (1972–79)	Neg. sett	✓	✓	✓	

case study accounts of the negotiation process provide of the order in which security-related issues have been debated and institutions constructed.[5] However, of the forty-nine negotiated agreements examined in this study, twenty-eight contain a provision mandating the sharing or dividing of military power, thirty-five include a measure focused on the distribution of political power, and twenty-two and nineteen agreements, respectively, include measures designed to address issues regarding the distribution of territorial power and economic resources. We consider this finding to indicate that one cannot a priori assume that adversaries emerging from civil war necessarily view any single power-sharing or power-dividing dimension as more important or desirable than any other.

EXPLANATORY VARIABLES

Nature of the Conflict

Our first category of explanatory variables relates to the nature of the conflict. Our central suggestion is that combatants will prove willing to contem-

5. See, for example, Child 1992, Msabaha 1995, and Byrne 1996.

plate the idea of sharing and dividing government power if they are convinced that they are embroiled in an interminable war that imposes substantial losses. How might combatants know that they are involved in a conflict that is both unwinnable and costly? Or, borrowing the terminology of I. William Zartman, how do enemies know when they are locked in a mutually hurting stalemate?[6] We identify three measures that could provide those involved in the fighting with the most intuitive indications of the conflict's trajectory and their prospects for victory.

The first factor relates to the stakes of the conflict. Scholars often suggest that civil wars centered on identity issues such as ethnic, religious, racial, and linguistic differences are less amenable to compromise than those conflicts focusing on ideological disagreements.[7] Chaim Kaufmann develops this claim in the following terms:

> Civil wars are not all alike. Ethnic conflicts are disputes between communities which see themselves as having distinct heritages, over the power relationship between the communities, while ideological civil wars are contests between factions within the same community over how that community should be governed. The key difference is the flexibility of individual loyalties, which are quite fluid in ideological conflicts, but almost completely rigid in ethnic wars.[8]

Hutu cannot easily become a Tutsi, but a left-leaning politician has the potential to become more conservative or recognize shared policy priorities with her political competitors. Based on this logic, we expect that combatants will view the possibilities of engineering power-sharing and power-dividing arrangements as greater when the war centers on ideological rather than identity-based issues. We represent the *stakes of the conflict* in our statistical test by using a dichotomous indicator that is scored as a "1" if a war is based on divisions associated with identity and a "0" otherwise.

A second indication of the conflict's nature is the length of time that hostilities have persisted. A war that has endured for years without any side gaining a clear upper hand is a powerful indication of the futility of continued conflict; in this sense, lengthy wars have an advantage in encouraging mutual enemies to contemplate the possibility of abandoning the battlefield

6. Zartman 1993.
7. Gurr 1990, Licklider 1993, Kaufmann 1996.
8. Kaufmann 1996, 138.

in favor of sharing and dividing power with their adversaries. Guatemala's civil war, which took place between the years 1963 and 1996, is a case in point. Although the parties to the conflict generally acknowledged that the government's forces were stronger than those of the Guatemalan National Revolutionary Unity (URNG), the army's inability to defeat the rebels led to the longest civil war in our data set—one that ended only when the relevant parties agreed to enter into negotiations.[9] As a reflection of conflict duration, we adopt a measure specifying the number of months between the start of a conflict and its conclusion.

A third aspect of the conflict's nature we consider is the intensity of the war. If a war's persistence indicates that combatants have fought one another to an unproductive stalemate, the number of deaths associated with the violence reflects how costly the conflict has become for the parties involved. The reason for contemplating a negotiated compromise based on the principle of power sharing when parties are embroiled in intense wars yielding high numbers of battle deaths is straightforward: it provides an opportunity to end the carnage without the need for further violence. The civil wars that make up our data set range widely in terms of intensity, from an average low of eighteen battle deaths per month in Mali's civil war to an average high of 27,904 battle deaths per month in one of India's intrastate conflicts. To reflect conflict intensity we use a measure of the number of monthly battle deaths experienced during the conflict.[10]

To summarize, we use these measures—stakes of the conflict, conflict duration, and conflict intensity—based on the view that they define the nature of the conflict and thus the desirability of a negotiated settlement based on the principles of sharing or dividing government power. Our theoretical expectation is that conflicts with the characteristics most conducive to achieving a negotiated settlement are long and costly wars in which the divisions among groups are based on ideological disagreements.

Conflict Environment

While combatants may have a mutual interest in constructing power-sharing and power-dividing institutions, they could still face an environment in which constructing these mechanisms proves quite daunting. This is espe-

9. The URNG, a united front of armed Guatemalan rebel groups, was established in 1981.

10. Note that this measure of conflict intensity is distinct from our indicator for duration, as we operationalize intensity as the average number of deaths in a month rather than the total number of casualties over the course of the entire war. Thus civil wars of longer duration may receive relatively low scores for the conflict intensity measure.

cially likely if the conflict environment is defined by actors inexperienced with the processes of compromise and who perceive negotiations to be challenging in their complexity. To account for factors that could facilitate or discourage the creation of power-sharing and power-dividing mechanisms, we identify four separate indicators that define the crucial characteristics of the conflict environment. Two concern aspects of the domestic environment; the remainder relate to factors that originate beyond the borders of the state emerging from civil war.

The first domestic factor we consider relates to the likelihood that actors involved in the negotiation process will prove amenable to the compromises inherent in the development of a peaceful resolution to conflict. We suggest that countries in which the populations have a previous experience with democracy should have a greater potential to agree to compromises based on sharing or dividing state power. In general, research has indicated that democratic states are less prone to violent domestic conflict, which has been interpreted as demonstrating that democracies have established a norm of bargaining among competing interests that favors peacefully resolving disputes.[11] While a preference for compromise over violence clearly has broken down with the emergence of civil war, an earlier experience with democracy should still enhance the prospects of a successful conclusion to negotiations by ensuring that parties to the emerging peace are familiar with the value of mutually accommodating one another's interests through institutionalized rules of conflict management.

Not all democracies are equivalent to one another in terms of the means by which they channel broad popular grievances or the level of freedom they afford their populations. Recognizing that these differing experiences with democratic governance are likely to impact the degree to which people have a meaningful prior experience with accommodating competing interests, we operationalize the concept of *previous level of democracy* for states emerging from civil war as a measure derived from the Polity IV data set.

The second domestic influence we consider is the level of economic development of the state emerging from war. The rationale for including this

---

11. Gurr 1994, Krain and Myers 1997, and Krain 1998. Regarding the issue of war-proneness, evidence exists of an inverted U–shaped relationship in which consolidated autocracies and consolidated democracies are among the least prone to war (Hegre et al. 2001). We do not control for this relationship in our model because we are interested in norms of bargaining, not war-proneness. We anticipate that the relationship between level of democracy and bargaining norms should be linear, as we have no reason to believe that consolidated autocracies behave like consolidated democracies in terms of fostering a norm of bargaining among competing interests.

measure is based on the recognition that constructing a postwar peace is expensive. More precisely, creating power-sharing and power-dividing institutions often comes with a substantial price tag attached. Whether integrating militaries, expanding the bureaucracy, or providing resources to a previously underprivileged group, each requires prolific spending of government funds. As one example, the Italian government, which played a significant role in helping to broker Mozambique's 1992 General Peace Agreement, called for financial support on the order of $402 million to help implement the military and political power-sharing components of Mozambique's peace accord.[12]

Given that creating power-sharing and power-dividing institutions generates substantial expenses, only countries that are relatively wealthy should have the resources available to produce a substantial array of these mechanisms. At the bargaining table, combatants that reside in poorer states may view the creation of these institutions as being simply beyond their means. As our proxy measure of the *level of economic development* of a country we use the life expectancy among the population in the year following the end of the war. This measure has been used by others to indicate development based on the logic that those countries that are capable of ensuring both the nutrition and health of their populations are typically among the wealthiest states.[13]

Conditions that define the conflict environment are not limited to what occurs within the borders of a state. Here we seek to account for influences originating outside the country that also have the potential to shape the conflict environment and thus influence the degree of ease or difficulty enemies face in efforts to construct power-sharing or power-dividing agreements through a bargaining process. The two factors we consider are the presence of peacekeepers and the structure of the international system.

Turning to the influence of peacekeepers, there is a growing consensus among scholars that introducing foreign troops into a country emerging from civil war is an effective means of addressing the pervasive security concerns that define these states. Peacekeepers are seen as discouraging a return to war by guaranteeing the safety of all parties to the conflict.[14] We

12. The funds, which the Rome government solicited from the international donor community, were slated to be used to support demilitarization and the electoral process. In addition, some were to help fund general emergency assistance requirements. The international donor community ultimately agreed to provide $308 million of the money that had been requested (Alden 1995, 105).

13. Doyle and Sambanis 2000.

14. Walter 1997, 1999, 2002; Doyle and Sambanis 2000; Hartzell, Hoddie, and Rothchild 2001; Hartzell and Hoddie 2003.

expect the promised introduction of peacekeepers to have an impact even before the force's boots hit the ground in the state emerging from war by influencing collectivities' perceptions concerning the feasibility and value of establishing a power-sharing or power-dividing arrangement. Specifically, we anticipate that a group's leaders will be more amenable to participating in the bargaining process and more willing to cede positions of power if there is an attendant realization that they will not immediately bear sole responsibility for providing for the collectivity's security. Feeling that they can rely on peacekeepers to ensure their safety, parties to the conflict should prove less reluctant to work alongside their former adversaries. The indicator we use to reflect the *use of peacekeeping troops* is a dichotomous variable scored with a "1" if peacekeeping troops were introduced following the end of the conflict and a "0" otherwise.

A second factor originating outside the state that we take into consideration is the structure of the international system. Specifically, we are concerned with whether the conflict took place during or after the years of superpower confrontation associated with the cold war. Earlier studies typically have found that the end of the cold war has improved the prospects for the peaceful termination of civil wars based on principles of mutual compromise and accommodation. Informed speculation as to why this proves to be the case has centered on outside powers' refusal to fund proxy wars and competitively arm the warring parties since the end of the East-West conflict.[15] Echoing this perspective, we expect that the end of the cold war will also mean a lessened complexity to negotiations as the superpowers are unlikely to have a vested interest in the results of the war and thus a reduced motivation to become active players at the bargaining table. The presence of the great powers during negotiations, if it is felt at all, will be limited to serving as a mediator or guarantor to the emerging peace.

The civil war in Cambodia, lasting between 1978 and 1991, illustrates the importance of the end of the cold war for improving the prospects for generating negotiated settlements founded on the principles of sharing or dividing state power. Michael Doyle characterizes the outside influence on this civil war in the following terms:

> The Cambodian civil war also resembled the international proxy wars of the cold war. Each of the factions depended on a foreign patron, which waged war against the other patrons over Cambo-

15. Hampson 1990, Wallensteen and Sollenberg 1997.

dian soil. The United States had backed the republican forces (now become KPNLF); Russia backed the SOC; China, the Khmer Rouge; the Europeans, the princely faction, FUNIPEC. To a significant extent the civil war was an international war; and the international war was "civil"—a war among ideologies to determine not just who but what "way of life" would govern Cambodia. The international community, which in the post–cold war period is promoted as the solution to the security dilemmas of civil wars, was here its cause.[16]

Only after the cold war reached its conclusion were the major powers willing to serve the interests of peace in Cambodia by participating at the bargaining table as facilitators of an agreement rather than as allies of interests within the state. To capture this important transformation in the relationship among the major powers, we measure the *international system structure* in our statistical tests with a dichotomous variable that is scored as a "0" for conflicts ended during the period of the cold war and "1" if the war concluded after the era of superpower competition.

   In summary, we argue that two conditions play a critical role in shaping the potential that a country will conclude its civil war through a negotiated agreement emphasizing the sharing or dividing of state power. Factors defining both the nature of the conflict as well as the domestic and international wartime environments determine whether combatants will view the creation of power-sharing or power-dividing institutions as both desirable and possible. We offer an outline of the variables examined in our tested models in table 4.

The Issue of Third-Party Mediation

We have chosen to omit the influence of third-party mediators from our list of factors originating outside the state with the potential to encourage the adoption of power-sharing and power-dividing arrangements at the end of civil war. At first impression, this might appear to be an important oversight, given that a wide array of case studies has pointed to the central role of mediators in bridging the divide among competing interests at the bargaining table. Prominent among these studies are those pointing to the critical importance of British mediator Lord Carrington in moving forward the

16. Doyle 1999, 192.

Table 4 Summary of variables used to predict the number of power-sharing and power-dividing institutions after civil war

Variable	Operationalization	Expected relationship
Nature of the conflict		
Stakes of the conflict	Identity-based civil war	−
Conflict duration	Months war endured prior to settlement	+
Conflict intensity	Monthly casualty rate of the war	+
Conflict environment		
Domestic Conflict Environment		
Previous level of democracy	Level of democracy associated with the prewar government	+
Level of development	Life expectancy in the postwar state	+
International Conflict Environment		
Peacekeeping operation	Introduction of a peacekeeping force	+
International system structure	War concluded in the Cold War or post–Cold War era	+

negotiations in Rhodesia (present-day Zimbabwe) that finally led to the end of the civil war between the black majority and governing white minority.[17]

Yet two unrealistic assumptions would have to be made to argue that mediators should be included in our statistical analysis. First, we would have to assume that mediators have a consistent concern in encouraging the sharing and dividing of political power among competing interests following civil war. This is a decidedly problematic belief—just as divisions exist within the academic community concerning the assessment of the value of sharing and dividing power, there are disagreements among policy-makers about whether such mechanisms are a legitimate means of conflict management.[18] In this sense, the presence of mediators is no guarantee that they will necessarily push for the option of introducing new power-sharing and power-dividing institutions.

A second necessarily problematic assumption tied to including a variable reflecting the role of mediators is the suggestion that we could identify all intermediaries involved in the peace process. This becomes challenging be-

17. See Rothchild 1997 for a discussion of tactics mediators might employ in facilitating a settlement. Walter 1997 cites the following studies of the negotiations to end civil war in Rhodesia: Vance 1983, Davidow 1984, and Stedman 1991.

18. We discuss critics of the power-sharing solution to civil conflict (most prominently Donald Horowitz and Philip Roeder) in the Conclusion of this book.

cause mediators are often interested in keeping a low profile and thus limiting the potential that they would themselves create distractions from the task at hand. It is thus often quite difficult to nail down whether a mediator was actually present and exactly what role this actor played in the peace process. For example, how would one interpret the role played by President Bill Clinton's effort in the final year of his presidency to facilitate the end of civil conflict in Burundi? At the request of former South African President Mandela, Clinton made his presence felt at the peace talks though a brief video conference call. Is this action sufficient to define Clinton as a "mediator" involved in the conflict's resolution?[19]

Testing the Argument

We now turn to tests intended to determine whether influences associated with both the nature of the conflict and the civil war environment have a measurable impact on the adoption of power-sharing arrangements. Our tests consider all civil wars ended between 1945 and 1999. The initial dependent variable takes the form of the number of power-sharing and power-dividing provisions specified in a settlement at the end of each civil war with values ranging between "0" and "4." Recall that a "0" reflects instances in which no power-sharing or power-dividing arrangements were established with the end of the conflict; scores between "1" and "4" reflect the total number of types of institutions associated with sharing and/or dividing the political, military, territorial, and economic bases of state power created at the conclusion of a civil war.

We adopt an ordered probit model for our analysis. The choice of this statistical approach is based on an expectation that an underlying continuous measure to power sharing can be observed through the four separate aspects of political, military, territorial, and economic power-sharing and power-dividing institutions. Using this statistical methodology is also consistent with our theoretical argument that including multiple types of power-sharing or power-dividing institutions enhances the prospects of ensuring a stable postwar peace.[20]

19. Walter 1997 includes a measure of mediation in her statistical study of factors associated with the negotiated end of civil war; she finds that this variable is only weakly associated with a peaceful end to conflict. She notes that the measure is inadequate to the task of reflecting the role of mediators—coded as whether or not any mediator was present at negotiations.

20. The adoption of this methodological approach distinguishes this chapter from previous

We test our hypotheses regarding the factors that predict the content of a given settlement in two different ways. In the first instance, we seek to predict only the content of fully negotiated political settlements of civil wars. Our reason for focusing on this type of settlement in isolation is that these agreements are unique in the sense that adversaries have chosen to directly address the question of who controls state power in the war-ending bargain. In this first test, we effectively discount the implications of power-sharing and power-dividing institutions that may be agreed to as part of a negotiated truce by assigning the eleven civil wars concluded in this fashion scores of "o" for the dependent variable.[21]

In our second test of the factors that predict settlement content we relax our definition of the kinds of arrangements that might be considered instances of power sharing and power dividing, broadening them to include negotiated truces as well as fully negotiated political settlements of civil war. We could plausibly argue that this is actually the most appropriate specification for our test as it includes all institutions developed at war's end that require sharing or dividing power among former combatants. Although in the case of negotiated truces the original intention behind creating these institutions is that they have a temporary existence, in quite a number of instances they effectively have performed the functions of conflict management for extended periods of time. This has proved to be the case, for example, in the unexpectedly durable negotiated truces that have persisted in the state of Georgia between the government and the regions of Abkhazia and South Ossetia. In this test of our model we allow the score on the dependent variable to vary from "o" to "4" for both negotiated political settlements and negotiated truces.

The second and third columns of table 5 display the results of the test in which we predict the content of negotiated civil war settlements. The overall model proves statistically significant and has a pseudo-R^2 value of 0.17. Among the seven independent variables included in the test, three indicators

---

work concerning the resolution of civil wars. For example, in her statistical study, Walter (2002, 100–101) finds that both the duration of the civil war and the presence of a third-party security guarantee are statistically significant predictors of reaching a power-sharing pact. The approach we adopt in this chapter differs substantially from Walter's in that we do not operationalize our dependent variable as either the presence or absence of a power-sharing agreement. Instead we focus on the odds of adopting any of four possible types of power-sharing or power-dividing institutions: the political, military, territorial, and economic bases of state power.

21. Because civil wars ended via a military victory are also assigned scores of "o" for the dependent variable, in this first test the only settlement type for which the score on the dependent variable varies from "o" to "4" is the fully negotiated political settlement.

Table 5 Predictors of settlement content after civil war

Ordered probit model

Variable	Predicting content of civil war settlements		Predicting content of civil war settlements and truces	
	Coefficient	Percent change in odds for standard deviation increase	Coefficient	Percent change in odds for standard deviation increase
Nature of the conflict				
Stakes of the conflict	−0.19 (0.28)	−0.09	0.004 (0.27)	0.002
Conflict duration (logged)	0.41*** (0.11)	0.81 (.1)	0.37***	0.74
Conflict intensity (logged)	−0.14* (0.08)	−0.27	−0.16** (0.08)	−0.32
Domestic conflict environment				
Previous level of democracy	0.02 (0.03)	0.12	0.03 (0.02)	0.17
Level of development	−0.01 (0.01)	−0.07	0.01 (0.01)	0.11
International conflict environment				
Introduction of a peacekeeping operation	0.98*** (0.29)	0.47	0.78*** (0.27)	0.37
International system structure	0.2 (0.28)	0.1	0.62** (0.27)	0.31
Cut 1	0.51 (1.01)		0.98 0.98	
Cut 2	0.81 (1.01)		1.44 (0.99)	
Cut 3	1.36 (1.01)		2.09 (0.99)	
Cut 4	2.15 (1.03)		2.83 (1.01)	
N	106		106	
Log likelihood	−97.36		−106.7	
Prob > chi²	0.0000		0.0000	
Pseudo R²	0.17		0.2	

Values in parentheses are standard errors. All tests are two-tailed.
***p < 0.01
**p < 0.05
*p < 0.1

prove to have a statistically significant influence on shaping the odds that a post–civil war state will develop power-sharing and power-dividing institutions.

In terms of the variables we categorize as defining the nature of the conflict, both the indicators reflecting the duration and intensity of the war have a demonstrable effect on the settlement's content. A standard deviation increase in the war's length increases the odds that power-sharing provisions will be specified in an agreement by 81 percent. This confirms Zartman's expectation that wars that have dragged on for extended periods of time encourage combatants to contemplate the possibility of compromise with their enemies.

Although only statistically significant at the 0.1 level, the conflict intensity variable also appears to influence the number of power-sharing and power-dividing institutions specified in an agreement. This finding, however, is contrary to our initial expectations. Recall that we had hypothesized that wars defined by higher numbers of monthly casualties should increase the willingness of combatants to compromise by creating power-sharing and power-dividing institutions in order to quickly stop the killing. The results indicate, however, that settlement architects actually prove *less* inclined to design provisions for sharing and dividing state power when wars yield substantial monthly casualties. A standard deviation increase in the number of war dead reduces the odds of power-sharing or power-dividing institutions being present in an agreement by approximately 27 percent. What accounts for this relationship? We interpret it to indicate that a higher monthly casualty rate establishes a sense of mutual grievance and suspicion among combatants that challenges any efforts at mutual compromise. Having lost friends and relatives to the war, individuals are understandably wary about the idea of compromise and interaction with those they know to be responsible for the killing.

A further finding of the test is that conditions associated with the domestic conflict environment have no apparent effect on the odds that negotiators will agree to power-sharing or power-dividing arrangements at war's end. Neither the variables associated with the ease of negotiations and compromise (as reflected in the country's previous experience with democracy) nor those that might encourage negotiators to consider the creation of new, costly institutions as viable (as reflected in the state's level of development) prove influential in determining the number of power-sharing and power-dividing arrangements.

Finally, a single variable related to the international conflict environment has a statistically significant impact on the odds that provisions for power-sharing and power-dividing will appear as part of a negotiated settlement. The promised introduction of peacekeepers increases the odds of power-sharing and power-dividing provisions appearing within a settlement by approximately 47 percent. We emphasize here that we *do not* interpret this as indicating that third-party actors are themselves encouraging the adoption of power-sharing and power-dividing institutions. Rather, by reducing the commitment problem associated with negotiated settlements (specifically, the fear that one's adversaries may defect from the settlement with negative consequences for the security of one's group), the presence of peacekeepers appears to encourage groups to have a greater willingness to construct power-sharing and power-dividing institutions.

We turn now to the test in which we seek to predict the content of negotiated agreements—the thirty-eight negotiated political settlements of civil wars plus the eleven negotiated truces that succeeded in ending intrastate conflicts for at least some period of time. The results of this test appear in the fourth and fifth columns of table 5. In this instance, the statistically significant model has a pseudo-R^2 of 0.2 and four of the independent variables we test prove to have a statistically significant effect on the content of the negotiated agreements.

With this specification of the dependent variable, the findings concerning the nature of the conflict are largely consistent with the first set of results. The variable reflecting the number of months a war has endured proves statistically significant with a standard deviation increase in the conflict's duration heightening the odds of power-sharing and power-dividing provisions appearing in a negotiated agreement by approximately 74 percent; conversely, a standard deviation increase in a war's monthly casualty rate decreases the odds of power-sharing and power-dividing provisions appearing in an agreement by approximately 32 percent.

As with the original test, none of the variables associated with the domestic conflict environment have a statistically significant influence on the specification of power-sharing or power-dividing institutions in a settlement. Among factors associated with the international conflict environment, the test identifies both the variables reflecting the introduction of peacekeepers and the international system structure as affecting the number of power-sharing and power-dividing institutions specified in an agreement. The presence of a peacekeeping operation increases the odds of power-sharing and power-dividing provisions in a settlement by 37 percent. A settlement or cease-fire negotiated since the end of the cold war has a 31 percent chance of power-sharing or power-dividing provisions being specified within its text.[22]

Conclusion

What conclusions might be drawn from the foregoing analysis? First, the findings do point to the importance of the nature of the conflict in determining the degree to which power-sharing and power-dividing institutions appear at the conclusion of civil war. This should have important policy implications for mediators who might want to encourage the use of power-sharing and power-dividing mechanisms as a means of managing conflict. Specifically, the environments in which mediators' efforts have the strongest potential for gaining traction and meeting with success are those in which the war has proved enduring enough to indicate to each side the limited prospects for military victory while simultaneously yielding a number of casualties that is sufficiently small to minimize any sense of bitterness among contenders for state power.

Also notable is that the factors defining the domestic conflict environment failed in each test to influence definitively the number of power-sharing or power-dividing institutions adversaries agreed to construct as part of a civil war settlement. To a certain extent, this is good news for those who seek to foster power-sharing and power-dividing institutions within post–civil war states. Even if a state's inhabitants are inexperienced with the practices of democratic compromise and lack the wealth to finance the development of new initiatives, they can still develop institutions that could encourage cooperation with former enemies. In short, the conditions that define a country's level of political and economic development are not determinants of their capacity to agree to sharing or dividing state power.

Finally, and perhaps most surprising, factors originating from the international conflict environment do play an important role in conditioning the prospects for sharing and dividing power within a state. The most consistent important outside influence is the introduction of peacekeepers. Our results suggest that the international community's promised deployment of an in-

22. In order to evaluate the robustness of our results, we also performed these two tests using the alternative model specification of negative binomial regression. When using this count model, the substantive results prove entirely consistent with the findings we report in the text. The same variables prove to have a determining effect on the specification of power-sharing and power-dividing institutions at the negotiated end to civil war.

ternational peacekeeping force may play the previously unanticipated role of motivating adversaries to construct power-sharing and power-dividing institutions. We suggest that they have this effect based on their capacity to foster an environment of security in which constructing arrangements appears to be less of a risk. In this sense, the international community may want to further consider the question of whether the most significant role these forces can play with respect to civil wars is that of peacemakers, peacekeepers, or some continuum that involves these and other roles for these actors.

Having addressed the question of factors associated with the creation of power-sharing and power-dividing institutions, in the next chapter we seek to demonstrate the value of employing these mechanisms in the aftermath of civil war. Specifically, we consider how these institutions facilitate an enduring peace among former combatants still suspicious of their former adversaries' intentions and concerned about maintaining the collectivity's security.

3

INSTITUTIONALIZING AN ENDURING PEACE

Successfully negotiating a peace agreement to end civil war does not ensure that the peace former foes have constructed will prove enduring. Among the forty-nine negotiated civil war peace agreements established in the post–World War II era, eighteen eventually collapsed and experienced a reinitiation of hostilities. What accounts for the difference between peace agreements that last and those that fall apart? If most of these settlements have in common a call for the creation of power-sharing and-power dividing institutions, what explains why some stick and others break down? These questions are pressing ones in light of continuing efforts to secure an enduring peace in the many states still plagued by civil war.

The argument we develop in this chapter is that the durability of peace agreements to end civil wars is enhanced by creating greater numbers of power-sharing and power-dividing institutions. Holding all other influences constant, the agreements most resistant to collapse require sharing or dividing power across all four dimensions of state power—political, military, territorial, and economic. While earlier research has suggested that a relationship exists between particular aspects of power sharing and an enduring peace, the argument we advance here is unique in emphasizing the value of employing such mechanisms across as many different dimensions of state power as possible.

In order to demonstrate the validity of this claim, we report the results of a series of statistical tests focusing on states emerging from civil war by the process of negotiated agreement since the end of the World War II. In each of these tests, one finding remains consistent and robust—greater numbers of power-sharing and power-dividing institutions enhance the prospects for an enduring peace among former adversaries. We interpret this relationship between power sharing and peace to indicate that these mechanisms have the desired effect of reassuring former combatants that they will be neither marginalized nor threatened by their former adversaries in the context of the postwar state.

Theoretical Perspective

Conflict is present in every society.[1] If this conflict is to be expressed through means other than the use of force, however, institutions must be constructed that clarify exactly how groups are expected to interact and compete with one another. This is particularly important in a postwar environment in which the institutions that had previously existed for the management of conflict have been under siege and, in some cases, may even have ceased to function.

When civil wars end by military victory, the winners presumably have the power to both establish the new conflict-management institutions they favor and to enforce the rules of the game. Although the losing side may dislike the victor's choice of institutions, and may even feel that the new governing structures could threaten their safety and livelihood, a painful awareness exists that they are not in a position to prevent the establishment of these institutions.[2] In contrast, if parties to a civil conflict elect to end hostilities via a fully negotiated settlement or negotiated truce, new conflict-management institutions must be constructed through mutual consent. Requiring the accommodation of competing interests, creating new governing institutions through the process of negotiation will almost always prove challenging, but the need to ensure that these institutions function in a manner that is acceptable to all groups is imperative, given that no party to the conflict has experienced a defeat that decisively excludes them from the political arena.

What are the most appropriate sets of institutions for preserving peace following the negotiated conclusion of civil wars? As we argued in Chapter 1, the concerns of antagonists that the postwar state may fall under the con-

1. Coser 1956.
2. Defeated powers can, of course, regroup at some point following the end of a war and contest these new rules using a variety of means, including the reinitiation of conflict. Focusing on interstate wars, Suzanne Werner (1999) concludes that belligerents are most likely to resume a conflict when changes, including the distribution of power among the former opponents, alter the perceived value of the original arrangement.

trol of a single collectivity hostile to their interests are best addressed through the creation of power-sharing and power-dividing institutions. Institutions that share, divide, or balance power among competing groups can help foster a sense of security among groups that would be unlikely to exist if power were concentrated in the hands of a single faction.

More than simply agreeing to share or divide power, we view former combatants as best served by settlements that specify power-sharing and power-dividing mechanisms across as many of the four dimensions of state power as possible. Agreements to share or divide power across the political, military, territorial, and economic dimensions offer four distinct advantages for antagonists as they emerge from the hostilities generated by civil war. First, and most intuitive, power-sharing and power-dividing mechanisms provide each contending group with a degree of influence within government that it would lack in the absence of the negotiated agreement.[3] With each additional power-sharing dimension specified in an agreement, a group's vested interest in maintaining and enforcing the terms of the settlement increases based on the recognition that its current level of influence within the postwar state is dependent on the continuing maintenance of peace. Groups also have the potential to use the range of powers ceded to them as part of an agreement to check any efforts by their competitors to win full control of the apparatus of the state; it is hard to imagine that there is any stronger deterrent to the idea of expelling your adversaries from the legislature than the fact that their co-partisans retain positions within the military.

Second, different dimensions of power-sharing or power-dividing institutions have the potential to reinforce one another. Territorial autonomy, for example, can be used to help reduce the stakes of competition among rival groups in a divided society by enabling a collectivity to rise within its own state bureaucracies and educational systems. This effect is likely to be reinforced if a settlement requires economic power-sharing measures that guarantee the allocation of resources to the same group that has been granted territorial autonomy. Malaysia's 1956 civil war settlement, which called for precisely this combination of power-dividing and power-sharing institutions, proved sufficiently reassuring to secure a peace that has now endured for more than forty years.

Third, extensively institutionalized settlements can also help enforce a set-

3. Combatants certainly hold less power than they would have had they won the war. As we suggested in Chapter 2, that they have initiated negotiations to conclude hostilities suggests a realization among the leadership of the respective groups that they are incapable of achieving monopoly control of the state.

tlement and foster long-term peace by serving as a source of protection for groups should any single power-sharing provision of the settlement not be implemented. Former adversaries' failure to follow through with creating the institutions to which they agree as part of the terms of a settlement can occur for a variety of different reasons. In some instances, parties may simply negotiate a settlement in bad faith—agreeing to create power-sharing or power-dividing institutions they have little or no intention of implementing. In other cases, groups may have every intention of carrying out the provisions of the agreement but confront obstacles that stymie progress toward fulfilling those obligations. This might occur because of miscommunication or misinformation regarding the expectations associated with the implementation process or a simple lack of financial resources that would allow them to establish and fund the institutional mechanisms outlined in an agreement.

Economic constraints appear to be at the heart of the problems associated with the implementation process in Nicaragua following the signing of the 1989 civil war settlement by the government and rebels. With the cessation of hostilities, the government was frustrated in its efforts to fund its postwar promises by both the slow release of foreign aid funds by the United States as well as pressures from the International Monetary Fund to undertake structural adjustment measures intended to reduce government spending. Given limited funds, President Violeta Barrios de Chamorro was unable to purchase land promised to the contra rebels for the creation of development "zones" intended to provide a form of territorial autonomy. That the Nicaraguan settlement did not collapse despite the failure to follow through on this commitment may in part be attributed to the settlement's call for three other forms of power-sharing and power-dividing institutions that also helped provide some measure of security for the parties to the agreement.

Finally, the act of agreeing to an extensive array of power-sharing and power-dividing mechanisms can itself help stabilize peace by demonstrating the adversaries' willingness to recognize and accommodate one another's interests. As described in the Introduction, group leaders incur costs by agreeing to a settlement containing power-sharing and power-dividing measures. These arrangements effectively end the pursuit of monopoly control of the state that often motivates the initiation of civil war and exposes elites favoring conciliation to charges that they are "selling out" to the enemy.

Settlements that consist of an extensive array of power-sharing and power-dividing institutions prove the most costly as they place the sharpest constraints on each group's authority and provide the clearest indication of the settlement's costs to potential critics. As a result, leaders who agree to design extensively institutionalized settlements are sending their adversaries a clear signal of their commitment to the agreement through their willingness to pay a steep price in the interest of peace.[4]

This certainly proved to be the case for Nur Misuari, leader of the Moro National Liberation Front, following his signing of a settlement intended to end more than two decades of war in the Philippines. Reactions to Misuari's acceding to the agreement ranged from challenges to his leadership from within his own ranks to the formation of new rebel groups committed to establishing a separate Muslim state in Mindanao. Misuari's willingness to withstand these costly challenges convinced the central government in Manila of his sincere interest in a peaceful end to war.

Explanations for the Endurance of Peace Following Negotiated Agreements

Promises by formerly warring groups to respect one another's security in the postwar environment, demonstrated through the mutual creation of power-sharing and power-dividing mechanisms, should help ensure an enduring peace. The degree to which peace agreements include such provisions is not, of course, the only factor that may account for the longevity of a civil war's negotiated settlements. In what follows we explore three distinct, but not mutually exclusive, explanations for the duration of post–civil war peace. These three explanations highlight in turn the importance of the nature of the conflict, the postconflict environment, and the terms of the settlement. Careful readers will note that the indicators we consider here, with the exception of the terms of the settlement, parallel those discussed in Chapter 2.

THE NATURE OF THE CONFLICT

The first explanation for differences in the length of time that peace endures following the signing of a negotiated agreement focuses on the nature of the conflict at the heart of each war. A number of scholars suggest that the particular attributes of some civil wars not only make them more difficult to end than others but, once concluded, may also make them more prone to a rapid return to conflict. Specifically, conflicts associated with the greatest

4. This suggests that the process of agreeing to an extensive array of power-sharing and power-dividing mechanisms may itself reflect a predisposition for abiding by an agreement. In this sense, power-sharing and power-dividing institutions serve to communicate, and perhaps reinforce, the desire among former enemies to allow peace to endure.

ongoing security concerns among belligerents at the termination of the war are the ones thought to be the most fragile and potentially short lived. Worried not only about threats to their interests but also to their very physical safety, collectivities emerging from conflicts characterized as high risk in nature are believed to be predisposed to interpret potentially innocuous actions by their opponents in the worst possible light, reacting in a fashion that may contribute to the breakdown of the settlement.

Such a process appears to have been at work in the case of the Sudan, for example, when, some years after civil war ended via settlement in 1972, President Gaafar al-Nimeiry imposed Islamic *sharia* law upon the entire country, including the formerly secessionist south. Viewing *sharia* as a harsh legal system that violated the human rights and cultural autonomy of the largely non-Muslim peoples of the south, the formerly rebellious region of the Sudan interpreted this move on the part of the government as a symbol of the north's weakening commitment to the terms of the peace settlement. Within months of the imposition of *sharia,* as well as a series of other acts on the part of Nimeiry's government, guerrilla activities resumed in the southern part of the state.[5]

The nature of civil conflict may shape the security concerns of former belligerents and thus affect the duration of peace in three principal ways. The first is in terms of the issues thought to be at stake in the civil war. A number of scholars suggest that identity conflicts (e.g., wars that hinge on ethnic, racial, religious, and linguistic differences) are less conducive to compromise and resolution than are civil wars centered on ideological issues (e.g., conflicts between adherents to capitalist and communist ideologies).[6] The logic of this claim is based on the view that while ideologies may be amended or moderated in the spirit of mutual accommodation, locating middle ground is more difficult when issues tied to largely fixed and unchanging identity differences are the focus of dispute. In the context of the postwar state, differences centered on ideology may blur or even fade as memories of the conflict become more distant; conversely, identity differences are often inescapable and mark every interaction among communities. Thus, we expect that identity-based civil wars will be associated with greater overall security concerns given that members of the competing communities are continually reminded of the differences that formed the basis of the conflict. As a result, peace should be of shorter duration following the nego-

5. Rothchild and Hartzell 1992.
6. Gurr 1990, Licklider 1993, Kaufmann 1996.

tiated conclusion of conflicts rooted in identity issues. We use the same indicator for stakes of the conflict that we adopted in Chapter 2—a dichotomous variable scored as a "1" for all wars based on issues of identity and a "0" otherwise. Twenty-three of the thirty-eight civil wars (60.5 percent) we examine that were ended via fully negotiated settlements were identity based in nature, whereas nine of the eleven intrastate conflicts (82 percent) in which the fighting was brought to a halt via negotiated truce were conflicts of an identity nature.

Civil conflicts may also further differ in two ways with the potential to impact former adversaries' security perceptions. One of these is the duration of the conflict. Lengthy civil wars provide parties to the conflict an opportunity to gather information concerning their chances for victory.[7] Should a war grind on for many years, belligerents are likely to become increasingly pessimistic about the prospects of defeating their adversaries on the battlefield. Not only should this make a negotiated settlement appear as an attractive alternative to continuing the war, it may also underscore the importance and value of working to nurture and protect a nascent peace once it is established. If battlefield experiences convince enemies that they cannot prevail in war, adversaries may well conclude that their interests and security have the greatest potential to be augmented through cooperation with wartime opponents. Peace should thus prove more durable if the negotiated agreement ends a conflict that lasted for an extended period of time. To analyze the effect that civil war duration has on the longevity of peace agreements, we use the same measure of the indicator conflict duration as appeared in Chapter 2—the number of months that transpire between the start of a conflict and its conclusion. The duration of the conflicts in our data set ranges from three months, in the case of the 1995 civil war in Croatia, to 406 months, or nearly thirty-four years, in the case of Guatemala's 1963–96 civil war.

Finally, the intensity of a civil war, or the number of deaths associated with the violence, can also affect combatants' sense of security once the war ends. We expect wars characterized by high casualty rates to produce the most profound security concerns and the lowest levels of trust among the relevant actors. The levels of violence involved in these conflicts and the seemingly unrelenting nature of the violence are likely to foster particularly intense concerns about future interactions with former enemies. In aggregate, these concerns should mean that former opponents will have limited enthusiasm for cooperating to manage future conflict. Because wars charac-

7. Mason, Weingarten, and Fett 1999.

terized by high casualty rates erode antagonists' commitment to peace, these conflicts are less likely than wars of lesser intensity to be followed by an enduring postsettlement peace. Our analysis of the effects of civil war intensity on the duration of peace agreements uses the same measure of the indicator *conflict intensity* as appeared in Chapter 2—the number of monthly battle deaths experienced during the course of the civil war. The conflicts in our data set range in intensity from an average of twenty-six deaths per month in the case of Djibouti (1991–94) to 27,904 deaths per month during India's civil war (1946–49).

THE POSTCONFLICT ENVIRONMENT

Civil wars and the processes by which they are resolved do not take place in a void. These conflicts are instead played out within a variety of environments, each of which holds the capacity to shape the likelihood of war initiation, the manner in which conflict transpires, the possibilities of settlement, and the longevity of peace. Here we focus on two parameters of what we refer to as the postconflict environment—the domestic and international circumstances in which the nascent peace develops. With respect to the domestic environment, we explore conditions that should make committing to a stable peace in the wake of a negotiated agreement to end a civil war easier for some countries but not others. In particular, we focus on how former regime type and present level of economic development affect the duration of peace. At the international level, we investigate the effects that both the decision by outside actors to introduce a peacekeeping force and the structure of the international system may have on civil war adversaries' commitment to an enduring peace.

Students of civil wars have considered a wide range of factors associated with the domestic environment in an effort to address a variety of questions related to the conflict process.[8] The measures we elect to include in this study are selected based on our theoretical emphasis on the security concerns former antagonists face at the end of a civil war. As we detail below,

---

8. In their study of the determinants of civil war onset for the period 1945–99, for example, James Fearon and David Laitin (2003) analyze the influence of factors such as the size of a state's population, its level of ethnic diversity, geographical features (e.g., whether or not the terrain is mountainous), a country's trade openness (i.e., the extent to which trade accounts for a share of the country's gross domestic product), and the percentage of a country's exports that is composed of primary commodities such as oil and diamonds, among other variables. Michael Doyle and Nicholas Sambanis (2000) focus on many of the same variables in their study of peacebuilding success following civil war.

both a previous experience with democracy and higher levels of economic development can mitigate the doubts groups may have regarding the capacity of a negotiated civil war agreement to ensure their future safety.

Negotiated peace agreements constructed by actors with previous experience with the institutions of democracy should have an advantage in maintaining peace in comparison to states unfamiliar with the practices of open political competition. Generally speaking, individuals residing in countries that were democratic prior to the outbreak of civil war tend to have more experience with accommodating competing interests than do citizens of authoritarian regimes. Familiarity with democratic processes, particularly the practices of communication and compromise, should augment former antagonists' sense of trust that the institutions they have designed will foster cooperation among former competitors. With some fifty years of experience with democratic institutions, for example, the architects of Costa Rica's negotiated settlement fully expected that the institutions they designed would regulate conflict in a peaceful manner, much as had been the case before the outbreak of armed conflict in 1948.[9] In sum, the more democratic a country's political regime was prior to the outbreak of civil war, the greater the potential that the country will experience an enduring peace following the war's end. In keeping with our use of the variable *previous level of democracy* in Chapter 2, we operationalize this concept using a measure derived from the Polity IV data set.

Following a civil war, economic conditions in some countries may prove more conducive to helping to stabilize peace than is the case elsewhere. Countries with higher levels of economic development are in a better position to promote reconstruction, provide jobs for unemployed soldiers, and direct resources to previously neglected regions that may have been popular recruiting grounds for rebel soldiers.[10] In the case of negotiated peace agreements emphasizing the creation of power-sharing and power-dividing institutions, countries with greater wealth should have an easier time creating and maintaining the institutions mandated by the settlement. The ability to implement these commitments should not only allay the security concerns they were originally designed to address, but should, in turn, help foster an

9. The authors of Costa Rica's settlement did not, however, rely solely on the presence of majoritarian democratic institutions to stabilize peace. Rather, they designed power-sharing and power-dividing measures that included abolishing the national army in order to guarantee that no single party would be able to control that institution and use it to threaten the interests of others.

10. Krishna Kumar (1997) posits that those settlements that are best able to engage in rehabilitation of this nature are the ones that have a higher likelihood of being followed by an enduring peace.

increased sense of confidence in and commitment to the agreement that ended the civil war. Based on this logic, we expect a more durable peace to follow negotiated agreements that end civil wars in countries characterized by higher levels of economic development. The most intuitive and frequently used measure of a country's wealth is its gross domestic product (GDP) per capita—the value of goods and services produced by a state in a single year divided by the size of the population. Because data related to the economy for many of the countries we consider simply do not exist, we instead use an alternate measure, also used by other scholars, as a means of gauging the overall strength of the economy.[11] Our indicator of the *level of economic development* is the average life expectancy at birth among the population for the first year following the end of the civil war. The performance of the countries in our data set with respect to this measure ranges from a low of thirty-seven years of life expectancy in Sierra Leone in the wake of both of its civil wars (1992–96, 1997–99) to a high of seventy-three years following the end of the civil war in Bosnia (1992–95).

Turning now to the international dimension of the conflict environment, we focus on the effect that factors originating in the international system may have on adversaries' sense of security and thus on the likelihood they will behave in a manner conducive to fostering an enduring peace. First, a number of scholars have found that civil war settlements are unlikely to prove stable unless the terms of the agreement are enforced by a third party.[12] Third parties are called upon to "guarantee that groups will be protected, terms will be fulfilled, and promises will be kept."[13] Introducing peacekeepers committed to intervene in order to provide for the safety of former belligerents is meant to reassure actors that their pledges to abide by the negotiated peace agreement will not leave them vulnerable. Settlements calling for the presence of peacekeepers to reinforce peace should thus be more likely to produce a durable peace than those making no provision for the introduction of such actors. In keeping with our discussion of the variable *peacekeeping operation* in Chapter 2, the indicator we use to represent this concept is a dichotomous variable that is scored as a "1" if some form of peacekeeping force was introduced following the end of the conflict and "0" otherwise. Twenty-six of the thirty-eight (68 percent) fully negotiated

11. Life expectancy serves as an effective proxy for measuring economic development in the sense that wealthier states tend to have a greater capacity to ensure the nutrition and health of their populations. Doyle and Sambanis (2000) use this measure as an indicator of development as well.

12. Touval 1982; Doyle and Sambanis 2000; Walter 1997, 2002.

13. Walter 1997, 340.

settlements constructed to end civil wars saw the presence of peacekeeping forces of some type while six of the eleven (54.5 percent) truces negotiated as a means of stopping the fighting saw peacekeepers deployed.[14]

Second, we account for perhaps the most significant change that has taken place at the international level during the period under consideration—the end of the cold war.[15] Our expectation is that the end of the cold war will favor increasingly durable settlements. During the years of superpower confrontation, both the United States and the Soviet Union actively channeled arms to existing and potential allies; antagonists within a country thus held the reasonable expectation that they could always count on the support of one of these powers should they back out of a settlement. In contrast, with the end of the cold war, intrastate rivals are decidedly less confident that they will have ready access to arms and resources from abroad. In this sense, the security of all parties to the agreement should be enhanced by the recognition that fewer resources are available to threaten the safety of any particular group or that would facilitate a return to war. In keeping with our discussion of the variable *international system structure* in Chapter 2, the indicator we use to represent this concept is a dichotomous variable that is scored "0" for all conflicts that ended during the period of the cold war (i.e., through the end of 1989) and "1" if the war concluded after that period. Twenty of the thirty-eight (53 percent) negotiated settlements of civil wars were agreed to in the post–cold war period as were ten of the eleven (91 percent) negotiated truces of intrastate conflicts.

TERMS OF THE SETTLEMENT

The final explanation we examine for differences in the duration of peace following negotiated agreements to end civil wars focuses on the terms to which belligerents agree as a condition for ending the civil war. Interestingly enough, very little attention has been paid to the impact that the content of an agreement may have on the duration of peace. The failure to focus on this issue almost seems to suggest that scholars and policy-makers commonly believe that a country's ability to secure an enduring peace following civil war rests on factors (such as natural resource endowments, level of

14. We have concerns regarding the effectiveness of peacekeepers' abilities to foster stability in the post–civil war environment. We discuss this in detail in Chapter 4.

15. A number of scholars have been interested in the effects the transition from a bipolar confrontation to the post–cold war system in 1990 may have had on a number of questions regarding civil conflict. See, for example, Crocker and Hampson 1996 and Wallensteen and Sollenberg 1997.

ethnic heterogeneity, and level of economic development) that are either beyond domestic actors' control or not particularly amenable to policy manipulation. While we acknowledge that a number of these conditions are likely to influence the stability of peace following civil war, in our view an important prerequisite toward securing a long-lasting peace is the design of institutions that enhance groups' sense of security and clarify the new rules by which future conflict is to be managed. Civil war settlements that spell out a number of these rules are most likely to produce an enduring peace.

As our earlier discussion suggests, our main concern regarding the settlement is the power-sharing and power-dividing institutions adversaries design as part of an agreement to end a civil war. Our expectation is that the most extensively institutionalized settlements should produce the longest-lived peace. We operationalize the concept *settlement institutionalization* by using a composite measure designed to reflect the four separate categories of power-sharing and power-dividing institutions that may appear in a peace agreement: the political, territorial, military, and economic bases of government power. The measure, which varies in value from "0" to "4," is ranked one unit higher for each dimension of power-sharing or power-dividing provision that a peace agreement specifies.

A potential objection to how we operationalize this variable is its treatment of each individual dimension of sharing and dividing power as having an equal influence over shaping the potential for an enduring peace. It certainly seems conceivable that some elements of sharing or dividing power might have heightened value to the resolution of civil wars relative to others. For example, given a recent experience with armed violence, sharing or dividing military power might have a greater potential to address immediate security fears in comparison to economic power-sharing and power-dividing institutions.

The most obvious means of addressing this potential concern would be to introduce a weighting scheme to our aggregate measure that reflects the different degrees of influence that each dimension of sharing and dividing power has on future peace. Yet even if we considered one power-sharing dimension as having a greater impact relative to others, what theoretical or empirical reasoning we might use for specifying our weights is not clear. On what basis could we claim that military power-sharing and power-dividing institutions should be considered precisely two times more important than other aspects of power sharing? Why not three or four times as significant? Based on this reasoning, we rejected the idea of adopting a weighting scheme out of a concern that it would introduce a false precision into the analysis.[16]

---

16. In the Appendix we present and discuss the results of statistical tests with the settlement institutionalization variable disaggregated into its four component parts.

We offer an outline of the variables we use in our models in table 6. The table indicates how each variable is operationalized and specifies the relationship we expect will hold between each independent variable and the dependent variable in question—the duration of peace.

Testing the Argument

We now turn to an evaluation of these explanations for the duration of peace through a series of tests focusing on all civil wars resolved via the bargaining process between 1945 and the end of 1999. We use hazard or event history analysis to examine the effects of the independent variables (representing the nature of the conflict, the postconflict environment, and terms of the settlement) on the duration of peace following a negotiated civil war agreement. Event history models are specifically designed to consider factors that might increase or decrease the length of time before a particular event occurs. In these tests, the event of interest is the failure of a

Table 6 Summary of variables used to predict the durability of negotiated agreements to civil wars

Variable	Operationalization	Expected Relationship with Duration of Peace
Nature of the conflict		
Stakes of the conflict	Identity-based civil war	−
Conflict duration	Months war endured prior to settlement	+
Conflict intensity	Monthly casualty rate of the war	−
Postconflict environment		
Previous level of democracy	Level of democracy associated with the prewar government	+
Economic development	Postwar life expectancy	+
Peacekeeping operation	Introduction of a peacekeeping force	+
International system structure	War concluded in Cold War or post–Cold War era	+
Terms of the settlement		
Settlement institutionalization	Total number of power-sharing dimensions specified in a settlement	+

civil war settlement, as indicated by the return to war. The model thus considers the duration of an episode of peace until (or if) the settlement fails.[17] Our dependent variable consists of the number of months peace endured following the signing of a settlement through December 31, 1999. A settlement is considered to have failed if civil war breaks out again in the country in question. In the terminology of hazard analysis, December 31, 1999, is the *censor date* for the statistical tests we perform in this chapter. Because we consider all negotiated civil war agreements signed between the beginning of 1945 and the end of 1999, the more recent agreements that remained in force at the end of 1999, e.g., Congo/Brazzaville (November 1999), Kosovo (June 1999), and Sierra Leone (July 1999), make but a brief appearance as stable settlements in the data set because they are censored from the data set soon after they are signed.

We use two sets of cases to test our hypotheses. In the first instance, we limit our tests to the thirty-eight cases of *fully negotiated settlements of civil wars.* These are the cases that, in addition to reaching decisions regarding the types of power-sharing and power-dividing institutions they will opt or not to construct, have seen settlement architects grapple with explicitly political issues, including the shape of and rules regarding the exercise of power in the postwar state. We expect settlement institutionalization to have the most meaningful impact on the duration of peace within the context of these negotiated political agreements. These are not, however, the only types of negotiated agreements belligerents have used to bring an end to the fighting where civil wars are concerned. Negotiated truces have also succeeded in a number of instances in stopping the killing for at least some period of time and thus merit inclusion in our analysis. Because these truces are relatively few in number (there are only eleven negotiated truces in our data set), we cannot analyze them alone. Therefore, we analyze them as part of the subset we refer to as *negotiated agreements*—forty-nine cases that include the thirty-eight negotiated settlements and eleven negotiated truces.[18]

17. We employ a Cox proportional hazards model to analyze the data. Agreements that remained intact as of December 1999 are considered "censored" from the data set, meaning that the event of interest never occurred. For further discussion of hazard models, see the Appendix.

18. We ran one version of our test of the forty-nine negotiated agreements of civil wars including a variable we called *political settlement*. This variable, which is meant to distinguish between the thirty-eight negotiated settlement cases and the eleven negotiated truces, was coded "1" if the settlement was a negotiated settlement and "0" if it was a negotiated truce. The coefficient for the variable was negatively signed, indicating that when contrasted with negotiated truces, negotiated settlements of civil wars lower the risks of the conflict recurring. The variable was not, however, statistically significant.

Tables 7 and 8 display our initial test results of the various explanations for the duration of peace following the negotiated agreement of civil wars. The second and third columns of table 7 show the results for all thirty-eight cases that are fully negotiated political settlements of civil wars. The second and third columns of table 8 indicate the relevant figures for the forty-nine negotiated peace agreements. The overall model for each of these cases proves statistically significant. In addition, of the eight independent variables included in each test, the same three indicators—economic development, settlement

Table 7 Hazard analysis of determinants of peace duration after negotiated settlements of civil war, 1945–1999 *fully negotiated*

Variable	Coefficient	Hazard ratio	Change	Revised hazard rate/ base hazard rate
Nature of the conflict				
Stakes of the conflict	0.95 (0.80)	2.59 (2.08)	1 to 0	0.39
Conflict duration (logged)	−0.20 (0.27)	0.82 (0.22)	to Min to Max	2.05 0.65
Conflict intensity (logged)	−0.03 (0.24)	0.97 (0.24)	to Min to Max	1.10 0.91
Postconflict environment				
Previous level democracy	−0.05 (0.06)	0.95 (0.06)	to Min to Max	1.37 0.51
Economic development	−0.10* (0.06)	0.91 (0.05)	to Min to Max	5.03 0.14
Peacekeeping operation	−1.42* (0.79)	0.24 (0.19)	1 to 0	4.15
International system structure	0.42 (0.89)	1.52 (1.35)	1 to 0	0.66
Terms of settlement				
Settlement institutionalization	−0.72** (0.28)	0.49 (0.14)	to Min (= 0) to 1 to 2 to 3 to Max (= 4)	5.20 2.53 1.23 0.60 0.29
Subjects	38			
Failures	13			
Time at risk	4355			
Log likelihood	−28.51			
Wald chi²(8)	41.77			
Prob>chi²	0.0000			

Values in parentheses are robust standard errors. All significance tests are two-tailed.
**p < 0.05
*p < 0.1

Table 8 Hazard analysis of determinants of peace duration after negotiated agreements to end civil war, 1945–1999 *negotiated + truces*

Variable	Coefficient	Hazard ratio	Change	Revised hazard rate/base hazard rate
Nature of the conflict				
Stakes of the conflict	0.97	2.63	1 to 0	0.38
	(0.62)	(1.63)		
Conflict duration	−0.23	0.79	to Min	2.22
(logged)	(0.20)	(0.16)	to Max	0.58
Conflict intensity	0.11	1.12	to Min	0.72
(logged)	(0.20)	(0.22)	to Max	1.50
Postconflict environment				
Previous level	−0.04	0.96	to Min	1.26
of democracy	(0.05)	(0.05)	to Max	0.59
Economic development	−0.05*	0.95	to Min	2.59
	(0.03)	(0.03)	to Max	0.40
Peacekeeping operation	−1.16*	0.31	1 to 0	3.19
	(0.60)	(0.19)		
International system	0.69	1.99	1 to 0	0.50
structure	(0.76)	(1.5)		
Terms of settlement				
Settlement	−0.52**	0.60	0 Min (= 0)	2.99
institutionalization	(0.21)	(0.13)	to 1	1.78
			to 2	1.07
			to 3	0.64
			to Max (= 4)	0.38
Subjects	49			
Failures	18			
Time at risk	4831			
Log likelihood	−48.47			
Wald chi^2(8)	27.71			
Prob>chi^2	0.0005			

Values in parentheses are robust standard errors. All significance tests are two-tailed.
**p <0.05
*p < 0.1

institutionalization, and the presence of a peacekeeping operation—emerge as those exercising a statistically significant influence on the duration of peace following mutually constructed agreements to end a civil war.

In table 7, which accounts for only the thirty-eight fully negotiated political settlements, none of the variables we identify as characterizing the nature of the civil conflict prove to affect the duration of peace as indicated by the failure of any variables to attain statistical significance. Turning to table 8, the same finding is evident for this particular explanation of the duration of peace in the case of the forty-nine agreements (both settlements and cease-fires) intended to end civil war. Again, the statistical results indicate that each of the three variables fails to definitively affect durability of peace.

A curious finding among the factors tied to the nature of civil conflict is the contradictory results regarding the *conflict intensity* variable. The test related to fully negotiated settlements suggests that wars with greater casualty rates are associated with a reduced risk of a return to war; conversely, when all agreements are taken into account, higher casualty rates increase the risk of hostilities being reinitiated. These results suggest that the dampening effect that high casualty rates have on the duration of peace may be mitigated in some way by constructing a fully negotiated political settlement. Whether this is because negotiating a political settlement differs in some significant way from designing negotiated truces (the former process, for example, may provide more opportunities to discuss war-related casualties and their implications than the latter) or because negotiated settlements, but not negotiated truces, include provisions for which we do not account, such as truth and reconciliation commissions that enable society to better cope with the implications of casualties, is hard to say.[19] Nevertheless, the results with respect to this particular variable suggest one important way in which negotiated settlements may have an edge over negotiated truces in helping to foster an enduring peace.

The conflict environment explanation for the duration of peace following negotiated agreements to end civil war fares better than the explanation emphasizing the nature of the conflict. In the cases of both the negotiated political settlements (table 7) and the negotiated agreements (table 8), the two variables that attain statistical significance are the indicators reflecting the level of economic development and the presence of a peacekeeping operation.[20] As hypothesized, higher levels of economic development reduce the risk of a return to war. Turning to the fifth column of tables 7 and 8, we can assess the impact that changes in this particular variable have on the duration of peace. In the case of the negotiated political settlement of civil wars

19. For a number of reasons, we have opted not to include "truth" commissions as one of the types of institutional arrangements that may be constructed as part of a negotiated agreement to end civil war. In the first place, as these are a relatively recent phenomenon, there might well prove to be colinearity between a variable accounting for the presence or absence of this institution and our *international system structure* variable. Second, the relevance this particular institution bears to the security concerns we argue former opponents face following a civil war's end is not as clear as in the case of the four other institutional arrangements we examine.

20. These variables, we should note, achieve statistical significance at only the $p < 0.1$ level.

(table 7), decreasing economic development to its minimum observed value (thirty-seven years of life expectancy at birth for the year following the end of both civil conflicts in Sierra Leone) increases the likelihood that civil war will break out again by 403 percent, while increasing the variable to its maximum observed value (seventy-three years of life expectancy at birth for the year following the end of the conflict in Bosnia) reduces the risk of renewed combat by 86 percent.[21] The effect is less pronounced in the cases of all negotiated agreements reached to end civil wars. Decreasing economic development to its minimum observed value for the cases in our data set on negotiated agreements to end civil wars, for example, increases the risk of a return to war by 159 percent. On the other hand, increasing economic development to its maximum observed value reduces the probability of a return to war by 60 percent.[22]

The negative sign associated with the coefficient for *peacekeeping operation* suggests that settlements calling for a peacekeeping operation to be put in place have a higher likelihood of producing an enduring peace than those failing to include such a mission. This variable's effects can best be judged by altering the variable in our analysis from its modal value of "1" to "0." Doing this produces an increased risk of a return to civil war by 315 percent for the negotiated settlements (table 7) and 219 percent for the negotiated agreements (table 8). By agreeing to field a peacekeeping operation, former antagonists improve the chances that long-term peace will prevail.

With respect to the other two conflict environment variables whose influence we test, although neither is statistically significant, only one— *previous experience with democracy*—is signed in a manner in keeping with our hypotheses for these two variables. Insofar as the variable *international system structure* is concerned, our expectation was that civil conflicts that had ended during the post–cold war period would be at a reduced risk for

21. The minimum and maximum values for the variable economic development are the same in tables 7 and 8. Having been concluded via negotiated settlements, the conflicts in Sierra Leone and Bosnia appear not only in table 8 but also as a subset of the agreements negotiated to end civil wars that appear in table 7.

22. We calculate the substantive impact of continuous variables such as *conflict duration, conflict intensity, previous experience with democracy,* and *economic development* by dividing the "revised" hazard rate (i.e., the hazard rate with the variable in question increased or decreased from its mean or mode value) by the "base" hazard rate (i.e., the hazard rate for the model for which all the variables are held at their mean values, if they are continuous variables, or mode values, if they are dichotomous variables). Following Werner (1999), "[i]f the variable has no substantive effect, the ratio [between the revised and base hazard rates] will equal 1.0 because the 'revised' hazard rate and the 'base' hazard rate are the same. The deviation of the ratio from 1.0 thus indicates the variable's substantive effect" (924).

renewed war. The positively signed coefficient indicates that this variable does not perform in the manner predicted by our hypothesis; rather, conflicts that ended during the post–cold war era have a greater likelihood of experiencing war again. One explanation we can offer for this unexpected result is that with the end of the cold war, the international system actually appears to have experienced an increase in the volume of arms flowing across international borders. This may have heightened actors' security concerns regarding potential adversaries' capacity to access weapons and reinitiate hostilities. In this respect, the end of the cold war may have undermined the sense of security we view as the crucial prerequisite to durable peace.[23]

We now turn to our explanation for post–civil war peace duration based on the terms of the settlement. The variable *settlement institutionalization* has a negatively signed coefficient associated with it, indicating that higher levels of settlement institutionalization lower the risk of a return to civil war.[24] This variable's effects on the duration of peace are, in fact, quite marked as indicated by assessing the impact produced by changes in the levels of settlement institutionalization. Beginning with table 7, we see that the effects of *settlement institutionalization* on the duration of peace are quite pronounced in the case of negotiated political settlements of civil wars. Settlements that fail to include any power-sharing or power-dividing institutions face an increased risk of a return to civil war by 420 percent. Including more types of power-sharing and/or power-dividing institutions in the negotiated settlements reduces the risk of a return to civil war. While agreeing to construct only one power-sharing or power-dividing institution increases the risk of a return to civil war by 153 percent, this represents a reduction in the risk level associated with excluding all power-sharing and/or power-dividing institutions from a negotiated settlement. Incorporating two such types of institutions increases the likelihood that civil conflict will reemerge by the lower figure of 23 percent. A breaking point of sorts appears to be reached when settlement architects include three or more different types of power-sharing and/or power-dividing institutions in a settlement. Former adversaries who succeed in designing three variants of power-sharing or power-dividing institutions see the probability of a return to war reduced by 40 percent, while those who agree to craft all four types of power-sharing

23. Hartzell and Hoddie 2003.

24. The variable *settlement institutionalization*, it should be noted, reaches the highest level of statistical significance (at $p < 0.05$) of the three variables that prove statistically significant in tables 7 and 8.

or power-dividing institutions see a 71 percent reduction in the likelihood of war breaking out again.

Turning to table 8, we can observe that in the case of negotiated agreements the effects of settlement institutionalization on the duration of peace are somewhat less pronounced. Negotiating an agreement that makes no provision for any power-sharing or power-dividing institutions increases the risk of a return to war by 199 percent. Including one type of power-sharing or power-dividing institution raises the likelihood of a renewed war by 78 percent, while designing two of these types of institutions increases the risk of a return to war by only 7 percent. By agreeing to construct three different types of power-sharing or power-dividing institutions, architects of a negotiated agreement lower the probability of a return to war by 36 percent. In those instances in which former foes agree to include all four types of power-sharing and power-dividing institutions we consider, the risk of a war breaking out again is reduced by 62 percent.

One of the interesting points to emerge from the foregoing analysis is that our test results prove remarkably robust across the two sets of civil war settlement cases we examine. The same three sets of independent variables prove influential—at the same level of statistical significance—across these cases. This strikes us as particularly remarkable for the *settlement institutionalization* variable. As we noted earlier in this chapter, we had reason to believe that extensively institutionalized negotiated political settlements of civil wars would be particularly likely to produce an enduring peace. In addition to finding support for this proposition we discovered that negotiated agreements—that is, negotiated settlements *and* negotiated truces— that are extensively institutionalized help structure a stable peace. This suggests that designing an array of rules for sharing and dividing power generates significant positive effects on the duration of peace, even when those rules are not part of a fully negotiated political settlement. By providing former foes with a sense of security, these institutions allow the signatories of both negotiated settlements and negotiated truces to avoid having to resort again to the use of arms. To the extent that power-sharing and power-dividing institutions succeed in helping to ensure peace, such rules, even when originally created as temporary measures meant to help stop the killing until a more developed political settlement can be reached, may take on a life of their own, accruing a certain degree of legitimacy and permanence. This appears to have taken place in countries such as Georgia, for example, where more than a decade after truces were negotiated the communities of that divided land have developed routines that allow them to engage in routinized politics despite the absence of a full settlement of the conflicts that have prevailed there.

Conclusion

Our analysis suggests that one of the most powerful explanations for the duration of peace following the negotiated agreement of civil wars centers on the terms of the settlements that former adversaries construct as a means of ending the conflict. By agreeing to construct a series of institutions that provide for their mutual security, as well as clarifying the rules by which conflict is to be regulated in the future, former foes have the capacity to structure a lasting peace. This result holds true not only for the negotiated settlement of civil wars but also for cases extending to negotiated truces. Although in the case of the latter type of agreement former adversaries may not actually have settled on a final set of rules for conflict regulation, we speculate that the very success of power-sharing and power-dividing institutions in helping to stabilize peace can lead these institutions to often take on a life of their own.

The support our tests provide for the important role played by settlement type is encouraging since, among the competing explanations for the longevity of peace, it stands alone as genuinely amenable to policy manipulation. Clearly, domestic and international actors can do little to change factors such as the stakes of a conflict, a country's previous experience with democracy, or the structure of the international system when a conflict ends. Even factors such as a country's level of economic development are very difficult to alter much over the short term. Actors can, however, affect the terms of a settlement. In fact, this may be the one area in which the actors that have been in conflict have a large role to play.[25] Former foes may be more likely to have a stake in peace when they themselves have played a role in designing the terms of that peace. By the same token, these same groups

25. It is not at all clear, for example, how much of a say belligerents have regarding the peacekeeping operations that are sent to their countries. For one thing, as cases such as Kosovo make clear, the decision regarding whether to have a peacekeeping operation deploy in a country is not always in the hands of the architects of a negotiated settlement. Secondly, decisions regarding the number of troops that will be deployed, the type or level of the mission involved, and how long peacekeepers will remain in the country tend to be made outside of the country that is the site of the peacekeeping operation.

are more likely to play by a set of rules in whose construction they have participated.[26]

Former foes can and have cooperated to institutionalize an enduring peace following the end of civil wars. If the message of Chapter 2 was that some conditions make it easier or more compelling for groups to agree to these institutions than do others, the point of this chapter has been to show that power-sharing and power-dividing institutions play a role in helping to foster a stable peace. In Chapter 4 we turn from the process of agreeing on and designing these institutions to an examination of whether and how former adversaries make these institutions work. Do former belligerents in fact implement the institutions they have designed? Do they do so fully, to a limited extent, or not at all? What factors affect the process of implementing these institutions? And, finally, does implementation or failure to implement these institutions affect the stability of peace? We seek to provide answers to these questions by focusing on military power-sharing and power-dividing measures.

26. That certainly has been the hope of the international community with respect to recent postconflict environments such as that in Afghanistan. Following the U.S.-led coalition's military defeat of the Taliban, the international community was deeply involved in helping broker the power-sharing agreement on a transitional government signed in Bonn in December 2001, yet the participation of delegates from four Afghan factions in Bonn and, later, of a *loya jirga* (or traditional assembly) charged with electing the transitional government was considered a crucial part of the process of helping build a lasting peace.

4

IMPLEMENTING POWER-SHARING AND POWER-
DIVIDING AGREEMENTS

Up to this point, we have been concerned with the process through which power-sharing and power-dividing mechanisms are established in the aftermath of civil war and how the development of these institutions enhances the prospects of an enduring postwar peace. In this chapter, we shift our attention from the postwar institutions themselves to focus on the behavior of former enemies operating under the constraints and expectations of a signed agreement. We seek to address the following question: How do the actions of competitors in the postwar state facilitate or hinder the continuing efforts to establish a lasting and self-enforcing peace?

The behaviors we consider consist of efforts by former enemies either to support or derail the process of implementing the provisions of a peace agreement. Our central finding is that the established peace will more likely remain undisturbed when former combatants ensure the full implementation of a settlement's provisions mandating the creation of power-sharing or power-dividing institutions. We interpret this relationship between implementing an agreement's power-sharing provisions and maintaining peace as reflecting that former enemies monitor one another's behavior closely for signals of intentions. By implementing the provisions of an agreement, signatories indicate to one another that they have a genuine interest in furthering their newly established cooperative relationship; conversely, the failure to act in accordance with the expectations outlined in a settlement signals that the reneging party cannot be trusted to act as a partner in the peace effort.

Earlier Research Concerning the
Implementation of Civil War Settlements

On first impression it may appear intuitive to suggest that the good-faith efforts of former combatants to implement a civil war settlement further the potential for an enduring peace. This has been the conventional wisdom in the literature on this subject, which has found that an immediate postwar environment of uncertainty and distrust makes the full implementation of settlements a challenging but crucial prerequisite to peace. Implementation is characterized as vital because it provides reassurances during the transition from war to peace that former opponents value stability over conflict and remain steadfast in their support of the peace process.[1] In short, implementation is thought to be significant because it makes the adversaries' commitments to maintaining peace credible.[2]

While the central findings of this chapter confirm expectations regarding this association between full settlement implementation and the maintenance of peace, they also enhance our understanding of this dynamic in two ways. First, our findings offer a new theoretical explanation as to exactly *why* the process of settlement implementation favors an enduring peace. Implementing peace agreements, particularly ones that call for the sharing or dividing of power by former adversaries, we argue, generates significant costs for a group's leaders through the compromises mandated by the agreement as well as the attendant loss of political support among those disenchanted with the peace process. Only by demonstrating a willingness to endure these costs do signatories send credible signals to their competitors emphasizing the integrity of the commitments they have made to peace.

Second, the research we present in this chapter joins only a handful of other studies in offering a systematic, cross-national investigation of the significance of the implementation process.[3] Most previous studies of peace-agreement implementation have taken the form of country-specific case studies rather than systematic, cross-national investigations. While the case

---

1. For studies that offer this perspective regarding the importance of peace-agreement implementation, see de Soto and del Castillo 1994, Hampson 1990, Stedman and Rothchild 1996, and Stedman 1997.

2. See Leeds 1999 and Walter 1997, 2002 for a discussion of the importance of credible commitment in postwar states.

3. Other studies include those by Stedman, Rothchild, and Cousens 2002 and Walter 2002.

study approach has provided a wealth of insights regarding the peace processes in individual states, it has inhibited the development of a generalizable
theory about how implementation relates to the durability of peace. The
value of the cross-national approach we adopt in this instance is its capacity
to reveal common patterns among cases that might remain obscured, if not
isolated, from the minutiae of a particular peace process.

Implementation and the Role of Third Parties

The post–civil war environment is defined by uncertainty. New postwar
governing institutions are typically embryonic in form and have not yet
demonstrated a capacity for resolving conflicts peacefully. Given this unset-
tled environment, parties to the dispute have little guarantee that war will
not return beyond a faith that their former enemies hold a preference for
peace over war. In the absence of evidence that further supports this hope,
however, former combatants may remain wary and reluctant to support a
peace process with the potential to leave members of their collectivity at
risk. No leader would take the gamble of issuing an order to disarm his
soldiers unless confident that his former enemies will follow suit. The risk
of being left vulnerable to attack is simply too great. How then might parties
genuinely interested in ending war move beyond this concern and work
together toward a self-enforcing peace?

A growing consensus suggests that third parties acting as the enforcers of
an established agreement may provide the sense of security and confidence
necessary to both fully implement a settlement and secure the emergent
peace.[4] Successful efforts to guide the peace process include those by international organizations (such as UN interventions in Cambodia and Mozambique) and states acting alone or as members of a coalition (such as NATO
intervention in the former Yugoslavia). The value of third-party enforcement is attributed to its capacity to minimize any sense of risk associated
with engaging in the peace process; as groups divest themselves of the ability
to provide for their own self-defense they can instead rely on the protection
offered by an outside force.

Third-party troops present during the latter stages of the peace process
may also serve the valuable function of facilitating communication among

---

4. See, for example, Walter 1999, 2003 and Stedman 1997.

former adversaries. Trusted by both sides because of their neutral status, third parties can observe and verify compliance with the requirements outlined in a settlement. This bridges any gaps in information that might contribute to the persistence of mistrust.[5]

The empirical record provides support for the view that third-party enforcement enhances the potential for a successful end to the peace process, a conclusion echoed by the findings we presented in the previous chapter. Yet reasons still exist for uncertainty about the capacity of third-party enforcement to serve as a panacea to the dilemmas associated with ending civil wars. One basis for this skepticism is the demonstrated lack of political will, at least among the leaders of states most capable of carrying out such operations, to come to the rescue of countries emerging from civil war.

In her study of international intervention in the aftermath of civil war, Virginia Page Fortna finds that international peacekeeping forces were deployed following 41 of 115 civil wars that concluded during the period 1947–99, or slightly more than one-third of the time. This figure drops even further when one examines the number of peacekeeping missions during this period that were carried out by the United Nations; only in thirty cases (26 percent) did UN troops intervene to attempt to stabilize peace.[6] In other words, there is little guarantee that peacekeepers will be available for those states in need of assistance.

Among those cases in which the United Nations has mustered sufficient support among its membership to authorize a peacekeeping operation, the majority of troops voluntarily contributed to these efforts have in most cases not come from the permanent members of the Security Council but instead represent countries of the developing world. The lack of both training and appropriate equipment for many of these soldiers has resulted in some well-publicized embarrassments for the UN, including a case in 2000 in which peacekeeping troops were briefly taken hostage and held for ransom in Sierra Leone.[7]

Equally notable is that in those instances in which countries of the industrialized world have decided to include their troops in peacekeeping missions, their commitment to those operations has proved to be easily shaken when confronted by local opposition. The 1993 killing of eighteen U.S. sol-

5. Walter 1999, 137.

6. Fortna 2004.

7. Considering the involvement of regional peacekeepers in the Liberian civil war, Herbert Howe finds that "an inadequate peacekeeping force may instead prolong a war and weaken regional stability" (1996, 146).

diers participating in a UN peacekeeping mission in Somalia provided sufficient motivation for President Clinton to order the withdrawal of all U.S. forces from the state and further served as the impetus for issuing a new directive limiting the scope of U.S. involvement in any future peacekeeping efforts;[8] similarly, it took only one week after the murder of ten Belgian peacekeepers in Rwanda for that country to recall all of its troops and the UN to initiate the process of removing all but a token force from the country.[9]

This reluctance to become involved or remain engaged in purely humanitarian missions has undoubtedly been compounded in recent years by the focus among states of the developed world on the "war on terrorism." At a time when the U.S. military has invested most of its resources in confronting a new threat, it has shown little interest in managing other states' civil conflicts. Even in instances in which a minimal U.S. contribution would have served the interests of peace, such as having troops assist in the 2003 removal of President Charles Taylor from power in Liberia or ending the genocide underway in the Darfur region of the Sudan in 2003 and 2004, the administration of George W. Bush has remained steadfast in its refusal to provide assistance. Thus it appears that, for the foreseeable future, states emerging from civil war may be increasingly responsible for maintaining domestic stability in the absence of substantial support from the international community.

Beyond the issue of political will, a second reason for a degree of pessimism concerning the ability of third parties to resolve civil conflicts is the issue of their capacity to perform consistently and capably the function of monitoring and verifying each parties' compliance with an agreement. Barbara Walter characterizes the advantages enjoyed by foreign peacekeepers in the following terms:

> Outside states are more likely to have sophisticated technology such as satellites and airplanes to monitor the agreement, can more easily distribute observers throughout the country without threatening either party, and are more likely to obtain access to sensitive military sites in order to observe behavior. The information collected under these circumstances is likely to be far more dependable than

---

8. This order took the form of Presidential Decision Directive 25 (Power 2002, 342).

9. A larger UN force was introduced into the state after most of the killings associated with the genocide had already taken place.

that which combatants can gather themselves, and is therefore more likely to elicit the desired behavior.[10]

Yet there are genuine reasons to doubt that peacekeepers will have the omniscient powers that Walter ascribes to them. As we have already noted, most peacekeepers come from less-developed countries. The most recent UN estimates report that the three largest contributors of personnel to peacekeeping operations are Pakistan, Bangladesh, and Nigeria. U.S. contributions of personnel to these missions account for just over 1 percent of the total.[11] Given these circumstances, it requires a heavy degree of optimism to expect that developing countries, which often view peacekeeping operations as little more than a means of keeping their soldiers occupied and employed, would have access to "sophisticated technologies" for use in these missions.

Even wealthy states' abilities to monitor conflict situations accurately may also be quite limited, which is perhaps best illustrated by the ongoing U.S. intervention in Iraq. Information failures have come to define this conflict—ranging from the inability to find the weapons of mass destruction that were the initial impetus for the war to the unexpected difficulties with identifying and eliminating sources of resistance within the local population. While far from a peacekeeping operation, that a force of more than 100,000 soldiers has confronted these problems in its efforts to pacify a decidedly weaker state suggests that information gathering under even the best of circumstances is challenging. This proves to be the case even when the last remaining superpower marshals all of its strength toward this one goal.

By noting these concerns related to both the willingness and capacity of third parties to act as the enforcers of peace agreements, we do not mean completely to discount outside actors' ability to perform a useful and valuable function during the implementation process and the transition to a self-enforcing peace. As we have already noted, past experience confirms that former enemies are far better off with this assistance than in its absence. Instead, these concerns suggest the need to identify strategies that might further the interests of postwar stability in two environments common to states emerging from civil war: (1) instances in which assistance from the international community is not forthcoming and former combatants must navigate the peace process alone, and (2) cases in which third-party en-

10. Walter 2002, 26–27.

11. Estimates for April 2004. Troop estimates for current missions available at http://www.un.org/Depts/dpko/dpko/contributors/index.htm.

forcers on the scene lack either the military muscle or resources to ade-
quately perform the tasks associated with their mission.

Costly Signals as a Mechanism for Generating Security

We seek to develop the claim that the process of implementing peace-agreement provisions related to the creation of power-sharing and power-dividing institutions offers an opportunity for former combatants autonomously
to overcome mutual distrust and lay the foundations for an enduring peace.
By engaging in behaviors that are in keeping with the requirements outlined
in a settlement, collectivities signal to one another their continuing commitment to the peace process. What makes these actions credible signals of
intentions are the burdens inextricably tied to carrying them out; these costs
make these commitments to peace believable.

In this sense, we derive our central argument from James Fearon's observation that any commitment is only likely to be perceived as credible "when
the act of sending it incurs or creates some cost that the sender would be
disinclined to incur or create if he or she were in fact *not* willing to carry
out" the obligation.[12] Below we describe exactly what costs a group, and
more specifically a group's leadership, incurs when participating fully in
the implementation of power-sharing and power-dividing institutions. We
suggest that these costs have the potential to take two forms—the establishment of limits on the ability of some group to exercise state power unilaterally and endurance of the objections of militants unhappy with the
trajectory of the peace process.

SETTING LIMITS ON ACCESS TO STATE POWER

As we have emphasized throughout this book, power sharing is a common
feature of negotiated settlements to civil war. The logic of creating power-
sharing and power-dividing institutions is that these mechanisms minimize
the capacity of any one party to control the postwar state and potentially
use this position of influence to threaten the interests or survival of their
rivals. While this provides a certain sense of safety to all of the relevant
parties, obtaining such a benefit also requires a concession. Establishing
power-sharing or power-dividing institutions means ending the pursuit of

12. Fearon 1997, 69.

what is typically the main objective of the war: monopoly control of the state. By committing themselves to abide by power-sharing and power-dividing institutions, participants are establishing a set of rules and norms that will by virtue of their very existence limit their capacity to unilaterally shape the postconflict society. The simple act of signing the peace agreement commits a collectivity's elite to this eventual loss of power; what makes the implementation stage of the process unique is that the true costs associated with an agreement cease to be an abstraction and instead become painfully apparent to everyone involved. Stephen Stedman and Donald Rothchild suggest the ambiguity linked to the peace process prior to efforts at implementation in the following terms: "[T]he pay-offs of implementing peace agreements are not common knowledge: no one knows for certain the rewards and costs associated with making peace or returning to war."[13] This uncertainty regarding the price to be paid for stability ends as implementation moves forward; both benefits and costs become increasingly apparent with each step forward in constructing the new institutions of the postwar state.

Thus the implementation of the 1996 accord between the government of the Philippines and the rebel MNLF made the compromises readily apparent for both the signatories to the agreement and their followers. The national government was no longer the sole authority throughout its entire territory but was instead required to share political power with a regional government representing the country's Muslim minority based on the island of Mindanao; for its part, the MNLF was forced to abandon its aim of becoming a separate state and to recognize Philippine sovereignty over its homeland.

ALIENATING SUPPORTERS

In addition to the costs of sharing power with rivals for state dominance, implementing a power-sharing or power-dividing settlement may enhance the credibility and stature of critics who decry the peace deal as "selling out" the vital interests of the collectivity.[14] Voices of protest may arise at any stage of the peace process, but militants emphasizing the dangers of compromise are likely to garner the most attention and new adherents as implementation moves forward and the comprises made for peace become increasingly apparent. This forms the second cost endured by a group's leadership as they

13. Stedman and Rothchild 1996, 20.
14. Fearon (1997, 1998) describes this phenomenon as audience costs.

implement a peace deal: carrying out a settlement's provisions fosters an environment in which leaders are likely to become vulnerable to the criticisms of militants who will use the arrangement as the basis for challenging their authority.

This second cost associated with implementation is also apparent in the peace process carried out in the Philippines. Once the agreement had been reached, the government of Fidel Ramos faced violent protests in which the president was accused of failing to protect the island's Catholic minority from the predations of the Muslim population; similarly, rebel MNLF leader Nur Misuari endured criticism from within his own organization for failing to secure independence for the island. Many MNLF followers critical of compromise left Misuari's side to join other groups (including Abu Sayyaf and the Moro Islamic Liberation Front) whose leadership had vowed to continue their armed resistance to the national government.

Pierre Atlas and Roy Licklider present further evidence to suggest that the development of fissures within a once cohesive collectivity is a frequent occurrence with the implementation of a peace agreement. Based on an examination of postsettlement politics in the Sudan, Zimbabwe, Chad, and Lebanon, the authors note a common pattern:

> Post-settlement tensions often arise, not from reopening fissures between former foes but deepening divisions among former allies. . . . Certain groups or factions feel that they have not received their just deserts from the settlement or that the terms of the settlement threaten their interests or security. This tension mounts until either the former allies resort to violence against one another or the settlement supporters are forced to change policy and violate the settlement.[15]

The willingness of an agreement's architects to endure and combat the challenges to their authority that emerge as a settlement moves forward thus serves as a costly signal of intentions. If a group's leadership can remain steadfast in its support of an agreement despite the best efforts of critics to derail the implementation process, it clearly indicates that they remain strongly committed to nurturing the emergent peace. Conversely, leaders who seek to mollify their critics by either distancing themselves from the

15. Atlas and Licklider 1999, 37.

peace process or inhibiting its progress are exposed as unreliable supporters of the agreement.

THE PROCESS OF COSTLY SIGNALING

How might the process of costly signaling work in practice? To a large extent this will depend on the settlements themselves, as each group's actions are assessed based upon how faithfully they perform the tasks assigned to them in the text of the agreement. Each incremental step taken by one party toward establishing the power-sharing and power-dividing institutions outlined in an agreement increases the confidence of those scrutinizing these behaviors that the implementing group's commitment to peace is genuine, as reflected by a willingness to absorb the costs tied to these efforts.

That power-sharing and power-dividing institutions serve as one of the main mechanisms through which costly signals may be exchanged reinforces one of the central premises of this book—that states emerging from civil war through a process of negotiation are best served by specifying as many dimensions of power sharing as possible. With the successful fulfillment of each provision observers have information that enhances their confidence that peace will hold. These opportunities would be more limited if the settlement called for only one or two power-sharing or power-dividing institutions. In this sense, each additional mechanism of power sharing mandated by an agreement provides another chance to signal intentions among former combatants.

Can Costly Signaling Work? Considering Three Objections

At least one scholar has indicated a substantial degree of skepticism about the value of signaling among former combatants as part of efforts to end civil wars. Barbara Walter has offered three reasons why signaling should fail as a mechanism for enhancing confidence in the peace process among former combatants. We consider and provide a response to each of her objections in turn below.[16]

The first criticism of the signaling approach that Walter offers is its failure

16. There is an important distinction between Walter's discussion of signaling and the one we present. Walter's discussion focuses exclusively on the process of disarmament; in contrast, we consider the potential for signaling to take place during the mutual creation of power-sharing and power-dividing institutions.

to include a mechanism for punishing uncooperative behavior. If one group reneges from some part of the agreement, she asks, how might others sanction such behavior when already disarmed?[17] The problematic assumption tied to this criticism is that the only means of indicating concern or displeasure with a rival's behavior is by exercising military power. In fact, the use of force is among the most perilous means of getting a stalled peace process back on track, given the attendant risks of reinitiating hostilities. Other tactics do exist with the potential to call to account a defector from an agreement without requiring a resort to arms; punishments falling short of violence that Walter does not consider include delays in implementing aspects of a peace agreement considered vital to a rival's interests, the use of public diplomacy to generate domestic and international condemnation of the reneging party, and threats to withhold material benefits connected to implementation of peace. For example, the threat to embargo funds in the amount of $15 million promised by international donors to the rebel group RENAMO (Mozambican National Resistance) in order to facilitate its transformation into a political organization was used to great effect in persuading the group to implement the Rome Accords agreed to in 1992 as a means of ending Mozambique's decade-long civil war.[18]

Second, Walter suggests that credible information is rare in postconflict environments and that limited resources mean that "combatants will find it difficult to sustain demobilization using their own monitoring and verification schemes."[19] Yet it is notable how often peace agreements include provisions designed precisely with the intention of allowing each party to observe the actions of its rivals. These mechanisms include establishing joint commissions, as seen in the cases of El Salvador and Mozambique, and exchanging observers, as was part of the cease-fire to end the South Ossetian conflict in Georgia. Such observers could be perceived as a particularly reliable source of information for their collectivity, especially in comparison to impartial third-party observers, given that their primary interests rest with protecting their own group rather than ensuring that the peace process proceeds unhindered.[20]

17. Walter 2002, 24–25.
18. Alden 1995.
19. Walter 2002, 25.
20. Walter suggests that the use of observers representing each party might actually heighten security concerns, given that the monitoring and verification responsibilities of soldiers could place them behind enemy lines. While it is certainly possible that the monitors may fear for their own safety while discharging their responsibilities, it is not clear why this would also heighten the sense of insecurity among other members of the relevant groups.

Third, Walter makes the point that "costly signaling is relevant only when groups are uncertain about an opponent's readiness to cheat on an agreement. In civil wars it is highly unlikely that either side would choose *not* to cheat if given the chance."[21] The postsettlement environment, however, differs fundamentally from the period during which the war is occurring. Once an agreement has been reached, former combatants must weigh the benefits of the settlement in hand against the risks of restarting a conflict that participants know they were incapable of winning in the past. In this sense, cheating may not always seem as desirable an option in comparison to cooperating toward a sustainable peace. This is reflected in our earlier finding that negotiated settlements ending prolonged civil wars tend to prove more durable than those resolving relatively brief conflicts. In part, this may be interpreted as indicating that groups from an enduring conflict place a greater value on maintaining a settlement as opposed to cheating and the associated risk of restarting hostilities.

In summary, we view Walter's critical discussion of costly signaling as a valuable means of pointing to some of the risks and limitations associated with relying on this process for facilitating cooperation among former rivals. But these critiques do not make the case that costly signaling cannot assist in fostering peace; rather they point to means by which the value of costly signals might be further strengthened and enhanced. In particular, they suggest the importance of ensuring that implementation processes include mechanisms to monitor implementation efforts among former combatants and that parties prove willing to use the pressures and incentives they have at their disposal to make defections from an agreement costly.

AN EMPIRICAL INVESTIGATION

In earlier chapters we focused on four types of power-sharing and power-dividing institutions: the political, military, territorial, and economic aspects of state power. Our approach differs in this chapter in that we focus solely on military power-sharing and power-dividing institutions. Both substantive and practical reasons exist for this change in emphasis.

The substantive basis for this focus is the significance of the rival militaries to the implementation process in a postwar state. Prior to the signing of a settlement, a collectivity's army provides the greatest degree of security for a group as well as the most obvious source of leverage vis-à-vis its adversar-

---

21. Walter 2002, 25.

ies. In most cases, implementing a military power-sharing or power-dividing arrangement requires collectivities to forego the capacity to protect their own interests and instead entrust their security to the newly established institutions of the postwar state.[22] Thus intense feelings of insecurity and resistance have the strongest likelihood of emerging as implementation moves forward. Centering our analysis on this challenging aspect of many peace processes most clearly indicates how efforts to implement settlements influence the prospects for maintaining stability.

The practical justification for focusing on military power sharing is the lack of data we typically confronted when seeking to chart progress in the implementation process. Analysts of postwar states, unfortunately, tend to consider maintaining peace itself a sufficient demonstration that the settlement has been implemented. Given this constraint, we are as a matter of necessity limited to focusing on power-sharing aspects that tend toward a lack of ambiguity. The advantage of considering the implementation of military power-sharing provisions is that it is linked to the readily observable movements and behaviors of soldiers within the postwar state.[23]

SELECTING CASES

In order to substantiate that a relationship exists between the implementation of military power-sharing arrangements and durable peace, we identified all negotiated civil war agreements reached between the years 1980 and 1996 that specified the establishment of military power-sharing or power-dividing institutions. We chose not to investigate agreements signed prior to 1980 because of difficulties in obtaining reliable data on the implementation of older peace settlement provisions. The interest of academics and policy-makers in questions related to peace-agreement implementation has developed only in recent years. For this reason, the more time that has elapsed since the signing of the agreement, the greater the likelihood that information on implementation processes will be incomplete or unreliable. We se-

22. Among the eighteen negotiated agreements we consider, only three (Azerbaijan, Chechnya, and Georgia–South Ossetia) do not require any integration of the militaries. These three agreements, we note, are all negotiated truces, not fully negotiated political settlements. Yet even in these three instances, the armies are required to cooperate in one form or another following the settlement to monitor the actions of their rivals.

23. A further benefit of concentrating on military power sharing is the availability of annuals that track the size and actions of armed forces around the world. Two particularly valuable resources in this regard are the International Institute for Strategic Studies' *Military Balance* and *Strategic Survey*.

lected 1996 as the last year in which settlements could be included in the data analysis so that there would in all cases be a significant period of time in which efforts at implementation might have taken place.

Recall that we designate an agreement as including military power-sharing or power-dividing provisions if it calls for any of the following: (1) the creation of the state's security forces through the integration of former antagonists' armed forces on the basis of a formula representative of the size of the armed groups; (2) the creation of the state's security forces on the basis of equal numbers of troops drawn from the antagonists' armed forces; (3) the appointment of members of armed faction(s) that do not dominate the state, or of weaker armed factions, to key leadership positions in the state's security forces; and (4) the retention by antagonists of their own armed forces or the creation of their own security forces. A total of eighteen of the twenty-nine negotiated civil war resolutions reached between 1980 and 1996 included provisions consistent with this definition.

CODING

Our dependent variable is settlement success, defined as the absence of a recurrence of sustained, violent civil conflict. We code settlements that have endured to 2003 without a return to war as long-term successes. The independent variable is the degree to which the military power-sharing and power-dividing arrangements called for in the eighteen peace settlements were implemented within five years following the signing of the agreement.

Our logic for focusing on the initial five-year period following the settlement is twofold. First, implementing some of the measures to which opposing sides agree as part of a settlement often takes an extended period of time. Analyzing implementation efforts for a period shorter than five years would involve the risk of missing former adversaries' genuine efforts to follow through on settlement commitments. Second, the value of implementation as a costly signal of conciliatory intent is likely to attenuate over time as peace proves durable. For this reason, implementation efforts following the first five years should appear less significant than those occurring immediately after the end of the war.

We define settlements as fully implemented if former combatants had fulfilled all of the military power-sharing and/or power-dividing requirements outlined in the original agreement by the end of the five-year period. Although efforts at demobilization or the creation of joint armies may have suffered delays during the five-year period, as long as parties were in compliance with the measures by the end of that time they were coded as having fully implemented their agreements regarding the exercise of military power. The Mozambican case is instructive in this respect. Mozambique's settlement called for government troops and RENAMO's rebel forces to integrate in order to form a new national army. RENAMO initially delayed sending students to officer training for the new joint army, and the demobilization of RENAMO and government troops was not completed until nearly two years after the peace agreement was signed. Ultimately, however, demobilization by both groups proved so successful that in 1995 President Joaquim Chissano announced that conscription would be necessary in order to get the newly integrated Mozambique Democratic Armed Forces up to full strength.[24]

We designated implementation as partial in those instances in which all parties to the settlement made some effort to follow through on their commitments but failed to implement them fully within five years. Two accords intended to end the civil war in Angola provide examples of partial implementation of military power-sharing provisions. The Bicesse Accords signed in 1991 called for the creation of an army, totaling 40,000 men, which would be evenly divided between government and UNITA troops. Although UNITA did send some of its troops to assembly points for disarmament and demobilization, tens of thousands of guerrillas and their arms were concealed in remote areas. By the time elections were held in September 1992, only 45 percent of government troops had been demobilized and 24 percent of the forces assembled by UNITA had given up their weapons. Angola's Lusaka Protocol, signed in 1994, also called for the creation of a unified national army, this time with a strength of approximately 90,000 troops. Although the integration process was deemed to have concluded in 1998 and UNITA claimed at that time to have completed the demobilization process, UNITA was reported to have 25,000 to 30,000 fully equipped troops that had not been demobilized.[25]

Finally, we defined settlement implementation as failed in those cases in which either some or all of the parties refused to live up to their commitments or no forward momentum took place regarding the measures to be implemented. The Cambodian settlement constitutes a case of failed implementation of military measures. The Paris Agreement, signed in 1991, called for the cantonment and disarmament of at least 70 percent of the forces of

24. *The Military Balance* (various years).
25. *Strategic Survey* and *The Military Balance* (various years).

each of the four warring factions—the communist Cambodian government, the forces under Son Sann, Sihanouk's forces, and the Khmer Rouge—with the remaining 30 percent to be incorporated into a new national army. Although the Phnom Penh government and the two noncommunist factions cooperated to some extent in this operation, the Khmer Rouge refused to regroup and disarm its forces.[26]

Based on these criteria, we assess groups that fully implement the military measures to which they have agreed as having engaged in the most costly form of signaling regarding their commitment to the negotiated settlement. Groups that partially implement the military agreements signal a lower degree of commitment to the settlement, while groups that fail to implement the agreed-to terms may end up signaling something different all together—a marked lack of commitment to the settlement in whose construction they have participated.

Table 9 summarizes our assessment of the level of success at implementing the military power-sharing or power-dividing bargains specified in the eighteen settlements; the narratives for each case provided in the Appendix

Table 9 Assessment of implementation efforts for eighteen peace settlements with provisions to share or divide military power, 1980–1996

Conflict settled	Assessment of implementation*	Settlement outcome
Angola (1989–91)	Partial	Return to war
Angola (1992–94)	Partial	Return to war
Azerbaijan (1990–94)	Failed	Maintenance of peace
Bosnia (1992–95)	Complete	Maintenance of peace
Cambodia (1978–91)	Failed	Maintenance of peace
Chad (1989–96)	Partial	Maintenance of peace
Chechnya (1994–96)	Complete	Return to war
Djibouti (1991–94)	Complete	Maintenance of peace
El Salvador (1979–92)	Complete	Maintenance of peace
Georgia SO (1989–92)	Complete	Maintenance of peace
Lebanon (1975–89)	Partial	Maintenance of peace
Mali (1990–95)	Complete	Maintenance of peace
Mozambique (1982–92)	Complete	Maintenance of peace
Nicaragua (1981–89)	Complete	Maintenance of peace
Philippines (1972–96)	Complete	Maintenance of peace
Rwanda (1990–93)	Failed	Return to war
Sierra Leone (1992–96)	Failed	Return to war
South Africa (1983–94)	Complete	Maintenance of peace

*Within five years

26. *Strategic Survey* (various years).

briefly outline the basis for the individual coding decisions. A relatively good distribution of implementation successes and failures exists among the eighteen negotiated civil war agreements that required military power sharing among former combatants. We find that four states failed to implement these provisions, another four only partially fulfilled their commitments, and ten states fully implemented their plans to share or divide military power.

METHOD

Because there are only eighteen cases in the time frame we examine we cannot use a statistical methodology to demonstrate the relationship between implementing and maintaining peace. We instead rely on a form of analysis described by both Arend Lijphart and Neil Smelser as appropriate for the study of small data sets, the comparative method.[27]

In contrast to individual case studies' attention to detail, the comparative method shares with statistical methodologies a concern with identifying causal patterns among variables.[28] A chief weakness of the comparative method relative to more sophisticated approaches is the inability to statistically control for the influence of other potentially important variables.[29] This limitation is apparent in this study as we are unable to control for other factors, such as the intensity of the conflict prior to settlement, the potential participation of third-party actors in maintaining stability, or even the effects of efforts to implement other aspects of the peace agreement not associated with military power sharing, likely to influence the prospects for a durable peace following civil war. Due to this absence of statistical controls, this chapter's findings should be interpreted as suggesting (rather than definitively demonstrating) a relationship among variables.

FINDINGS

We present our findings using the comparative method in table 10. The table indicates a strong relationship between successful efforts at implementing

27. Lijphart 1971, 1975; Smelser 1973.

28. See Lijphart 1971, 1975; Smelser 1973; and Jackman 1985. For a discussion of the value of the case study approach as a means for testing the validity of theories, see Eckstein 1975 and King, Keohane, and Verba 1994.

29. In the words of Lijphart (1971, 684), "The comparative method should be resorted to when the number of cases available for analysis is so small that cross-tabulating them further in order to establish credible controls is not feasible." Also see Lieberson 1991 for a discussion of other problems associated with the comparative method.

Table 10 Implementation of military power sharing or power dividing and the maintenance of peace

Level of implementation	Return to war	Peace	Total
None	2 (50%)	2 (50%)	4 (100%)
Partial	2 (50%)	2 (50%)	4 (100%)
Complete	1 (10%)	9 (90%)	10 (100%)
Total	5	13	18

an agreement's military power-sharing or power-dividing provisions and maintaining peace. Combatants eventually returned to war in four of the eight instances in which former combatants either reneged on their commitments or only partially fulfilled expectations. In contrast, peace proved durable in nine of the ten cases in which post–civil war states with agreements requiring military measures fully implemented this aspect of the settlement. Chechnya is the single instance of a return to conflict following the full implementation of military power sharing. This case stands out as one in which the military arrangements required by the settlement were particularly limited, including joint Russian-Chechen patrols and checkpoints manned by the opposing sides. That these operations did not require substantial efforts by the warring parties may have limited their value as signals of a commitment to peace.

This distribution among cases suggests that once an agreement has been reached requiring the sharing or dividing of military power among former combatants, the prospects for continuing stability are enhanced by faithful implementation of the arrangement. Peace proves much more durable if groups make good on the promises made at the negotiating table, with almost all states that have implemented military power-sharing or power-dividing mechanisms maintaining stable intergroup relations. This is a significant contrast to those instances in which former combatants prove unwilling to fulfill their commitments to share the coercive instruments of the state, with only half of those states continuing to enjoy peace.

We interpret this finding as validating the claim that implementing an agreement is a costly signal of conciliatory and cooperative intent. Former combatants monitor their adversaries' behavior for evidence that signatories are still committed to stability and peaceful coexistence once the costs associated with a successful compromise have been clarified for both leaders and followers. Evidence of a failure to act in a manner consistent with the agreement's provisions increases the likelihood that groups will lose faith in their competitors' good intentions and will opt for a return to conflict. This option often proves preferable to having cooperative actions abused for advantage by an unreliable partner to the settlement.[30]

Factors Associated with the Successful Implementation of an Agreement

Given that carrying out a civil war settlement's provisions appears vital to sustaining peace, do particular factors improve the prospects for implementing a successful agreement? Below we consider two conditions that could enhance former rivals' capacity to carry out the provisions of a settlement and thus signal their enduring commitment to the nascent peace.

THIRD PARTIES AND THE IMPLEMENTATION PROCESS

As we have discussed previously in this chapter, third parties acting as guarantors of peace agreements enhance the prospects for implementation success following the signing of a peace agreement by creating a secure environment and by facilitating communication among collectivities still harboring suspicions about their former adversaries' intentions. Countries emerging from civil war are thus much more likely to enjoy an enduring peace if they are fortunate enough to host an external force of sufficient capacity and commitment to assist them in establishing the postwar state.

We should emphasize, however, that we do not interpret this to mean

---

30. We considered the possibility that the relationship we identify between implementing civil war settlements and maintaining peace is spurious. One factor that may condition both implementation and peace is the casualty rate of the conflict the settlement is designed to resolve. The relatively benign environments associated with low-intensity wars might predispose former combatants toward genuine implementation efforts and a willingness to allow the nascent peace to endure unchallenged. The existing literature on the durability of civil war settlements has demonstrated that a relationship between higher casualty rates and settlement failure exists (Hartzell, Hoddie, and Rothchild 2001). Do higher casualty rates also dim the prospects for settlement implementation? Our analysis of the eighteen cases included in this study suggests that this is not the case. For the nine settlements of conflicts with casualty rates below the median value for this indicator, five fully implemented their settlements. The same proves true for those conflicts settled with casualty rates above the median value, with five of nine agreements to share or divide military power being fully implemented. This suggests that the intensity of the war is not a central determinant of the prospects for implementing a peace agreement.

that third parties are the crucial prerequisite to maintaining peace in countries emerging from civil war through a process of negotiation. While certainly outside the dominant trend, instances exist in which a negotiated accord has been implemented and peace has endured in the absence of third-party enforcement. Both South Africa and the Philippines are examples in which former combatants proved to have an autonomous capacity for keeping the peace process on track. We take this to indicate that costly signaling during efforts at implementation can forge cooperative relationships with or without external assistance. This suggests that the possibility remains for an enduring peace even in the far-too-common scenario in which a negotiated agreement is reached and third-party enforcers are either absent or prove incapable of performing the tasks required of them.

In those instances in which an external force is present, what role should it play within the postwar state? At times, advocates of a third party-role in peace processes have emphasized the coercive capacity of third parties. Walter, for example, discusses the role of external actors in minimizing the potential for cheating during the disarmament and demobilization of soldiers in the following terms:

> Third parties can verify compliance with the terms of demobilization and warn of a surprise attack, they can guarantee that soldiers will be protected as they demobilize, and they can become involved if one or both sides resume the war. Third parties can thus ensure that the *payoffs from cheating no longer exceed the payoffs from faithfully executing the settlement's terms.* Once cheating becomes difficult and costly, promises to cooperate should gain credibility and cooperation should become more likely.[31]

In a similar vein, Stedman outlines a set of three strategies (inducement, socialization, and coercion) that third parties might deploy in order to manage and control spoilers seeking to derail progress toward peace once a settlement has been reached.[32] In this sense, both Walter and Stedman suggest that third-party actors are most effectively deployed as enforcers of the agreement during the implementation stage of the peace process. Their role is not only to identify potential spoilers to an agreement but also to impose high costs on settlement violators so that they have no choice but to return to behaviors consistent with the original compromise.

31. Walter 1999, 46 (emphasis added).
32. Stedman 1997.

Our concern with focusing on this third-party role is its potential to mask the intentions behind the actions of parties to the agreement. In other words, the presence of an external actor performing the role of agreement enforcer will often mean that parties to the settlement will not have the opportunity to assess whether behavior consistent with the signed agreement is based on a genuine desire for peace or simply expedient behavior intended to placate interested third parties. Because actions that could signal conciliatory behavior will likely be discounted if they are perceived as a reaction to third-party demands, the establishment of trust among former combatants becomes less probable and peace may prove less durable once the external power leaves the scene. Based on this logic, we believe that the most appropriate role for a third-party actor is simply that of an intermediary among former combatants that communicates its findings as it monitors and verifies progress toward implementation.[33] Indications that a third party intends to enforce an agreement mean that the value of the signal that comes with implementation is lost.[34]

ECONOMIC DEVELOPMENT AND THE IMPLEMENTATION PROCESS

In a study of the resolution of post–World War II civil wars, Michael W. Doyle and Nicholas Sambanis find a positive association between higher levels of economic development and the maintenance of peace.[35] Doyle and Sambanis's reasons for believing that this association exists are most plainly stated as a hypothesis: "More developed economies with lower levels of poverty should be both better able to rebuild after war and less susceptible to wars stemming from economic grievance."[36]

Our understanding of peace processes mutually signaling conciliatory intent offers a different explanation for why more economically developed states emerging from civil war via bargained settlements may enjoy greater success in maintaining peace. The financial resources of wealthier states give the participants in peace processes a stronger capacity to implement the

33. This view regarding the role of third-party actors as monitoring rather than forcing compliance is articulated in Stedman and Rothchild 1996.

34. We are suggesting that third parties limit their actions to observers of agreement implementation, but this would not prohibit them from taking a more active role and intervening if parties engaged in large-scale acts of violence. Once mass violence has emerged, the issue of whether costly signals of conciliatory intent have been made by parties to the agreement is obviously no longer relevant.

35. Doyle and Sambanis 2000.

36. Ibid., 785.

programs first outlined in peace settlements. Alvaro de Soto and Graciana del Castillo note that the costs of implementing a peace settlement can often prove overwhelming to a developing country and calculate the costs for implementing the Salvadoran Accords for a single year in the following terms: "For 1993 alone, El Salvador needed about $250 million to reintegrate ex-combatants into society (through purchase of land, agricultural credit, housing, credit for small enterprises, pensions for the disabled, etc.) and to promote democratic institutions (National Civil Police, National Public Security Academy, human-rights activities, and activities related to the coming elections)."[37]

This suggests that countries need substantial financial resources to implement peace settlements. As a result, participants in peace processes within wealthier countries are often at an advantage to offer the conciliatory signals associated with faithfully agreeing to implementation.

Evidence exists that higher levels of economic development are associated with a greater capacity to implement the military power-sharing or power-dividing aspects of settlements. Using life expectancy following the end of the war as a proxy measure of development, our previous work identifies a relationship between economic development and implementation success among the eighteen cases with settlement provisions for sharing or dividing military power. Rather tellingly, two of the four cases of complete implementation failure are among the poorest states: Rwanda and Sierra Leone.[38]

Because signals of conciliation associated with agreement implementation are often costly, states transitioning from civil conflict to peace should have ready access to international assistance that would facilitate their meeting the expectations outlined in the settlement. Without such assistance, failing to carry out settlement provisions as a result of resource scarcity may be misperceived as an act of bad faith by former adversaries and could reignite hostilities.

Conclusion

This chapter offers two contributions to the literature concerning the implementation of civil war settlements. First, we have offered a theory to explain exactly why settlement implementation is important for building an endur-

37. De Soto and del Castillo 1994, 72.
38. Hoddie and Hartzell 2003.

ing peace in states emerging from violent civil conflict via negotiated settlement. By implementing the provisions of an agreement, leaders of the compromising groups are unambiguously signaling their genuine commitment to peace. These signals are understood to be credible because they are associated with heavy costs to the implementing parties in terms of both an immediate loss of political power vis-à-vis their competitors in the war as well as the likely loss of support among the more militant members of their own groups. The willingness to endure these costs in an effort to demonstrate a preference for stability allows former antagonists to surmount security concerns and move toward a self-sustaining peace.

A second contribution of this study relates to its methodology. This chapter joins only a few works in undertaking a systematic, cross-national examination of the effect that peace-agreement implementation has on settlement durability. Although case studies of agreement implementation have helped identify particular characteristics of the implementation process as well as challenges associated with fulfilling settlement obligations, this literature has yet to develop generalizable theories regarding the peace process.

In the next chapter we make an effort to illustrate the value of the statistical findings presented thus far by using them to interpret the peace processes in two states: Angola and the Philippines. Our discussion focuses on the central importance of power-sharing and power-dividing institutions in shaping the prospects for constructing a self-enforcing peace. We consider the bargaining, creation, and implementation of these arrangements and how they create a sense of security among former combatants in the postwar state.

5

NEGOTIATING FOR PEACE IN ANGOLA
AND THE PHILIPPINES:
CASE STUDIES OF FAILURE AND SUCCESS

In the previous three chapters of this book, we used a cross-national approach to consider the role that power-sharing and power-dividing institutions play during the process of negotiating an end to civil war. Here, however, we move beyond analyzing civil war resolution through the columns and rows of data sets and instead offer detailed descriptions of both successful and unsuccessful efforts at ending domestic wars through bargaining. Specifically, we provide historical analyses of peace processes as they played out in Angola and the Philippines.

These case studies are an opportunity to develop further claims first introduced in the earlier statistical analyses in two ways. First, they offer a means of moving beyond the sometimes abstract concepts represented by variables and indicate precisely how the concerns of armed combatants and the commitments they make to one another during negotiations shape the trajectory of the peace process. In other words, case studies allow us to flesh out our discussion of the factors that are central to establishing an enduring peace.

Second, and perhaps most important, describing these efforts at civil war resolution through case studies provides an opportunity to look at the relationship between different stages of the conflict-resolution process. Of necessity, previous chapters have analyzed each individual step of the peace process and its influence on the prospects for an enduring stability in isolation. Through detailed case studies, however, we can consider how these individual stages of (1) negotiating a settlement, (2) structuring the institutions that form the basis of the agreement, and (3) implementing settlement provisions fit together into a coherent narrative and collectively influence the prospects for establishing peace.

We consider Angola and the Philippines to be particularly effective cases to contrast with each other because they differ in terms of both the content of their negotiated settlements and the final outcome of their peace processes.[1] None of Angola's three separate attempts between 1975 and 1999 to establish peace through a negotiated settlement included provisions that required adversaries to share or divide state power across all four dimensions of government power—the political, military, territorial, and economic aspects of state strength. In contrast, the 1996 agreement reached among enemies in the Philippines included provisions that addressed every relevant aspect of state power identified in this volume.

Despite the assistance of third-party forces seeking to enforce the terms of the agreement following two of its negotiated agreements, Angola slid back into civil war after the signing of each of its settlements. Conversely, competitors in the Philippines, even in the absence of external support, proved able to maintain their agreement and establish a sense of security among signatories that allowed each side to lay down its arms and peacefully participate in the politics of the postwar state.

We construct the following narratives for each state by considering how initiating the negotiation process, designing institutions as part of an agreement, and implementing a settlement convey signals by former adversaries regarding their commitment to peace. We emphasize throughout our analysis that competitors are likely to view commitments to an enduring peace as credible when leaders prove willing to accept the costs associated with agreeing to establish power-sharing and power-dividing institutions, and then carry out the promises specified in the settlement. This newfound confidence that former enemies' intentions are nonthreatening is the foundation of a sustained and self-enforcing peace.

Angola

Angola has experienced only intermittent moments of peace since gaining its independence from Portugal in 1975. Each of these brief moments of stability, the longest of which lasted only four years, was preceded by the

---

1. For further discussion of case selection criteria, including those on which we draw below, see Van Evera 1997.

signing of a negotiated peace settlement. All told, warring groups within Angola have negotiated four civil war settlements in attempts to bring peace to their beleaguered country. Three of these agreements—the Gbadolite Accord, the Bicesse Accords, and the Lusaka Protocol—subsequently failed. The collapse of each of these agreements subjected millions of Angolans to more years of conflict and misery. A tenuous peace, established with the signing of yet another agreement in April 2002, remains in place at present.

Why, in the face of these repeated failures, do warring groups in Angola continue attempting to end armed conflict through bargained agreements? Why have the country's negotiated civil war settlements failed to establish enduring, peaceful relations among former enemies? This case study addresses these questions by analyzing the negotiation, establishment, and implementation of the three Angolan civil war settlements reached prior to the year 2000.

BACKGROUND

At the eve of independence in 1974, Angola had already experienced more than a decade of conflict as nationalists struggled for freedom from colonial rule by Portugal. Militarily weak and unwilling to reconcile their differences and work together, three movements—the National Front for the Liberation of Angola (FNLA), the Popular Movement for the Liberation of Angola (MPLA), and the National Union for the Total Independence of Angola (UNITA)—proved incapable of defeating the colonial power.[2] Only after a military coup in Portugal did the new government deem control of Angola more trouble than it was worth and grant independence.

With this unexpected decision, the three competing liberation movements were obliged to come together quickly and establish a common platform for independence talks with Portugal. This was achieved in a meeting held in Mombasa, Kenya, by the three groups in early January 1975.[3] Subsequently, on January 15, 1975, following four-party talks held in Alvor, Portugal, the FNLA, the MPLA, and UNITA signed the Portuguese-brokered Alvor Accord.

This accord, which called for Angola to become independent on November 11, 1975, stands as the country's first effort to create conflict-management

2. Not only did the groups refuse to join forces against the Portuguese but they also frequently fought each other for control over Angola's territory. For further details regarding the three movements during the period prior to independence, see Kambwa et al. 1999.
    3. Ibid.

institutions based on the principle of sharing power among contending groups. The agreement committed the FNLA, the MPLA, and UNITA to forming a transitional coalition government in which each group would have equal representation. Headed by a Portuguese high commissioner, a presidential council with a rotating chairmanship was expected to assist the government.[4] The accord also called for the formation of a National Defense Commission, which would integrate 8,000 troops from each of the independence movements. These troops, augmented by 24,000 Portuguese soldiers who would later withdraw, were to form the basis of the new country's unified army.

The transitional government established by the Alvor Accord faltered soon after the agreement was signed. The armed struggle was quickly reinitiated with each of the three liberation movements gambling that it might achieve dominance once the Portuguese left the scene. These groups' links to a number of external actors further complicated the process of determining who would control the Angolan state following independence.[5] Ultimately, following fierce fighting to control the capital of Luanda, and only a single day after the departure of the Portuguese, MPLA forces established control over the city and declared an independent People's Republic of Angola.

For the next two decades, the actions of foreign states would shape the trajectory of Angola's civil war, as well as the prospects for a peaceful settlement. During the 1980s, heightened attacks in Angola by South African Defense Forces (SADF) pursuing troops fighting for the independence of neighboring Namibia prompted a build-up of Cuban troops supporting the Angolan government army. Clashes between these two sets of external forces in 1988 prompted concerns that Angola's domestic war could escalate into an international conflict among allies of the United States and the Soviet Union. In an effort to head off this threat, negotiations were initiated with the participation of Angola, Cuba, and South Africa. The United States served as a site of the negotiations as well as the intermediary among the competing sides.

These talks resulted in the signing of an agreement in New York on De-

4. Hampson 1990.

5. The FNLA was initially supported by the United States, South Africa, and later by China. The group's regional patron was Zaire. Following the decline of the FNLA as a fighting force, UNITA, which had initially received its support from China, became the beneficiary of U.S. and South African support. The MPLA had the backing of the Soviet Union, Cuba, and, regionally, of the Congo (Brazzaville) and Zambia.

cember 22, 1988. The accord provided for the initiation of the independence process in Namibia on April 1, 1989, and required the withdrawal of all Cuban troops from Angola by July 1991. The agreement pointedly did not address a means of ending the ongoing armed conflict between the Angolan government and UNITA.[6] Nor did it commit any external actors, with the exception of Cuba, to ending their assistance to parties engaged in the civil war. Not until several months later would an attempt be made to negotiate a settlement among the domestic interests participating in the war.

THE GBADOLITE ACCORD

Stage One—Initiating Negotiations

Following the New York agreement of 1988, the MPLA and UNITA started low-level negotiations in January 1989. The substance of the talks was initially limited to an offer by the government to provide amnesty for UNITA soldiers who abandoned the armed struggle. Over the next few months, the government's position in the negotiations, guided by President Eduardo dos Santos, evolved to suggest that achieving peace was contingent on UNITA agreeing to the temporary exile of its leader Jonas Savimbi and integrating its civilian and military elements into the MPLA-led one-party state.[7] The government's negotiating stance, which essentially amounted to little more than a demand for surrender, proved fundamentally incompatible with the rebels' continuing insistence on power sharing and multiparty elections.

Given this apparent stalemate, many observers were surprised when dos Santos agreed in June 1989 to participate in a summit meeting focused on national reconciliation hosted by Zairian president Mobutu Sese Seko in Gbadolite, Zaire. What accounted for the Angolan government's willingness to make a new attempt at negotiations? In part, the MPLA appeared increasingly concerned about the imminent loss of international support that had, to this point, provided it with the resources necessary to prosecute the war. With Cuban troops in the process of withdrawing and the Soviet Union seeking to terminate financial commitments that it had made at the height of the cold war, dos Santos anticipated that his power, and thus his ability to shape the direction of negotiations, would only erode in the future.[8] This concern was reinforced by expectations that the United States would main-

---

6. The FNLA had ceased its participation in the conflict by the early 1980s.
7. Rothchild 1997.
8. *Facts on File World News Digest* 1989a.

tain its financial backing of UNITA. This, at least, was Savimbi's impression as he indicated in the following terms: "If America did not support UNITA, first UNITA could be weakened and you don't negotiate with weak people. It is because UNITA is strong that the MPLA (government) is talking."[9]

The agreement to initiate these negotiations produced uneven costs for the competing sides. The leader of the government, President dos Santos, was forced to concede the most by submitting to negotiations under the auspices of international mediators. UNITA came away from the agreement with an imprimatur of legitimacy that it had previously lacked. As noted by Jardo Muekalia, a Washington-based UNITA representative, through its agreement to a high-level meeting with UNITA, the MPLA had "gone from calling us bandits and terrorists to a handshake."[10] Dos Santos, on the other hand, faced the criticism of doctrinaire Marxists within his party who accused him of selling out their interests at Gbadolite.[11]

Stage Two—Designing Institutions and Signing the Settlement

No meaningful compromises regarding the design of institutions to manage conflict nonviolently were reached at the Gbadolite summit. Neither side proved willing to compromise positions that had been staked out prior to the conference. Savimbi remained adamant in his demand that the MPLA-led government share power with the rebels. The government, for its part, remained committed to leading a one-party state. At this point, although the civil war in Angola had dragged on for nearly fourteen years and produced approximately 26,000 deaths, each warring group, still believing it could prevail militarily, refused to contemplate the possibility of sharing or dividing state power with the other.

That any agreement at all was signed may have had more to do with the interests of Mobutu than participants in the war. The Zairian leader, scheduled to travel to Washington soon after the negotiations, appears to have wanted a diplomatic victory at the talks as a means of demonstrating his influence and importance in Africa. Observers at Gbadolite suggest that this may have led Mobutu, who acted as the intermediary between dos Santos and Savimbi when the two refused to meet each other, to mislead the belligerents about exactly what concessions each had made.[12]

9. Cited in Reed 1989b.
10. Reed 1989a.
11. *The Economist* 1990, 36. On the issue of the uneven costs felt by rebels and governments associated with the initiation of negotiations, see Hoddie and Hartzell 2003.
12. *Facts on File World News Digest* 1989b.

An unwritten settlement later issued in the form of a communiqué ultimately emerged from Gbadolite. Diplomatic sources were quoted as saying the settlement involved four points, which included a cease-fire, an ambiguous commitment to creating a "national unity" government, a two-year, self-imposed exile for Savimbi, and the monitoring of the agreement by leaders of Zaire, Congo, and Gabon.[13] Soon after the end of the summit, Savimbi dismissed claims that he had agreed to exile and called into question other elements of the settlement. With no real agreement on rules for managing conflict, peace prevailed for only two months before sustained conflict once again emerged. Implementing the agreement became a moot issue; not only was it unclear exactly what provisions there were to fulfill, but the rapid renewal of hostilities made following through on any aspect of the settlement impossible.

By failing to agree on the design of institutions for sharing or dividing power at the Gbadolite summit, Angola's adversaries signaled most clearly to one another their continued reluctance toward paying any costs in exchange for a peaceful resolution to the civil war. The two parties' lack of readiness to compromise regarding the question of how and by whom power was to be controlled at the center indicated that although each group may have been interested in peace, they were still unwilling to absorb any of the costs necessary to achieve this goal.

THE BICESSE ACCORDS

Stage One—Initiating Negotiations

A new round of talks between the MPLA and UNITA began in Portugal during April 1990. There was a heavy international presence at these talks, with Portugal serving as mediator and both U.S. Secretary of State James Baker and Soviet Foreign Minister Eduard Shevardnadze attending as "observers."[14] The negotiations engendered a series of compromises between the government and UNITA over the ensuing months. These included a promise by MPLA's central committee that the government would "evolve toward a multiparty system" and a commitment by UNITA to drop its demands for a role in a transitional government.[15] By September 1990, the MPLA and UNITA had also agreed that the United States, the Soviet Union, and Portugal

13. Reed 1989a.
14. Hampson 1990, 100.
15. Quoted in ibid., 99.

should monitor an eventual cease-fire. Shortly thereafter, the United States and Soviet Union indicated their willingness to police not only a cease-fire but also multiparty elections.[16]

Bolstering this progress was a series of moves taken by the leadership of UNITA and the MPLA to solidify support among their memberships of the peace process. Accordingly, UNITA held a conference on the negotiating process from December 28, 1990, through January 2, 1991. The meeting, which included members of the UNITA bureaucracy and of the supreme command of its armed forces, concluded with an expression of full support for continuing negotiations with the MPLA to peacefully resolve the war. The MPLA, for its part, conducted a military and cabinet reshuffle, presumably with the intention of removing from positions of influence any potential critics of conciliation efforts with UNITA.[17] Because UNITA and the MPLA took steps in full public view to bolster each movement's support for peace negotiations, these efforts by each group's leadership could signal to each other a willingness to bear the costs of confrontation with its own membership and thus a resolve to move the peace process forward.

While these signals were more costly for both sides than those occurring during the initiation of negotiations at Gbadolite, the context in which these actions took place limited their significance. At the time the Bicesse Accords were finally signed in May 1991, for example, the government and UNITA were still engaged in heavy fighting. The two parties' reluctant agreement to the accord appears to have been a reaction to pressure exerted on them by their respective sponsors. In fact, just prior to signing the accord, President dos Santos and the MPLA refused to recognize UNITA; the rebels also publicly challenged the political legitimacy of the MPLA.[18] As events would demonstrate, this was an inauspicious start to the newly negotiated settlement.

Stage Two—Designing Institutions and Signing the Settlement

The Bicesse Accords provided for a cease-fire that was to go into force on May 15, 1991. Many of the agreement's provisions were geared toward holding elections that would establish the new government. These included recognition by UNITA of the present government in power and a commitment by the MPLA to the principle of multiparty democracy. Elections were to be held on a timetable agreeable to the two parties, but not later than November 1992, and would be monitored by international observers.[19]

16. Ibid., 100.
17. Ibid., 102.
18. Ibid., 119.
19. Rothchild and Hartzell 1992.

The Bicesse Accords also included provisions consistent with two of the four power-sharing and power-dividing dimensions that form the focus of this book. The power-sharing rules adopted were both political and military in nature. Political power-sharing measures during the period of transition took the form of a variety of verification commissions on which both sets of belligerents were to be represented. These included the Political-Military Joint Commission (CCPM), a Mixed Commission for Verification and Super-vision (CMVF), and a Joint Commission for the Constitution of Armed Forces (CCFA).[20] Despite these commitments to sharing power in the transitional bodies, the elections that would determine the composition of the new government were to be decided based on a "winner-take-all" formula that would minimize the presence of those who failed to gain a plurality in elections.

With respect to military power sharing, the Bicesse Accords required the creation of a single national military force to be composed of soldiers drawn in equal numbers from the government and UNITA forces. Government and rebel troops, who had only recently sought to kill each other, were now expected to cooperate and serve together as the foundation of the state's security forces. Through this mechanism, neither UNITA nor MPLA forces would have a monopoly on the most unambiguous means of ensuring security in the postwar state.

By agreeing to these measures, the leaders of the government and UNITA demonstrated an awareness of how security concerns might affect the prospects for a continuation of peace once the war ended and the state became the sole center of power. Certainly the agreement to incorporate UNITA troops into the national armed forces, thereby making it more difficult to use the army against former UNITA supporters, indicated some sensitivity to the rebels' most immediate fears. These actions, and the limitations they placed on the capacity of either dos Santos or Savimbi to unilaterally control the direction of the postwar state, were critical for getting the two parties to acquiesce to the agreement.

Stage Three—Implementing the Settlement

Implementation of the Bicesse Accords was to take place in a series of phases. Once a cease-fire had taken hold, each side's military forces were to move to assembly points for disarmament and demobilization. This was to

20. Members of the so-called troika of observers—the United States, Soviet Union, and Portugal—would also participate in the CCPM, while the CMVF would include the same external observers, plus UN representatives.

be followed by the creation of a single national military and the enactment of electoral reform laws. The final step in the process was to be the national elections that would establish the new government.[21]

Although the cease-fire held, for the most part, troop assembly and demobilization did not proceed as expected. In part, this can be attributed to the logistical difficulties of getting troops to designated assembly areas. There were also indications, however, that rebel leader Savimbi began to balk when he confronted the escalating costs associated with adhering to the expectations of the peace process. He sought to delay the army's integration process and at one point put his troops in the assembly areas on alert, presumably as a precursor to sending them back into the bush in anticipation of returning to war.

These actions followed warnings by diplomats in Luanda during March 1992 that defections within UNITA were increasing. Whether these defections signaled unhappiness on the part of UNITA members with the compromises required by the accords and/or discontent with Savimbi's leadership style (including allegations that he had ordered the execution of children as well as two UNITA spokesmen in Washington) was not clear.[22] What was apparent, however, was that Savimbi, fearing challenges to his continued leadership as well as the growing possibility that he would not fare well in the upcoming elections, was contemplating resuming the war in a bid to maintain his control over UNITA.

Despite these discouraging signs of Savimbi's weakening commitment to the peace process, national elections were held on September 29 and 30, 1992. Monitored by the UN Angola Verification Mission (UNAVEM II), which had originally been deployed to verify that the joint monitoring groups fulfilled their responsibilities, the MPLA won the legislative elections with 54 percent of the vote as compared to UNITA's 34 percent. In the presidential elections, dos Santos received 50 percent of the vote against Savimbi's 40 percent. Because neither presidential candidate achieved a clear majority of the vote, electoral law required the two candidates to compete in a second round of balloting.

Despite the elections having been judged "generally free and fair" by Margaret Anstee, the UN secretary-general's special representative to Angola, UNITA claimed that its electoral defeat was the result of fraud. Savimbi followed these accusations with the withdrawal of UNITA troops, including

21. Hampson 1990.
22. Ibid.

eleven former UNITA generals, from the newly unified armed forces. Fighting soon broke out near major urban centers but ceased after a hastily negotiated cease-fire in early November.

Choosing to ignore clear indications that Savimbi was unwilling to abide by either the settlement provisions or the election results, dos Santos proceeded with plans to create a national unity government. He appointed his new cabinet on December 1, reserving five ministerial portfolios for UNITA members. In addition, the posts of the chief of the army general staff and deputy chief of the general staff were held for UNITA. These efforts, however, did not prevent the situation from deteriorating to the point that, by early February 1993, UN Secretary-General Boutros Boutros-Ghali advised the Security Council to withdraw all but a handful of UNAVEM II's 600 military observers out of concern for their safety. By the time the conflict was renewed, the Bicesse Accords had brought Angola little more than one year of fragile peace.

In the final analysis, the failure of the Bicesse Accords can be attributed to the continued unwillingness of Savimbi to bear the costs that his continued participation in the peace process would have imposed on both himself and his party. By holding the first round of elections, Savimbi realized that he would likely never become president nor would his party be in a position to control the postwar state. A loss of personal power would prove inevitable with the fulfillment of the settlement's terms. At the same time, Savimbi faced criticism and a loss of prestige within UNITA for failing to protect his group's interests during the peace process.

In short, the process of signaling between parties was aborted by the rebel party's unwillingness to absorb the costs that resulted from implementing power-sharing provisions. Through his actions, Savimbi demonstrated a preference for continuing war over the necessities of sharing power with a rival and facing down critics within his own party. The signal he sent while implementing the Bicesse Accords was that he still valued conflict and maintaining control over his own party to the more ambiguous rewards of peace.

THE LUSAKA PROTOCOL

Stage One—Initiating Negotiations

The negotiations leading to the signing of the Lusaka Protocol began a year after the collapse of the Bicesse Accords. The UN-mediated talks, which occurred between 1993 and 1994 in Lusaka, Zambia, were held against a backdrop of intense violence as the Angolan army launched a new offensive against UNITA in an effort to reclaim the territory occupied by the rebels (by some estimates, nearly 70 percent of the country's land).[23]

At this stage of the conflict, the leadership of UNITA and the government had different motivations for once again attempting to construct a bargained resolution to war. For his part, Savimbi had growing concerns that the power of his rebel group was weakening. Continuing divisions within his movement and the recent military successes of the Angolan army suggested that UNITA increasingly risked becoming marginalized within the state. There was also a growing sense of international isolation. Savimbi had come under criticism from foreign leaders for reneging on previous peace settlements; the Clinton administration had also announced that it was on the verge of approving the establishment of diplomatic relations with the MPLA-led government.

Since the Bicesse Accords, President dos Santos had enjoyed greater approval from members of the international community in recognition of his efforts to keep that peace process on track. He thus saw reinitiating negotiations as a means to bolster further his own status and the legitimacy of his regime. In addition, the risks to him of a challenge from within the MPLA were lowered by that group's demonstrated ability to triumph electorally at the legislative level as well as dos Santos's strong showing in the presidential elections. New negotiations and a renewed agreement to share power with UNITA thus came at very little cost to dos Santos as leader of the MPLA.

Given their shared history of failed agreements, it is unlikely that either the government or UNITA was particularly focused on the signals of intent made during the bargaining process leading up to the Lusaka Protocol. The costs of the talks themselves were minimal to both sides. The MPLA and UNITA had faced each other at the bargaining table a number of times before. In this sense, these two parties had already recognized each other as having a legitimate role in the governance of the postwar state.

Stage Two—Designing Institutions and Signing the Settlement

Under the guidance of a "coalition of mediators," among them UN special representative Alioune Blondin Beye, U.S. special envoy Paul Hare, and Portuguese and South African diplomats, the government and UNITA signed the Lusaka Protocol on November 22, 1994.[24] The protocol refined the roadmap

---

23. Rothchild 1997.
24. The phrase "coalition of mediators" is Rothchild's (1997, 136).

to peace developed during the Bicesse Accords. It also sought to take up where the Bicesse Accords had left off by requiring UNITA to accept the results of the previous elections and to agree to complete the second round of voting for the presidency.[25]

One key difference between the earlier Bicesse Accords and the Lusaka Protocol was that power-sharing and power-dividing institutions played a much more significant role in the latter than had been the case in the former. The Lusaka Protocol augmented the political and military power-sharing provisions that had appeared in the earlier agreement. At the same time, it expanded the number of power-sharing dimensions to be employed in the governance of Angola by addressing the issue of the territorial distribution of power.

In terms of political power sharing, the Lusaka Protocol moved beyond simply providing for mutual participation in verification committees and added the requirement that the MPLA and UNITA share executive power by allocating cabinet appointments. Although it did not constitute part of the final settlement, reports leading up to the signing of the protocol indicated that the government and UNITA had reached a "gentleman's agreement" that would secure a measure of personal power for Savimbi by guaranteeing him the title of vice president.[26] While this never became a reality, it does indicate how far the government was willing to go to secure peace.

The military power-sharing dimension in the new agreement was conceptually the same as it had been in the Bicesse Accords. The protocol once again called for integrating the armed forces so that they were composed of both government and UNITA soldiers. Substantively unique about this dimension of the Lusaka Protocol was that it extended the concept of sharing power among those wielding the state's coercive power to the country's police force. Having UNITA soldiers serve as part of the police force provided yet another means of ensuring that the most tangible aspect of state power would not be targeted against them.

Finally, a new power-sharing dimension was introduced in the Lusaka Protocol. A territorial power-sharing provision was included in the agreement by granting a number of key governorships to UNITA as well as guaranteeing them control over a significant number of municipalities.[27]

As was the case with the negotiations themselves, the history of failed

25. Kambwa et al. 1999.
26. Mwiinga 1994.
27. Rothchild 1997.

agreements seems likely to have diminished the significance of the signals of intention associated with the mutual commitment to share state power across a majority of dimensions. The Lusaka Protocol produced a set of power-sharing compromises that served as the strongest guarantee yet that neither the MPLA nor UNITA would be marginalized in the context of the postwar state. The remaining critical test was whether both sides would prove willing to absorb the costs associated with these compromises while implementing the agreement's provisions.

Stage Three—Implementing the Settlement

As with the Bicesse Accords, the implementation of the Lusaka Protocol was not left in the hands of the parties to the conflict. The role of UN troops in this instance was transformed from the rather straightforward verification mission they had performed earlier to one with powers of intervention. More than 4,000 UN troops (UNAVEM III) were deployed in Angola with the authority to enforce the settlement.

Over the next four years, the United Nations oversaw the 1994 Lusaka peace agreement at a cost of $1.6 billion. Progress toward the implementation of some key components of the settlement—including those requiring the quartering and demobilizing of UNITA soldiers—proceeded slowly. Despite these delays, it was agreed in 1997 that a coalition government incorporating UNITA would be put into place. As with prior agreements, Savimbi eventually refused to take the steps necessary to make peace a reality. His reneging on his commitments by maintaining his regional strongholds, holding onto his army, and retaking territory through force led the government to suspend coalition rule in September 1998. Shortly thereafter Angola once again found itself embroiled in civil war.

As had been the case with the two prior agreements, Savimbi was exposed during the implementation process as an unreliable partner in the peace process. Through his actions he signaled to the MPLA his reluctance to cede any degree of personal power to form a coalition government and a disinclination or inability to force critics of compromise to back down from their positions of intransigence.

ACCOUNTING FOR FAILURE

Three negotiated settlements were crafted in an effort to end two decades of civil war in Angola.[28] What explains the failure of each of these agreements

28. Angola is unique among our civil war cases in the number of efforts that have been made

to bring stability to the country? On its surface, the most straightforward explanation is rebel leader Jonas Savimbi's refusal to make the concessions necessary to fulfill the obligations required by the peace process. In this interpretation, Savimbi was simply a "spoiler" of these settlements who signed them with the intent of buying time until the next rebel offensive.[29]

While such a possibility cannot be completely discounted, it fails to address a related question—did the process by which these agreements were constructed or the substance of the settlements themselves in some way contribute to Savimbi's decision to act as a spoiler? In other words, is it possible to offer an account of the peace process that explains Savimbi's behavior as a rational response to conditions he confronted immediately following the signing of a settlement? Below we consider this possibility by examining how both the behavior of third-party actors and the settlement's content may have engendered conditions that unwittingly undermined the prospects of an enduring peace.

Third-Party Actors

A number of third-party actors, ranging from state leaders to international organizations, played a role in efforts to resolve the conflict in Angola. Despite the largely good intentions of these interventions, we suggest that their net effect was to minimize competing parties' potential to signal their true intentions to one another, which instead fostered an environment rife with suspicion.[30] Adversaries could never fully discount the possibility that their rivals' actions were reactions to the pressure applied by external forces rather than a sincere desire for peace.

The risks that signals of intentions among adversaries may be lost because of the behavior of third-party actors is perhaps best illustrated by the events leading up to the Gbadolite Accord. In this instance, President Mobutu pri-

---

to negotiate a settlement of what is essentially the same civil war (i.e., the same sets of issues, adversaries, and leadership of the parties in conflict were in place when the Gbadolite, Bicesse, and Lusaka settlements were negotiated). Because none of our other civil war cases shares this characteristic with Angola, we have opted not to include a variable controlling for previous failed efforts to negotiate an end to a civil war in our statistical analyses.

29. This is the interpretation of Stephen John Stedman (1997, 40): "In part, Savimbi's personality defined the conflict in all-or-nothing terms; a combination of racism, paranoia, and megalomania led him to believe that the MPLA had stolen the election from him and that he had the right to rule all of Angola." Based on this perspective, Stedman suggests that coercion, used to force UNITA to abide by its agreements, would have served as the most realistic means of moving the peace process forward.

30. See Chapter 4 for a more developed discussion of this perspective.

oritized his own interest in scoring a diplomatic victory above reaching a meaningful settlement between the competing groups. Only by ignoring or misrepresenting the positions of each side was Mobutu able to claim that the conflict between the MPLA and UNITA had been settled.

In hindsight, however, it seems clear that Mobutu's actions simply masked the true intentions and beliefs of the two sides—that each party still hoped it could win the war through armed force and that no shared vision existed concerning the management of conflict in the postwar state. By imposing a premature settlement on the parties to the conflict, Mobutu's actions resulted in an environment in which violations of the initial agreement were inevitable and any new efforts to resolve the conflict would have to contend with the fact that each side had experienced acts of bad faith by its rival. Interpreted in this light, Savimbi's "paranoia" as the leader of the weaker party instead appears as a set of well-founded concerns based on experiencing the failure of previous settlements.

Settlement Institutionalization

Angola's first two negotiated settlements provided only limited opportunities for power sharing among the competing groups. The Gbadolite Accord made no explicit calls for power sharing beyond vague references to a government of national unity. This agreement thus failed to guarantee each group access to state power that would enable it to secure its continued existence.

The Bicesse Accords did call for both political and military power sharing. But even the particular content of some of these power-sharing provisions suggested a limited embrace of establishing a state in which the competing groups had a substantial influence over its future. This is most notable in the political power-sharing provision that called for the mutual control of transitional bodies. To a large degree, this provision was overshadowed by another political institution: the decision, as part of the elections agreement, to hold winner-take-all elections. Not only did this particular institutional arrangement give those failing to achieve a plurality in the electoral contest little incentive to comply with the outcome, but it likely also proved particularly threatening to those in the minority, because it gave the winner an important element of state control.

By failing to include a wide array of power-sharing and power-dividing institutions at the outset, settlement architects missed an important opportunity for the adversaries to signal their commitment to a negotiated peace. Had they agreed to create a range of power-sharing and power-dividing

institutions in some of the earlier settlements, the costs associated with signing on to those institutions—the loss of power vis-à-vis a former enemy as
well as a potential loss of credibility or stature within one's own group—
would have sent a powerful signal of their commitment to building a stable
peace. By the time the more highly institutionalized Lusaka Protocol was
reached, the credibility associated with such signaling had been almost irre-
trievably damaged by the failure to follow through on previously established
institutional agreements.

RECENT DEVELOPMENTS

Recent events in Angola have provided another opportunity to negotiate an
end to its long-running civil war. The precipitating factor leading to new
negotiations was the death, in combat, of Savimbi on February 23, 2002. A
little less than a month after his death, negotiations were initiated under the
auspices of the United Nations.[31] A cease-fire agreement signed by government and UNITA representatives on April 4, 2002, committed both sides to
implementing the measures specified in the 1994 Lusaka Protocol.

At the time of this writing, the peace in Angola has held for nearly two-
and-a-half years following the implementation of the latest agreement. Angola's political landscape has changed in some significant ways during this
period. UNITA has reshaped itself into the country's main opposition party.
Civil society, under the leadership of the Catholic Church, has become an
increasingly active force for national reconciliation. Angola is now concentrating on postwar reconstruction and efforts to take advantage of its enormous economic potential. Given its disappointing past, whether Angola has
finally embarked on a peace that is both stable and self-enforcing remains
to be seen.

The Philippines

In contrast to Angola's multiple failed agreements, the Philippines appears
only once in our data set of bargained resolutions to civil wars and is an
example of a successful effort at ending conflict through a negotiated settlement. Despite earlier attempts to reach a bargained resolution between the
government of the Philippines and the Moro National Liberation Front

31. *AllAfrica, Inc., Africa News* 2002.

(MNLF), not until the signing of the 1996 agreement, informally known as the Davao Consensus, was a negotiated resolution to the war between the two sides finally achieved.[32]

As with our discussion of Angola's efforts at conflict resolution, our emphasis is on exactly how the particulars of the peace process shaped both the impressions and behaviors of former combatants. We attribute the success of the peace process in the Philippines to the mutual creation among adversaries of a highly institutionalized settlement that included provisions for sharing political, military, territorial, and economic aspects of state power. The willingness of each side's leadership to cede government power in the interest of creating a secure postwar environment, as well as to endure the criticisms of militants unhappy with these compromises, served as a costly signal that they preferred peace over continuing conflict. That this was achieved with the first fully negotiated settlement between the current leadership of the contending groups meant, in contrast to experiences in Angola, that parties were not primed for distrust based on a history of defections and failed agreements.

BACKGROUND

The conflict in the Philippines centers on religious differences within the population. The state is predominantly Catholic, with a Muslim minority that constitutes less than 5 percent of the country's total population and is concentrated on the southern islands of Mindanao.[33] Members of the Muslim population have sought greater levels of autonomy, and even independence, from the government in Manila in order to end what they perceive as systematic state discrimination and a lack of opportunities for local economic development. Among their most prominent concerns has been the high rate of migration into Mindanao by Filipino Catholics, which has led to a substantial reduction in the total number of localities in which Muslims are a majority.[34]

Armed opposition to President Ferdinand Marcos's government began in 1968 with the organization of the Muslim (Mindanao) Independence Movement.[35] Marcos responded to this resistance movement by co-opting

32. Peter Chalk (1997, 79) refers to the agreement as the Davao Consensus in reference to the Philippine city that served as a site of negotiations.

33. McKenna 2004.

34. Chalk 1997, 81.

35. This is not the first instance of the population of Mindanao taking up arms against the state. Inhabitants had also opposed efforts by Spain and the United States to extend their colonial administration to the islands (Quimpo 2001, 274).

many of its leaders into positions in the central state; for example, twelve former rebel leaders were commissioned into the armed forces.[36] Those seeking to continue hostilities formed the Moro National Liberation Front (MNLF), along with its armed contingent known as the Bangsa Moro Army, under the leadership of Nur Misuari.[37] As we describe below, two prominent efforts to secure an agreement between the government of the Philippines and the MNLF failed before a full settlement was reached.

THE TRIPOLI AGREEMENT

Stage One—Initiating Negotiations

Violence between the MNLF and the government of the Philippines escalated during the early 1970s; one estimate puts the number of Muslims that died as a result of the civil war during this period at 60,000.[38] In response to the heightened intensity of hostilities, Middle Eastern states represented in the Islamic Council of Foreign Ministers (ICFM) threatened President Marcos with an oil embargo if he continued to resist negotiations with the Muslim rebels.[39] Essentially forced to the bargaining table, the government and MNLF held negotiations in Saudi Arabia in 1975 and in Libya's capital city of Tripoli the following year.[40] Serving as mediators at the talks were Libyan President Muammar Qaddafi, the Organization of the Islamic Conference (OIC), and the ICFM.[41]

Marcos had previously sought to placate the Muslim minority through a series of unilateral actions ranging from building a mosque in the capital city of Manila to officially recognizing Islamic holidays.[42] Coerced into negotiations by foreign countries, the president only reluctantly absorbed the loss of authority and prestige that came with recognizing the MNLF as a legitimate voice for the state's Muslim interests. Given the international arm twisting necessary to get negotiations off the ground, it seems unlikely that the MNLF interpreted Marcos's actions as signaling a genuine change of heart concerning his intentions toward them.

---

36. May 1997, 343. For a discussion of the use of cooptation as a mechanism for resolving civil conflict, see Byman 2002, 81–99.
37. Islam 1998, 448–49.
38. Jones 1986.
39. Noble 1981, 1099.
40. Chalk 1997, 83.
41. May 1997, 344.
42. McKenna 2004.

Stage Two—Designing Institutions and Signing the Settlement

A preliminary settlement between the government and MNLF, termed the Tripoli Agreement, was reached in December 1976. Had the accord been finalized, it would have constituted a highly institutionalized settlement that provided for power sharing between the two parties across the political, territorial, and economic dimensions of state power. Political power sharing between the state and MNLF was to be guaranteed through a promise of Muslim representation in the institutions of central government. Territorial autonomy, the issue at the heart of the agreement, was to take the form of Muslim self-governance in thirteen of Mindanao's twenty-one provinces. This autonomy would have been embodied in the establishment of a regional legislative assembly, executive council, and Islamic courts. Finally, the provisional settlement called for economic power sharing by giving the regional government control over local finance and a "reasonable percentage" of the profits from mining on the island.[43] In return, the MNLF pledged an end to the armed struggle that intended to establish the entire island as a separate and sovereign state.[44]

Negotiations to resolve critical details associated with the settlement, including the structures of the autonomous state and the possibility of integrating MNLF forces into the government army, were to be held in the early months of 1977. Once the two parties returned to the bargaining table, however, the talks quickly collapsed into discord. A central cause of the deadlock was Marcos's insistence that the preliminary accord be ratified by a referendum among the affected provinces. When the vote was held on April 17 despite strong objections from the MNLF, Mindanao's Christian majority strongly rejected the idea of creating a fully autonomous Muslim government. Pointing to the referendum results, Marcos backed away from the commitments embodied in the Tripoli Agreement and talks between the two sides broke down that same month.[45] A return to armed hostilities followed in October.[46]

Beyond reinitiating conflict, the failure of the Tripoli Agreement shook the solidarity that had once existed among the Muslim rebels. Hashim Salamat, leader of the MNLF's Foreign Affairs Bureau, abandoned the party following its failure to secure a final settlement, accusing Misuari of corruption

43. Noble 1981, 1,100.
44. Chalk 1997, 83–84.
45. The fact that the ICFM had failed to follow through on its threat of an oil embargo may also have emboldened Marcos to reject the settlement. See Noble 1981, 1103.
46. Noble 1981, 1102.

and selling out Muslim interests over the course of the negotiations.[47] Since that time, Salamat's Moro Islamic Liberation Front (MILF) has become the more radical of the two major Muslim resistance organizations, which is reflected in its more intense religious orientation and nearly consistent advocacy of Mindanao's independence from the Philippines.[48] That the MNLF's unity foundered with the Tripoli Agreement suggests that the rebels endured the greatest costs with the provisional agreement to establish a power-sharing arrangement. While never having to actually cede any power to the government, the MNLF lost many adherents who viewed the leadership's efforts at conciliation with skepticism.

What accounts for the failure of the Tripoli Agreement? Parallel to Angola's experience at Gbadolite, the agreement appears to have gained initial assent among the relevant parties because of the heavy-handed influence of third parties intent on forcing through a settlement. Neither side was convinced that it was in its best interest to reach a settlement, and each interpreted the behavior of its enemies as nothing more than an expedient reaction to foreign pressure.[49] Engineering an opportunity to renege on his commitments through the referendum, Marcos abandoned the negotiations and reinitiated hostilities.

CREATION OF THE ARMM

Stage One—Initiating Negotiations

A second failed attempt to resolve the conflict between the government and the MNLF took place after the overthrow of the Marcos regime in 1986.[50] As part of an effort to establish its legitimacy, the newly elected democratic government of President Corazon Aquino sought to resolve disputes that had plagued the previous regime. To this end, the Aquino government restarted negotiations with the MNLF in the hopes of securing a peace settlement. The OIC again mediated these talks.[51]

As was the case with the bargaining prior to the Tripoli Agreement, negotiations centered primarily on the territorial scope of the autonomous Mus-

47. Islam 1998, 449–50.
48. Tan 2000, 273.
49. Noble (1981, 1102) suggests that the most straightforward reason for the failure of the agreement was the fact that "neither side was convinced that it would lose more by the resumption of fighting than it would lose in a settlement."
50. The MILF refused to participate in these talks (Tan 2000, 273).
51. May 1997, 345.

lim state. Misuari maintained that the regional government's authority should extend to the entire island of Mindanao. Aquino, in recognizing opposition to the negotiations from both the armed forces and the island's Christian population, sought to limit the promise of autonomy to those provinces and cities in which Muslims continued to constitute a majority. Facing this impasse, Misuari chose to end talks with the government in 1987 over accusations that the government violated the cease-fire.[52]

Despite the breakdown of talks, Aquino ensured that the post-Marcos constitution recognized the autonomy of "Muslim Mindanao."[53] Following a referendum held on the island in 1987, the government unilaterally established the Autonomous Region for Muslim Mindanao (ARMM) to encompass the four provinces in which Muslims retained a substantial presence. Declaring the territories designated as autonomous too limited, the MNLF and MILF chose to continue their armed opposition.[54]

The ability of militants on both sides of the dispute to derail the progress of the peace process is notable regarding this aborted attempt at negotiating a settlement. Aquino was constrained in the concessions she felt she could offer to the MNLF for fear that it would alienate her supporters among the military and Mindanao's Christian population. Misuari encountered both rhetorical and military attacks by the MILF that characterized the negotiations as a betrayal of Muslim interests. The inability or unwillingness of both Aquino and Misuari to face down their militant critics and save the peace talks indicated that both parties remained unwilling to bear the costs tied to a settlement that might signal their genuine interest in peace.

THE DAVAO CONSENSUS

Unlike previous attempts at conciliation, a new round of negotiations started in the early 1990s resulted in a negotiated settlement accepted by both the government and MNLF. This settlement has proved successful in fostering an enduring peace between these two parties.

Stage One—Initiating Negotiations—Tiptoeing on Barbed Wire

Negotiations that eventually led to the final settlement were initiated during 1993 in Jakarta, Indonesia, under the auspices of the Indonesian government and the OIC after the mutual commitment of President Fidel Ramos and the

52. Tan 2000, 273.
53. Bertrand 2000, 40.
54. Chalk 1997, 84–85.

MNLF to a cease-fire.[55] While the costs of the war had never again reached the zenith of the period associated with the early 1970s, one estimate places the total number of dead at the start of this new round of negotiations at 120,000.

The MNLF's attempt at peace almost immediately stirred reactions of opposition from individuals and groups both inside and beyond the rebel organization itself. Resistance from inside the MNLF became apparent when a number of its commanders refused to accept the cease-fire and sponsored sporadic attacks intended to end the negotiations. Outside the MNLF, it is notable that a new rebel group grew in prominence with the start of peace talks and offered an additional challenge to Misuari's authority. Abu Sayyaf, organized in 1991, was responsible for an upsurge of violence between 1993 and 1995.[56] Misuari interpreted the growing violence of this group, and in particular the attack on the predominantly Christian city of Ipil, as an effort to derail the peace process.[57]

These events demonstrate that the MNLF's leader, Nur Misuari, paid significant costs as a result of his decision to negotiate with the state. Challenges to Misuari's role as leader of the Muslim opposition intensified from within his own group as some members of the organization violated the declared cease-fire. Outside the MNLF, competing rebel groups enjoyed higher levels of support and prominence as Misuari was increasingly perceived as failing to represent the interests of Muslim Mindanao.

Stage Two—Designing Institutions and Signing the Settlement

The accord between Misuari's MNLF and the government of the Philippines was signed on September 2, 1996, in Jakarta.[58] The issue of the territorial reach of Muslim autonomy, which had proved to be an impasse in previous talks, was resolved through a novel arrangement. The settlement provided the MNLF with a degree of authority within the territory originally identified by the Tripoli Agreement as the scope of Muslim autonomy; a referendum would then be carried out within this territory three years after the settle-

---

55. Tan 2000, 274. Ramos had been elected as Aquino's chosen successor. "Tiptoeing on barbed wire" is the phrase Misuari used to describe the negotiation process and his efforts to manage and represent the diverse interests within the MNLF (Healy and Lopez 1996).

56. This group shares the MILF's interest in creating a separate Muslim state; the purposeful targeting of the Christian civilian population provides this organization its distinct identity (Tan 2000, 274–75).

57. Ibid., 275.

58. May 1997, 2.

ment to determine whether the population assented to continue the autonomy arrangement.[59]

The final peace settlement addressed all four potential aspects of power
sharing between the state and the MNLF. In terms of the political dimension
of state power, the agreement called for the creation of a Southern Philippine Council for Peace and Development (SPCD) composed of at least forty-
four MNLF representatives among its eighty-one total members. With Misuari acting as the organization's chairman, the SPCD's responsibilities included overseeing regional development projects and paving the way for the
autonomy referendum.[60] The territorial power-sharing aspect of the settlement recognized the SPCD's authority over the area originally identified in
the Tripoli Agreement and now designated as the Special Zone of Peace
and Development (SZOPAD). The military power-sharing dimension of the
agreement was its call for 7,500 MNLF soldiers to join the army of the Philippines. Finally, recognizing that the SPCD's main challenge was promoting
development on the island, the settlement provided for economic power
sharing by committing the government to increasing its expenditures in the
region.

For both sides in the conflict, the immediate cost of the final settlement
was conceding some of the objectives associated with the start of the war.
The government of the Philippines could no longer claim a monopoly on
government power. Instead, it would be forced to coordinate administra-
tively with a Muslim organization that had an equal or greater claim to the
loyalties of some of the local population. With the signing of the settlement,
the MNLF was also required to scale back its ambitions. The rebels had previously sought autonomy for all of the territories identified as Muslim
homelands in the Tripoli Agreement; the new settlement introduced substantial uncertainty about whether that goal would ever be achieved. Misuari
could only hold out hope that his administration would appear sufficiently
reassuring over the first three years and that the Christian population would

---

59. Exactly how long the provisional government would remain in place was an issue of
contention between the two sides during the negotiations. Healy and Lopez (1996) describe the
negotiations in the following terms: "During the three years of formal talks, Manila and the MNLF
clashed over what kind of administrative system should be installed in southern Mindanao.
Misuari originally demanded a 10-year provisional government; Manila's chief negotiator, retired
four-star Gen. Manuel Yan, offered one year. Misuari compromised on five years and Manila
came up to two. The talks stalled at that point. Then, Libya and Indonesia intervened to get
negotiations back on track. Indonesia was especially helpful, says Ramos. . . . Misuari and Yan
eventually settled on a three-year transitional council."

60. Chalk 1997, 85–86.

be willing to support the continuation of the territorial reach of the autonomy arrangement in the scheduled referendum.

The concessions associated with the peace agreement also led to intense criticism of the leadership by members of their respective constituencies. Both leaders were accused of betraying their collectivities' vital interests for little in the way of tangible benefits. The protests that followed soon after the settlement was announced provided the strongest indication of the dissatisfaction with the established agreement. MILF leader Hashim Salamat gave a voice to those within the Muslim collectivity critical of the compromise. Salamat condemned the agreement for failing to guarantee the territorial boundaries of the autonomous region and for providing only a façade of self-rule. Salamat was not alone in his criticism. Approximately 60,000 Muslims gathered in the town of Sultan Kudarat to protest against the agreement and reiterate their demands for a separate Muslim state.[61]

The reaction among some members of the Christian population indicated an equal degree of unease with the agreement. Protests among members of this collectivity greeted the Philippine president in Mindanao shortly after signing the settlement. The *Christian Science Monitor* reported: "In a two day tour through the region aimed at allaying the fears of the Christian population and explaining the controversial agreement, President Ramos was greeted with angry protesters and near riots. In Zamboanga last week, riot police held back an unruly crowd, estimated at over 10,000, which tore down the perimeter fence of the Edwin Andrews Air Base and rushed toward Ramos shouting 'No! No! No!' and 'Misuari stinks!' "[62] Even more ominous, three Christian militias within the region declared their intent to pursue armed resistance to the agreement.[63]

The mutual commitment of both Misuari and President Ramos to the agreement despite the prevalence of the protests enhanced the likelihood of peace by providing each side to the conflict with valuable information concerning the level of commitment of its former adversary to maintaining the emerging peace. The willingness to continue moving forward with the peace process, despite the protests their efforts elicited, suggested a genuine interest in resolving the conflict.

Stage Three—Implementing the Settlement

The final stage in the peace process we analyze is the implementation of the provisions associated with the 1996 agreement. On the basis of our assess-

61. Tan 2000, 275.
62. Tan 1996, 7.
63. Chalk 1997, 93.

ment we find that efforts at implementing the political and military aspects of the settlement have proved largely successful; this contrasts with the greater ambiguity concerning implementation of the agreement's territorial and economic dimensions.

The success of implementing the settlement's political dimension is apparent in the creation of the SPCD, with its membership including individuals representing the interests of both the central government and MNLF. A further indication of the transformation of the MNLF from rebels to participants in the peace process was Nur Misuari's offering himself as a candidate for the governorship of the ARMM "under the Banner of President Ramos's party" shortly after the agreement was signed.[64] Winning the election, Misuari served as the governor of the region between 1996 and 2001.

As with the political dimension of the settlement, implementing the military aspect of the accord appears to have been successful, with the integration of at least 6,750 MNLF soldiers (out of the 7,500 called for in the settlement) into special and auxiliary units of the armed forces and the Philippine National Police four years after the settlement was signed.[65]

In contrast to successes associated with implementing the political and military dimensions of the settlement, a significant degree of ambiguity remains concerning the carrying out of the provisions for territorial autonomy. While the SZOPAD is recognized as a legitimate entity by both the government and the MNLF, the referendum that was scheduled for 1999 to determine the territorial boundaries of the autonomous entity has not yet been held.[66] The question of whether the areas dominated by the Christian population but claimed by Muslims as their ancestral homeland will be permanently included as part of the autonomous region has not yet been resolved. For this reason, we consider implementation of the settlement's territorial provisions to be incomplete.

Turning to the economic provisions of the accord, MNLF representatives have been highly critical of what they perceive to be the government's far too limited financial assistance to Mindanao. Defenders of the government's efforts suggest that the funds provided have been squandered through the SPCD's mismanagement. As one observer notes:

> After [Misuari] became governor of the autonomous region, he had at his disposal, in addition to foreign aid, a development budget

64. Gutierrez 1999.
65. *Business World* (Philippines) 2000.
66. May 1997.

totaling nearly $600 million, allocated by the central government for the country's poorest region. Very little of this was spent on education or basic infrastructure projects such as roads. Instead, Misuari focused upon prestige projects, such as an international airport for his home island of Jolo. Worse still, money was spent to maintain a very comfortable lifestyle for the governor and his companions; it was reported that, on trips to Manila, Misuari would rent blocks of rooms at five-star hotels for himself and his retinue. This did not help to make him more popular in the autonomous region.[67]

Overall, both the government and the former rebels more often than not fulfilled the political, military, territorial, and economic commitments specified in the settlement. The peace process was far from flawlessly implemented, which is reflected in the failure to carry out the referendum on regional autonomy, but the actions of both sides indicated that they remained committed to peace and had no intention of reinitiating hostilities.

As with the earlier stages of the agreement, efforts to halt the peace process continued among those dissatisfied with compromises they perceived as marginalizing their interests. Both the MILF and Abu Sayyaf continued their armed resistance to the peace settlement. Also notable is that a new rebel group emerged in 2000 identifying itself as the MNLF-Islamic Command Council. Among their justifications for restarting the war against the government under the banner of the MNLF was that Misuari "had lost authority to lead the Moro people because he could not be in government and lead the jihad (holy war) at the same time."[68]

Consistent with the initial signing of the peace settlement, unavoidable costs were associated with efforts to implement the agreement. The government lost a monopoly on state authority, and representatives of the MNLF often received less local authority than had been anticipated during the war. Both sides continued to face both criticism and armed attacks from those who chose not to support the peace process. Yet the remaining commitment to this process despite these costs signals continuing conciliatory intent.

ACCOUNTING FOR SUCCESS

What accounts for the resolution of the conflict between the government and MNLF rebels in the Philippines? We attribute the success of the 1996

67. Gee 2002.
68. Fernandez and Balana 2000.

settlement to the ability of the two sides to provide convincing signals of their genuine interest in peace.[69] Their capacity to send these signals was enhanced by the restrained actions of third parties and the construction of a highly institutionalized settlement emphasizing the sharing of power between former adversaries.

Third-Party Actors

The first attempt by third-party actors to facilitate an accord between the Philippine government and MNLF rebels ended in failure. The Tripoli Agreement was tentatively reached because Middle Eastern states had threatened Marcos with an oil embargo if negotiations did not take place. Given that the settlement was the product of arm twisting, it had little meaningful value to the combatants as indicating preference for peace over continued conflict. This skepticism proved warranted when Marcos reneged on his commitments and war was soon reinitiated. As with Angola's Gbadolite Accord, the failure of the Tripoli Agreement illustrates that settlements forced upon enemies often do little to assuage security concerns or serve as a stable resolution of the conflict.

By contrast, the 1996 settlement was established with the meaningful participation and support of the conflicting parties themselves. Mediators, including Libya, Indonesia, and the OIC, were on hand during the bargaining. Yet nothing indicates that these third parties threatened to use sanctions to ensure government and MNLF participation. Because the negotiating environment was one in which the parties had no reason to doubt that the talks were motivated by anything other than an interest in peace, the talks themselves were a strong signal that the competing sides genuinely desired conciliation with the enemy. This offered a firm foundation of trust upon which to shape the agreement and begin the process of emerging from civil war.

Settlement Institutionalization

The 1996 settlement was the first fully realized agreement between the government and rebels. It also constituted the first and only effort at concilia-

69. Our assessment of the successful implementation of the 1996 agreement stands in sharp contrast to accounts that describe the accord as fragile or a failure (see, for example, Bertrand 2000). We think this difference has its roots in differing criteria for determining implementation success. Our focus is on whether the criteria outlined in the settlement have been fulfilled by signatories to the initial agreement and peace has endured. This contrasts with those who are critical of the settlement for failing to end the violence between the government and the armies of the MILF and Abu Sayyaf.

tion between President Fidel Ramos and MNLF leader Nur Misuari. In this sense, it is significant that the initial agreement between these two actors took the form of a highly institutionalized settlement in which the parties agreed to share or divide state power across political, military, territorial, and economic dimensions. Through this action, and in the absence of the history of failed agreements that weighed down conciliation efforts in Angola, the two sides proved capable of offering costly signals to each other concerning their genuine interest in maintaining peace. That they willingly endured both the loss of power and criticisms of their leadership inextricably linked to sharing and dividing power signaled that they were willing to pay a high price in order to maintain good relations with their former rivals. That peace was maintained without the assistance of third-party forces indicated the independent capacity of signaling between rivals to foster a secure and peaceful postconflict environment.

RECENT DEVELOPMENTS

While peace between the MNLF and government has remained intact, many of the players in the conflict itself have changed. Growing criticism of Misuari's misuse of government development funds culminated in his replacement as leader of the MNLF by Parouk Hussin in 2001. As Misuari was barred by law from running for election to governor more than once, Hussin was subsequently elected the new governor of the ARMM.[70]

Misuari did not fade quietly into political obscurity. In November 2001, prior to the scheduled governor's election to replace him, Misuari initiated an attack against government soldiers. Although one hundred people were killed during the incident, Misuari's actions failed to generate a great deal of support among rank-and-file members of the MNLF. Misuari was later arrested in Malaysia following his failed rebellion and was imprisoned in the Philippines.[71] More significant than Misuari's return to the use of violence is that it failed to restart the conflict between the MNLF and the government. This suggests the development of a degree of trust, and even mutual dependence between these two collectivities, that proved enduring even when it conflicted with the interests of an individual who had formerly been central to the peace process.

Beyond maintaining the 1996 accord, recent indications suggest that

70. Gee 2002.
71. Ibid.

progress is being made to end the continuing conflict between the government of the Philippines and the MILF.[72] Following the death of Hashim Salamat, a cease-fire between the two sides has been in place since May 2003. Negotiations supported by the United States are ongoing as of this writing.[73] Should these negotiations prove successful, it can at least be partially attributed to the recognition among the MILF leadership that the government has abided by its commitments to the MNLF and has demonstrated through these actions that it can behave as a reliable partner in peace processes.

Conclusion

The case studies in this chapter highlight a number of the points we have sought to emphasize throughout this book regarding the prospects for structuring a stable peace following the negotiated settlement of civil wars. Foremost among these is the difficulty of securing an end to a civil war in those instances in which the settlement provides few mechanisms for distributing or dividing state power among the parties to the conflict. Fearing for their future under conditions in which one group may come to dominate power and perhaps use it to the detriment of others, adversaries will not long abide by settlements that fail to include a number of measures for sharing and dividing state power among the formerly warring groups. In the absence of agreed-upon rules for nonviolently managing conflict, peace is not likely to prove enduring. This proved true in the case of Angola, where at least two of the country's three negotiated civil war settlements—Gbadolite and Bicesse—suffered from low levels of institutionalization. The high level of institutionalization of the Philippine settlement, however, seems to be an important reason peace there has held.

The cases of Angola and the Philippines also emphasize the limitations of a strategy that calls for third parties to act as guarantors of a settlement. However well-intentioned they may be, third parties may end up interfering with the process of signaling that communicates the credibility—or lack thereof—of rival groups' commitment to building a stable peace. In some cases, as with Mobutu and the Gbadolite Accord in Angola, this occurs because the third party is more focused on advancing its own interests than helping the civil war adversaries to address the types of bargaining failures

72. President Ramos left office in 1998 and was succeeded by Joseph Estrada.
73. Bayron 2003.

that make the peaceful resolution of war so difficult. In other cases, as with the UNAVEM forces that acted as guarantors of the Bicesse Accords, third parties seemingly become so committed to seeing a peace take hold that they fail to transmit information accurately regarding armed rivals' failure to follow through on the agreement.

Our focus on these two case studies has also illustrated connections among the different stages of the conflict-resolution process in a manner that our previous chapters' focus on the individual phases of the process did not allow. One of the points that emerges from this focus is that the types of factors associated with bargaining failures—e.g., a lack of knowledge regarding actors' preferences and the credible commitment problem—are not easily resolved at any single stage in the process. Convincing an adversary that the group one leads is truly committed to the bargained resolution of a civil war requires a leader to show her willingness to bear costs by recognizing and entering into negotiations with her rival, agreeing to a number of institutions that call for sharing and dividing state power, and pushing her followers to implement peace. Leaders that show a lack of will to bear these costs, as did Savimbi and, at times, dos Santos, should be seen as signaling a lack of real commitment to the conflict-resolution process. In these instances, as the case of Angola suggests, it may be better to allow the process of negotiating a civil war settlement to collapse than to undermine further the credibility of signals of peaceful intentions that may be transmitted in the future.

CONCLUSION

We began this book by describing the role power-sharing and power-dividing institutions played in facilitating the construction of an enduring peace in South Africa. Emerging from a war that had lasted nearly a decade, provisions for sharing multiple dimensions of state power fostered an environment in which people on both sides of the racial divide felt secure enough to allow the peace process to move forward. The success of this effort to negotiate the end of civil war is perhaps best symbolized by the 2004 dissolution of the white political party that had presided over the country's racist apartheid system. In an act that would have appeared treasonous during the years of interracial conflict, many members of the now defunct National Party have chosen to join their former rivals in the African National Congress.[1]

That South Africa's contending groups succeeded in constructing a political system in which competing interests are expressed without violence does not mean that power-sharing and power-dividing institutions were a panacea for all the problems that the country faced in the post–civil war era. In fact, a short three years after signing the peace settlement, the country adopted a new constitution that abandoned many of the power-sharing and power-dividing provisions that had formed the original basis for peace.[2]

---

1. Wines 2004.

2. Claiming that the new constitution included no provisions for sharing and dividing power would be an exaggeration. For example, guarantees of regional autonomy remained in place for the province of Kwazulu Natal. On a discussion of power sharing in the current governance of South Africa, see Sisk and Stefes 2005.

Having nurtured a sense of trust and security among former rivals, politicians felt sufficiently comfortable with one another to modify the political system so that it might address a new set of concerns. Chief among these new priorities was creating a political system efficient enough to quickly and effectively tackle the many challenges of governance still facing the state. The persistence of poverty, a daunting crime rate, and the rapid spread of HIV infection among the population all required the construction of a political system in which the government could operate with heightened efficiency, even if at times this meant failing to build consensus among the state's competing interests.

As the example of South Africa demonstrates, employing power-sharing and power-dividing institutions as the foundation of a political system brings with it both advantages and liabilities. This conclusion is intended to explore these different sides of power-sharing and power-dividing institutions. In the first section, we emphasize the value of these institutions as a tool for facilitating an enduring peace in states emerging from civil war via a process of negotiation. Toward this end, we summarize the central findings of our statistical analyses and advance the claim that negotiated settlements based on power-sharing and power-dividing principles are preferable to alternative means of ending civil wars. In the second section, we describe the problems and challenges inherent in any power-sharing or power-dividing arrangement. Specifically, we consider the inability of power-sharing institutions to foster a fully democratic state with the capacity to adapt to changing circumstances. We suggest that these limitations make the value of power sharing most apparent in the immediate aftermath of civil war. In a final section, we build on these and other insights to discuss the policy implications for those involved in efforts to resolve intrastate conflicts.

Power Sharing as a Means of Managing Conflict in Post–Civil War States

KEY FINDINGS OF THE BOOK

The statistical analyses that form the heart of this study each seek to illustrate the role that power-sharing and power-dividing institutions play during the process of peacefully ending civil war. Collectively, these findings indicate that the chances for an enduring peace are greatly enhanced when competing parties include power-sharing or power-dividing provisions for multiple dimensions of state power as part of their negotiated agreement to end civil war.

Factors Associated with Creating Power-Sharing and Power-Dividing Institutions

We initiated our consideration of the value of power sharing in Chapter 2 by identifying the conditions under which institutions requiring the sharing or dividing of the political, military, territorial, and economic aspects of state power might first develop. Taking into account all civil wars ending between 1945 and 1999, we conclude that the odds that a war would terminate with a power-sharing settlement is largely determined by factors related to both the nature of the conflict and the international conflict environment. In terms of conditions defining the nature of the conflict, civil wars with the strongest potential to end with a power-sharing or power-dividing arrangement are those in which the dispute has proved enduring and included relatively few casualties. Long-lasting wars encourage compromise based on power-sharing and power-dividing principles as each side realizes that it lacks the capacity to prevail on the battlefield; at the same time, lower levels of bloodshed facilitate bargaining success among adversaries by minimizing the mutual distrust and animosity that define civil war.

The only factor related to the international conflict environment that has demonstrated a capacity to increase the odds of reaching a power-sharing or power-dividing arrangement is the promised introduction of foreign peacekeepers into the state emerging from civil war. We do not interpret this statistical association as indicating that peacekeepers themselves encourage the adoption of these institutions. Instead, we view the commitment to introduce peacekeepers as influencing the bargaining process by sufficiently reassuring parties to the dispute about their security to enable them to contemplate potential compromises with their adversaries. Bargains to share or divide power with an enemy appear less risky when third-party troops are present to assist in developing new governing institutions and potentially protecting those left vulnerable through their participation in the peace process.

Linking these disparate influences together is their effect on the perceptions of those at the bargaining table. Only when outright victory seems beyond reach (as indicated by the duration of the conflict) and parties to the dispute feel that the potential remains for relatively low-risk compromise with their enemies (as reflected in low levels of conflict and the promised introduction of peacekeepers) does a heightened possibility exist for a bargained resolution to emerge based on the principles of sharing and dividing state power.

Power-Sharing and Power-Dividing Institutions as a Means of Institutionalizing Peace

In Chapter 3 we provided an empirical demonstration of the value of power sharing through a focus on the substantive content of all civil war settlements reached via negotiated agreement in the post–World War II era. Holding all other potential influences constant, we find that the prospects for peace remaining intact are enhanced with each additional power-sharing aspect included as part of the settlement to end the war. Agreements that include requirements for sharing or dividing the political, military, territorial, and economic dimensions of state power are far more likely to foster an enduring peace as compared to those agreements that fail to include these provisions among the settlement's terms.

We interpret the value of these arrangements to the peace process as being based on both the substantive and symbolic importance attributed to them by former adversaries. Substantively, agreeing to establish these mechanisms guarantees that no single group will monopolize state power and use this position of dominance to threaten the security of others. Each additional power-sharing and power-dividing dimension specified in a settlement increases confidence that abandoning a wartime posture will not place a collectivity's membership at the mercy of its former adversaries. Through these provisions, each group's leadership also receives a commitment that it will have its influence felt in some aspects of governance of the postwar state and that it can use this power to protect its membership's interests. In short, the substantive value of power-sharing and power-dividing institutions is that they provide each contending group with a level of state power, which, while inhibiting their ability to establish dominance, guarantees them a capacity to check the predatory actions of their rivals.

The symbolic significance of these power-sharing and power-dividing mechanisms is the costly indication of conciliatory intent embodied in the agreement to create institutions based on the principles of cooperation. Signing on to the establishment of power-sharing and power-dividing institutions requires that adversaries abandon the typical wartime aim of monopoly control of the government and instead work together in the context of the institutional arrangements of the new state.[3] In this sense, adversaries

3. Among the notable exceptions to this common emphasis on monopoly control of the government among civil war combatants are those instances in which a group seeks to partition the country and establish its own state. Yet even in this context, establishing power-sharing or

that commit themselves to the idea of sharing and dividing power have indicated to one another an interest in peace by virtue of their willingness to forgo priorities that seemed nonnegotiable at the initiation of hostilities.

The Significance of Implementing Power-Sharing and Power-Dividing Arrangements

In Chapter 4 we considered how the process of implementing the power-sharing and power-dividing commitments outlined in a peace agreement might further augment the prospects for maintaining post–civil war peace. In recognition of the limited information available concerning the postwar implementation process, we chose to focus solely on those states emerging from civil war between 1980 and 1996 that had committed to establishing military power-sharing and power-dividing institutions as part of their negotiated peace settlement. Our findings indicate that faithfully and completely implementing this aspect of a settlement's provisions substantially reduced the potential for a return to war in comparison to those cases in which combatants failed to fulfill these obligations. Only one of ten states returned to war following the full implementation of its military power-sharing arrangement; conversely, half of those agreements in which implementation was incomplete or failed led to the renewal of hostilities.

We account for the relationship between complete implementation and the maintenance of peace by again referring to the costly signals former enemies send to one another during the peace process. Group leaders that are successful at implementing military power-sharing and power-dividing provisions have demonstrated their genuine interest in peace by virtue of their willingness to absorb two categories of unavoidable costs. First, they have gone through with the commitments outlined in the original agreement and have participated in creating institutions that, by virtue of their existence, limit their own political power. Second, they have endured, and in many instances overcome, militant critics within their groups who emerge during the implementation of an agreement and charge the leadership with "selling out" the interests of the collectivity. By absorbing these costs inextricably linked to the implementation process, former adversaries indicate to one another their sincere commitment to maintaining the nascent peace. The new sense of security engendered through this process substantially reduces the risk of a return to war.

power-dividing institutions is a costly signal of compromise in the sense that the separatist movement acquiesces to remaining within the boundaries of the established state in exchange for concessions from the central government.

In summary, the findings of this book suggest that power-sharing and power-dividing institutions, when included as part of a negotiated settlement to end civil war, can play an important and positive role in fostering an enduring peace. Through their own efforts at developing these institutions, wartime adversaries foster a new sense of confidence that the postwar state will not be dominated by a single party with the intention of attacking the interests of its rivals.

ALTERNATIVES TO POWER-SHARING AND POWER-DIVIDING INSTITUTIONS IN RESOLVING CIVIL WARS

While this book has focused on the adoption of power-sharing and power-dividing institutions as a means to peacefully resolve civil wars, this is far from the only policy prescription that has been offered with the intent of definitively ending these conflicts. Below we offer a critical discussion of three alternative mechanisms that have been considered as a means to bring peace to states experiencing civil war; we suggest that the these paths to peace have inherent limitations that make them less desirable as mechanisms for securing stability when compared to the adoption of a negotiated settlement based on the principles of sharing and dividing state power.

Military Victory

The most common means by which civil wars are brought to an end is when one party to the dispute establishes its dominance on the battlefield and forces its enemies to surrender. While people rarely advocate this outcome openly, members of the policy-making community have often tolerated such an approach through their well-documented reluctance to commit troops and resources toward efforts that might end ongoing civil violence.[4] There is often a preference for allowing these conflicts to burn themselves out even when no immediate end to the war is in sight.[5]

The death and destruction that come with waiting for a definitive military victory are thought to be a price worth paying because wars decided on the battlefield unambiguously establish one collectivity's hegemony over the society as a whole. With victory, it has been argued, the organizational identities of any competing groups are effectively erased along with their capacity

4. One scholar who has commended the stabilizing and transformative effects of military victory as a means of ending armed conflict is Edward Luttwak (1999).
5. Power 2002.

to compete for the reins of power in the context of the postwar state.[6] Achieving peace does not require engaging in the often frustrating process of bargaining and compromise but is instead asserted by the only party that has demonstrated having sufficient power to impose its will on others.

Although a military victory can secure peace, reasons still exist to question whether such an outcome is desirable in most circumstances. As we pointed out in the Introduction, some of the costs associated with achieving a military victory are much greater than would have been the case if competitors had proved capable of reaching a mutually acceptable settlement. In addition, the perceived need to destroy the present and future capacity of defeated enemies to compete for political power encourages the continuation of mass violence even when the final outcome of the war is no longer in doubt. If civil wars resolved through negotiations provide a means for groups to live together within the context of a single state, wars ended through a military victory give the winning side the often employed capacity simply to eliminate their competitors.

Members of the defeated groups surviving the initial stages of defeat have little reason to expect that governance of the postwar state will favor their interests. While isolated instances may exist in which an especially magnanimous victor has prioritized accommodating the concerns of the losing sides, in most cases the defeated become marginalized politically and in other ways. This was the case in Rwanda, for example, where the Tutsi army that proved victorious in 1994 has since made little or no effort to incorporate the majority Hutu into the new government.[7]

In short, while military victories in civil war establish peace, they also foster an environment in which the grievances that formed the original basis for the conflict remain salient. The absence of violence within the state is solely a function of the continuing coercion of weaker parties.[8] In this sense, military victories may ensure stability, but they also tend to create a set of governing institutions unresponsive to the concerns of those on the losing end of the civil war.

Partition

A second prescription for resolving civil wars that has garnered a great deal of attention in recent years is the suggestion that these countries be parti-

6. Wagner 1993.

7. In fact, the state recently has sought to erase those identities that had formed the basis for the civil war from the society as a whole. The government has initiated a campaign seeking to eliminate loyalties based on the Hutu and Tutsi ethnicities and replace them with a shared identity as Rwandans (Lacey 2004).

8. See, for example, Lustick 1979.

tioned so that each competing group holds its own sovereign state. While a traditional emphasis on state sovereignty has meant that the international community has been reluctant to favor partition as a means of conflict management, the tactic has been employed for exactly this purpose both explicitly (e.g., East Timor's independence from Indonesia) and implicitly (e.g., the de facto partition of Cyprus).

Advocates of this method of ending civil wars suggest that the risks of a renewal of hostilities following partition are minimal given that each side holds its own territory and the ability to protect its own borders. By dividing groups into defensible states, partition establishes a sense that enemies can be kept at bay. Chaim Kaufmann has been among the strongest proponents of the partition solution to civil wars and suggests that the value of creating separate homelands is most apparent in wars among ethnic groups. In his words: "The safest pattern is a well-defined demographic front that separates nearly homogenous regions. Such a front can be defended by organized military forces, so populations are not at risk unless defenses are breached. At the same time, the strongest motive for attack disappears, since there are few or no endangered co-ethnics behind enemy lines."[9]

While at first impression the partition solution to civil wars might appear less costly in comparison to ending conflict through military victory, the historical record indicates that partitioning states has rarely been achieved without producing substantial numbers of casualties and refugees. The partition of India and Pakistan is just one example of an effort at conflict management using this mechanism that produced enormous human costs. This partition resulted in an estimated hundreds of thousands of deaths and millions of refugees.[10]

Evidence also calls into question whether partitioning provides an enduring solution to civil conflict. The recurrence of conflict between communities in the partitioned states of India/Pakistan and Ethiopia/Eritrea reflects the failings of this strategy. These examples do not appear to be the exception to the more general trend of stability following a state's division. In a statistical study of the effects of partition following civil war, Nicholas Sambanis finds that this tactic has largely failed as an enduring means of preventing intrastate violence.[11]

As with the prescription to allow civil wars to end in military victory, the

9. Kaufmann 1996, 149.

10. Kaufmann 1999, 230. Kaufmann suggests, however, that these problems could be minimized if third parties act to assist in the planned partition of states.

11. Sambanis 2000. Also see Kumar 1997 for a critical discussion of the partition solution to civil war.

costs associated with employing the partition solution often seem unaccept-
ably high in comparison to the negotiated resolution of these conflicts.
While less pronounced than a battlefield solution, partitioning imposes substantial population losses as the process of dividing the state takes hold;
partitioning also does little to encourage these groups to establish institutional mechanisms for peacefully managing the differences that formed the
basis for war beyond demarcating a border between enemies.

Creating Incentives for Moderation

A third and final prescription for resolving civil wars we consider suggests
that the interests of peace would best be served by establishing a set of postwar institutions that reward moderate behavior by a country's politicians.
This category of policy recommendations was initially developed as a critique of Arend Lijphart's advocacy of power sharing for managing conflict in
multiethnic states. It also sought to outline a viable alternative to Lijphart's
emphasis on guaranteeing each group a share of state power as the most
assured means of facilitating their continued loyalty to the national government.

The central criticism of Lijphart's position voiced as part of this perspective is that power-sharing institutions encourage people to cling to those
identities that are the original basis for conflict within the state. Because the
legitimacy of a claim to government power is dependent on meeting the
criteria defined within the context of the peace agreement or constitution,
people have a strong incentive to continue defining themselves and their
interests along those lines. Individuals will thus find it difficult to develop
new solidarities that cross-cut those linked to the war given that the state
neither recognizes nor privileges these alternative forms of identity.[12] In a
state governed by a power-sharing arrangement in which ethnicity is the
sole criterion for distributing influence and resources, competing sources of
loyalty that might bring wartime adversaries together, such as class, gender,
or regional identities, have little prospect of gaining saliency.

It has been suggested, for example, that the negotiated resolution to Bosnia's civil war demonstrates this liability associated with the use of power-
sharing and power-dividing mechanisms. The Dayton Accords established a
new central government that included, among other power-sharing provisions, guarantees of representation for each ethnic group (Bosnian, Serb,
and Croat) in both a bicameral legislature and rotating presidency. Susan L.

12. On this topic, see Barry 1975.

Woodward offers the following interpretation of how this affected Bosnia's postwar politics: "Rules for ethnic representation and voting encouraged caucusing by nation on most issues, discouraged voting on interests that crossed national lines, and hard-wired alliances, preventing the essential business of democracy and supporting an authoritarian approach to politics in which radicals had a natural advantage."[13]

With this critique of power sharing in mind, the alternative favored by those categorized within this perspective is to structure incentives in such a way that they encourage people to move beyond identities inextricably linked to the initial conflict. Most prominently, Donald Horowitz identifies a set of government institutions with the potential to encourage cooperative behavior among different groups by rewarding those politicians capable of reaching beyond their own base and incorporating former enemies as part of their coalition of supporters.[14] He suggests, among other things, that states divided by ethnic differences would best be served by using an electoral system in which candidates could only gain office if they proved capable of garnering a degree of electoral support from those outside their own community.[15] He also advocates adopting a federal system in which each of the country's states include multiple ethnic groups with the expectation that this would often force local politicians to seek support from the diverse collectivities that form their constituency.[16]

In a similar vein, Philip Roeder has advanced the claim that postwar institutions should be engineered toward the goal of encouraging individuals to move beyond wartime identities. He focuses on two sets of policies consistent with this goal. First, he suggests that issues particularly likely to be a source of identity-based conflicts should be placed beyond the authority of government. Second, he advocates constructing an institutional structure of checks and balances intended to prevent any single group from monopolizing the political system. Roeder identifies the United States as the prime example of this conflict-management system in practice.[17] The constitution's separation of church and state ensures that the contentious issue of religion

13. Woodward 1999, 105.

14. It should be noted that Donald Horowitz's focus is on the broader topic of ethnic conflict rather than only civil wars. As examples, see Horowitz 1985, 601–52; 1990b.

15. Timothy Sisk (1996, 55) notes that the method of electing the president of Nigeria, as outlined in the 1979 constitution, took a form consistent with Horowitz's prescriptions. In order to be elected president, a candidate "was required to garner a plurality of votes nationwide and at least 25 percent of the votes in thirteen of Nigeria's then nineteen states."

16. Horowitz 1985, 601–13.

17. Roeder 2005.

is kept outside the reach of government authorities who might seek to impose the views of the majority on religious minorities. At the same time, constructing a presidential system, bicameral legislature, and independent judiciary provides multiple points in the political system to challenge, and potentially stop, the passage or implementation of laws that do not have a substantial level of support (or at least acquiescence from) interested parties.

Could the institutions described by either Horowitz or Roeder facilitate an enduring peace in states emerging from civil war? Answering this question is simply impossible given the rarity with which the structures advocated by these scholars have been adopted in the aftermath of war.[18] While this does not serve as an indictment of this approach's value to conflict management, it does suggest its lack of appeal to former combatants as they transition from war to peaceful cooperation. In a situation in which individuals are emerging from sustained violence, it is clear that there is a preference for strong security guarantees that go beyond encouraging moderation or providing promises of institutional checks and balances. Power-sharing and power-dividing mechanisms, by ensuring access to different dimensions of state power, provide a straightforward and intuitive means of protecting collectivities' interests during a period of intense uncertainty and transition. For this reason, power-sharing and power-dividing mechanisms have become a common feature of negotiated settlements to end civil wars.[19]

Power-sharing and power-dividing institutions can reinforce wartime identities. In the immediate aftermath of conflict, however, anticipating that new identities and sources of cleavages would emerge in the short term seems premature. Identities that formed the basis for conflict in this environment are inescapable, and only after political institutions have demonstrated a capacity for providing security on the basis of those identities may people reach beyond them to a new set of loyalties.

The Limitations of Power-Sharing and Power-Dividing Institutions

Power sharing does not resolve all of the dilemmas facing a post–civil war society. Below we describe some of the pathologies that come with adopting

18. Concerning Horowitz's favored institutional mechanisms, Sisk (1996, 44) notes that few states have put them into practice as a means to manage conflict between groups. In his statistical demonstration of the value of the conflict management structures he advocates, Roeder (2005) considers *all* countries rather than those that have emerged from civil war.

19. As the recent cases of Afghanistan and Iraq demonstrate, power-sharing and power-dividing institutions are increasingly being used in an effort to stabilize peace following conflicts other than civil wars.

a power-sharing or power-dividing regime. We suggest that these costs are worth absorbing, at least in the immediate aftermath of civil war, in the interest of creating a sense of security among former enemies.

POWER SHARING AND INEFFICIENT GOVERNANCE

A problem that is almost always apparent immediately following the establishment of a power-sharing or power-dividing arrangement is the creation of a system in which government gridlock becomes unavoidable. By providing each wartime adversary a guaranteed share of political power, legislation is often blocked unless it meets with the approval of all interested parties. While this fosters a level of confidence that no group will be threatened by state actions that might compromise their security, it also makes responding quickly to the many challenges facing a state emerging from civil war exceedingly difficult for the government.

Bosnia's postwar experience demonstrates this problematic aspect of power-sharing and power-dividing arrangements. With a parliament divided among three collectivities, passing new legislation and autonomously moving the peace process forward have proved challenging for the government. Recognizing the difficulties inherent in reaching agreement among the contending groups, this task instead has been carried out by Bosnia's International High Representative, who has often opted to impose laws after they failed to receive sufficient support from elected officials.[20]

POWER SHARING AND UNCOMPETITIVE DEMOCRACY

A second dilemma confronting regimes based on the principles of sharing and dividing state power is that they typically offer very limited opportunities for a genuinely open and competitive democratic political system. For most power-sharing and power-dividing systems to operate as intended, a group's leaders must have a relatively free hand to bargain and compromise with the representatives of competing interests within the society. Gaining this enhanced capacity for compromise, however, often means that leaders must act in ways that are decidedly out of step with common expectations of politicians' behavior in the context of a democracy.[21]

20. See, for example, Kroeger 2002.

21. It should be noted that at least some scholars have indicated a concern that an emphasis on democracy may be ill advised for states when they are initially emerging from violent civil conflict. See, for example, Paris 1997, 2004.

While not initially considered in this light, we described exactly this type of antidemocratic behavior in our discussion of the costly signals that take place while implementing a peace agreement. Group leaders who ignore or suppress militant members of their own constituency in order to fulfill the obligations outlined in a settlement are indicating to their former adversaries that they have a genuine interest in peace. At the same time, however, this behavior silences and marginalizes those who would be most likely to articulate concerns with the direction in which leaders are taking the postwar state. This tendency to ignore the interests of their own constituencies in favor of focusing on the bargaining process with former adversaries suggests that the system tends toward an often elitist and antidemocratic orientation.[22]

THE INFLEXIBILITY OF POWER-SHARING ARRANGEMENTS

Finally, power-sharing and power-dividing arrangements are sometimes criticized for proving inflexible and unable to adapt to changing times. When established at the conclusion of the conflict, these arrangements distribute power among groups on the basis of their interests and relative power as they appear at that point in time. Yet if circumstances change within the state in the aftermath of the war, the existing settlement may come under attack as being inadequate to address current conditions. Conflict could reignite as parties maneuver to enhance or protect the role assigned to them in the original peace deal.

Lebanon's National Pact of 1943 is one example of the dangers inherent in the inability of power-sharing arrangements to evolve with changing times. Reached during a period when the country's Christian population was obviously in the majority, the provisions of the pact became progressively less acceptable to Muslims as the demographic balance of power shifted in their favor. This disjuncture between the provisions of an antiquated settlement and the realities within the state eventually led to a return to civil war.[23]

ADDRESSING THE LIMITATIONS ASSOCIATED WITH POWER-SHARING AND POWER-DIVIDING ARRANGEMENTS

Problems that may affect states that use power-sharing and power-dividing institutions to manage intrastate conflict take the form of the potential for

22. This perspective is voiced by Nordlinger 1972.
23. Sisk 1996, 58.

inefficient governance, limited prospects for open political competition, and arrangements that lack a capacity to evolve with changing times. With all of these inherent limitations, however, the fact remains that power-sharing and power-dividing institutions have a unique and demonstrated capacity to fulfill the one task that is essential to ensuring the successful transition from war to peace—guaranteeing that former combatants feel sufficiently secure to participate in establishing new governing institutions with the capacity to peacefully manage intrastate disputes.

It is perhaps expecting too much that these countries would prove able to establish governing institutions capable of addressing such diverse goals as promoting open political competition and ensuring efficient governance in the immediate aftermath of civil war.[24] The reality facing groups in a postwar state is that they place their highest priority on providing for their security. It thus makes perfect sense that the institutions that are most commonly employed are those with the demonstrated capacity to perform this task.

Because states with negotiated civil war settlements are most likely to have their institutional architecture characterized by power sharing for a number of years, it seems reasonable to ask whether any means of minimizing some of the limitations typically associated with these arrangements exist. Turning first to the problem of inefficient governance, little can probably be done with respect to this issue in a post–civil war environment. To a very real extent, institutional arrangements involve trade-offs between policy efficiency and the credibility of policy commitments. Institutions that disperse power, as is the case with power-sharing and power-dividing institutions, reduce the risk of unpredictable government action. By doing so, these institutions facilitate the emergence of a stable policy environment in which governments can make policy commitments that are credible into the future. As civil war adversaries who negotiate an end to a civil war place a premium on credible commitments of this nature, of less importance to them is that politically fragmented institutions of the type they have designed do not generally make for responsive and adaptable governments.[25] Faced with this trade-off, former rivals will tend to opt for inefficiency even

24. Even the strongest critics of power sharing would acknowledge that these goals are incompatible. By increasing the voices heard in governance, opening up the political process inhibits the capacity of elites to reach consensus on policy goals and actually implement legislation.

25. For an overview of the debate regarding this trade-off in the literature on institutions and governance, see MacIntyre 2003.

if they are aware that this may produce other problems in the future.[26] Under these circumstances, rivals may, at best, be aware of the trade-off they face and attempt, with the passage of time, to give greater emphasis to policy efficiency as a goal.

Along the same lines, groups may be able to do little regarding the limited prospects for open political competition that power-sharing and power-dividing institutions can produce beyond cultivating an awareness of this fact and attempting to address it at the margins. Particularly noteworthy in this respect has been the recent emergence of civil society in countries that have experienced civil war.[27] As groups emerge that are beyond the control of the leadership of the parties that have negotiated a settlement, the political landscape may slowly start to expand beyond the contours agreed to in the initial negotiated settlement.

Ultimately, if power-sharing and power-dividing arrangements have met the goal of fostering a sense of security among former adversaries, and new priorities have emerged that cannot be addressed under the current arrangements, the possibility remains that these institutions may be amended or discarded altogether.[28] Because institutions are "sticky," they are likely to leave behind traces. In the case of power-sharing and power-dividing arrangements, the institutional legacy one hopes these measures will produce includes an increased sense of security and the emergence of new norms of nonviolent conflict management. With these in place, alternative institutional futures are possible, as the case of South Africa makes clear.

Policy Implications

Two important sets of policy implications follow from efforts to employ an institutional approach to resolving intrastate conflicts. The first centers on

26. Paris (2004) argues that in the post–civil war period an emphasis on efficiency, at least in the form of market-oriented institutions, is misplaced and may end up leading to renewed competition and violence.

27. Civil society refers to intermediary institutions such as professional associations, religious groups, labor unions, and citizen advocacy organizations that give voice to various sectors of society, protect collective interests, and foster public participation in the political arena. A number of scholars have suggested that even in countries where political elites have been intent on efforts to expand political control and have shown no particular commitment to civil liberties, there has existed a political space in which associational life has taken root. For a review of some of these works, see Bratton 1989.

28. One way groups might attempt to limit some of the negative effects associated with power-sharing and power-dividing institutions is to negotiate a time-bound settlement, one that limits the number of years these institutions will be in place before making the transition to more competitive institutions. Colombia's National Front Agreement is an example of just such a

efforts to facilitate this process of conflict resolution. If highly institutionalized negotiated settlements are the best way of securing peace, how best can
adversaries be encouraged to design such settlements? The second set of
policy implications concerns the limitations associated with settlements institutionalized on the basis of power-sharing and power-dividing measures
and how some of these might best be managed or minimized. In discussing
these issues, we pay particular attention to the role third parties might play
in institutionalizing peace.

ENCOURAGING THE ADOPTION OF HIGHLY INSTITUTIONALIZED
NEGOTIATED SETTLEMENTS

Our findings in Chapter 2 regarding the impacts the nature of a conflict and
the international conflict environment have on the likelihood that adversaries will agree to adopt power-sharing measures suggest that third-party
actors can take steps to encourage belligerents to design highly institutionalized settlements. These include avoiding early intervention in a conflict,
helping to limit the overall casualty rate, and deploying peacekeepers. Because some of these policies can at times conflict with one another, we also
suggest other more straightforward measures that the international community can take to help encourage the adoption of institutionalized negotiated
settlements of civil wars.

It is ironic, given the frequent criticism received by the international
community for its perceived unwillingness to help end civil wars, that one
of the most important things third parties must do is refrain from intervening in a conflict before it is "ripe for resolution."[29] Long-lasting civil wars,
as we have found, are more likely to produce settlements that include a
range of power-sharing and power-dividing institutions in comparison to
short-lived conflicts. Efforts by third parties to bring a war to an end before
combatants have come to grips with the costs of the conflict may inhibit the
process of appropriate institutional design. A case in point is Mobutu's effort to force a settlement at Gbadolite when each party to the Angolan conflict still believed it could secure a military victory.

Seemingly at odds with the warning to third parties that they not inter-

---

settlement. By agreeing to share power for sixteen years, the Conservative and Liberal parties
sought to keep power-sharing institutions in place long enough to foster a sense of trust on the
part of each group that the other would not use state power to harm its interests once there was
a return to fully competitive democracy.

29. Zartman 1989.

vene too soon in a conflict is the need to limit the casualty levels that a civil war produces. Civil wars with a heavy human toll are unlikely to see former adversaries willing to negotiate highly institutionalized settlements. As casualty rates start to mount, outside actors might thus be motivated to intervene in the course of the conflict. Since these actors must take care not to end a conflict before its time, intervention of other types might be in order. These could take the form of a refusal on the part of the international community to sell armaments to the belligerents that are associated with high death tolls (and to punish, through sanctions or other measures, actors that continue to sell such weapons to the warring parties) and efforts to create safe havens for refugees fleeing the conflict.[30]

Once the international community promises to send peacekeepers into the conflict arena, it must be aware that the effect of their presence extends beyond helping to stop the killing by separating the belligerent parties. Settlements negotiated in an environment into which peacekeeping troops are expected to be deployed are more likely to be highly institutionalized than settlements designed in the absence of such promises. Although it is unlikely the peacekeepers themselves are encouraging the creation of these institutions, by sending in these troops third parties may provide a sense of security that gives adversaries the courage to design institutions that involve compromising over future control of the state. The international community may well want to factor in the effect the presence of peacekeepers has on levels of settlement institutionalization as it makes future choices about where to deploy these troops.

Somewhat less-complicated measures third parties can take to encourage the adoption of highly institutionalized settlements include increasing awareness of the relationship between such settlements and the stability of peace and providing incentives to encourage groups to design power-sharing institutions. Neither of these policy suggestions should be seen as encouraging the international community to take the lead role in designing the conflict-management institutions for a state attempting to emerge from civil war. As we have emphasized throughout this book, the institutional choices adversaries make as well as the efforts they make to implement them are important signals of the groups' commitment to peace. Third parties that impose institutions on a postwar society run the risk of interfering with this process of signaling intentions among former adversaries. However, third parties can play a productive role by educating antagonists who are

---

30. On the issue of creating safe havens to mitigate refugee crises, see Posen 1996, 98–104.

considering the adoption of power-sharing and power-dividing measures as part of a negotiated settlement about the relationship between high levels of institutionalization and the durability of peace.

The international community can also facilitate the adoption of a diverse range of power-sharing and power-dividing institutions by helping to provide resources the belligerents consider necessary to design or implement the institutions. In cases such as El Salvador, for example, financial commitments by outside actors appear to have played a key role in enabling the antagonists to agree to include economic power sharing as part of the settlement.

Summary

With wars now more common within states than among them, a pressing need exists to identify means of resolving these conflicts. By focusing on civil wars ended though a process of negotiation, the research we have presented in this book indicates that power-sharing and power-dividing institutions enhance the prospects of establishing a lasting postwar peace. Institutions that require former enemies to share or divide power have this demonstrated capacity to encourage peace because they go beyond simply requiring an end to the killing—they also establish a new set of rules and expectations intended to ensure that former antagonists can engage one another in political competition without threatening any collectivity's sense of safety. This unique capacity of power-sharing and power-dividing institutions to foster a sense of security, and sometimes trust, among former rivals allows them to serve as the foundations for an enduring peace.

APPENDIX

This Appendix contains details on the data sets and statistical methodology employed in Chapters 2, 3, and 4 of the book.

Chapter 2

In this part of the Appendix we present the coding rules associated with the data set we use in Chapter 2 and details related to the statistical methodology. We also present alternate specifications of the models tested in Chapter 2.

VARIABLE CODING AND SOURCES

We indicate below both the means by which the values of indicators used in this study were determined and our data sources.

Power-Sharing and Power Dividing-Provisions: The power-sharing indicator we include in this study varies in value from "0" to "4."[1] This composite measure is designed to reflect the four separate power-sharing categories that may appear in a peace settlement: political, territorial, military, and economic (the coding for each of these dimensions appears below). A settlement is ranked one unit higher for each power-sharing category that it includes. The coding for the composite power-sharing variable is based on the texts of the settlements themselves. If the text was unavailable, we largely relied on *Keesing's Contemporary Archives* and the annual *Yearbook of the Stockholm International Peace Research Institute* (SIPRI).

I. Political power sharing: Score as "1" if the civil war settlement in-

---

1. The composite measure we use reflects both power-sharing *and* power-dividing institutions. In what follows we use the term "power sharing" as shorthand for institutions devised for the purposes of either sharing or dividing power.

cludes any of the following provisions: (a) electoral proportional representation (settlement or discussion of settlement must specify its use and that it is not a revision to previous use of proportional representation); (b) administrative proportional representation (i.e., appointment of representatives of warring groups to courts, civil service, foreign service, and commissions); (c) executive proportional representation (i.e., appointment of representatives of warring groups to ministerial, subministerial, and cabinet positions).

II. Territorial power sharing: Score as "1" if the civil war settlement includes any of the following provisions: (a) divisions of political power among levels of government on the basis of federalism (either centralized federalism or decentralized federalism) or confederalism; (b) division of political power among levels of government on the basis of regional autonomy.

III. Military power sharing: Score as "1" if the civil war settlement includes any of the following provisions: (a) creation of state's security forces (e.g., army, navy, air force, state militia) through the integration of former antagonists' armed forces on the basis of a formula representative of the size of the armed groups; (b) creation of state's security forces (e.g., army, navy, air force, state militia) on the basis of equal numbers of troops drawn from the antagonists' armed forces; (c) appointment of members of armed faction(s) who do not dominate the state, or of weaker armed factions, to key leadership positions (e.g., general, commander, director, defense minister) in the state's security forces; (d) permission for antagonists to remain armed (i.e., settlement does not specify any disarmament measures); (e) permission for antagonists to retain their own armed forces.

IV. Economic power sharing: Score as "1" if the civil war settlement includes any of the following provisions: (a) specification of resource-distribution pattern by the state to disadvantaged groups, either on the basis of a percentage of resources to be allocated to those groups or on a financial amount to be directed to those groups; (b) specification of policies to be used to direct economic assets toward groups on the basis of their group membership or geographic location (e.g., policies associated with provision of land; control or administration of natural resources; scholarships and admissions to schools, training centers, colleges; creation and/or reservation of jobs, promotions; transfer of factories, capital, and credit; provision or creation of licenses to operate commercial enterprises and to practice professions or trades).

Stakes of the conflict: Score as "1" if the primary issue at stake in the conflict was ethnic, religious, racial, or linguistic; score "0" otherwise. In the majority of the cases, the coding for the conflict issue was based on Licklider's (1995) coding of the variable. In those cases in which the settlements postdate Licklider's study, or case study material raised questions regarding Licklider's coding of the material, statements by the parties to the conflict regarding the issues they believed to be at stake in the conflict were drawn upon, as well as Wallensteen and Sollenberg (1997), SIPRI *Yearbook* summaries of civil war cases, and case study materials were also consulted.

Conflict duration: The conflict's duration is based on the length of the conflict in months. This number was then logged to reduce variance. In the majority of the cases, the month and year the conflict started and ended are based on those identified in the Correlates of War (COW) civil war database. Where there were questions regarding the dates identified in the COW database or the conflicts were too recent to have been included in that database, *Keesing's Contemporary Archives* and case study material was used to identify the start and end dates of the conflict.

Conflict intensity: The number, in thousands, of war-related deaths was divided by the duration of the conflict in months. This number was then logged to reduce variance. In the majority of the cases, the month and year the conflict started and ended are based on those identified in the COW civil war database. Where there were questions regarding the dates identified in the COW database or the conflicts were too recent to have been included in that database, *Keesing's Contemporary Archives* and case study material were used to identify the start and end dates of the conflict. In the majority of the cases, the number of civil war deaths was drawn from the COW civil war database. These data were checked against those of Sivard (1996). Where discrepancies between the two sources existed, the annual SIPRI *Yearbook* was consulted and case study material was used.

Previous regime type: Based on the Polity IV data set. Measured as the five-year average of the Polity score [(Democracy − Autocracy) + 10] for the five years prior to the outbreak of war. See Marshall and Jaggers 2002; data set available at http://www.bsos.umd.edu/cidcm/inscr/polity.

Level of economic development: Operationalized using years of life expectancy at birth for the year following the end of the war. If a settlement fails in fewer than twelve months we use the life-expectancy figure for the year in which the war ended. We draw on the Doyle and Sambanis (2000) data set for this variable. Data set available at http://www.worldbank.org/research/conflict/papers/peacebuilding. We use the World Bank's *World Development Indicators* to fill in the values for cases not included in their data set. A select number of indicators and years are available online through the World Bank at http://web.world bank.org/wbsite/external/datastatistics/0,,contentMDK:20899413~menu PK:232599~pagePK:64133150~piPK:64133175~theSitePK:23941 9,00.html. More complete series can be accessed through some libraries or via individual subscription.

Peacekeeping operation: Score as a "1" if a peacekeeping operation was introduced into the state following the signing of a settlement; scored "0" otherwise. We draw on the Doyle and Sambanis (2002) data set for this variable. Data set available at http://www.worldbank.org/research/conflict/papers/peacebuilding.

International system structure: Score as "0" if the settlement was negotiated during the cold war years from 1945 to 1989 and "1" if the settlement was constructed in the post-cold war period from 1990 onward.

ALTERNATIVE SPECIFICATIONS OF THE MODEL EMPLOYED IN CHAPTER 2

Accounting for the size of the government army: A measure that is commonly used in studies considering factors leading to the end of civil wars is the size of the government army (see, for example, Mason and Fett 1996; Mason, Weingarten, and Fett 1999). We did not include such an indicator in this study for two reasons. First, we are concerned that this measure fails to capture what appears to us to be the most important aspect of government military power: the advantage (or disadvantage) the state holds relative to rebel armies. We acknowledge that such a measure cannot easily be included because reliable data simply do not exist concerning the relative power of the contending groups. Nevertheless, we are skeptical that a measure of the government army is meaningful in the absence of information concerning the group(s) in opposition.

Our second reason for not including such a measure is based on the results reported below. These tests replicate those found in the chapter's text, with the important modification that we now include a variable reflecting the size of the government army relative to the total population of the state. This new variable is logged in order to approximate a normal distribution of values. Table 11 below presents the results of these tests. What is most notable about these revised results is that even though they include

Table 11 Predictors of civil war settlement content, including a measure of the size of the government army

Ordered probit model

Variable	Predicting content of civil war settlements		Predicting content of civil war settlements and cease-fires	
	Coefficient	Percent change in odds for standard deviation increase	Coefficient	Percent change in odds for standard deviation increase
Nature of the conflict				
Stakes of the conflict	−0.14 (0.28)	−0.07	0.06 (0.28)	0.03
Conflict duration (logged)	0.38*** (0.1)	0.76	0.35*** (0.1)	0.7
Conflict intensity (logged)	−0.1 (0.08)	−0.19	−0.13 (0.08)	−0.25
Domestic conflict environment				
Previous level of democracy	0.03 (0.03)	0.13 (0.02)	0.04	0.2
Level of development	−0.02 (0.01)	−0.2	−0.01 (0.01)	−0.06
Government army as percent of population (logged)	0.3** (0.13)	0.38	0.38*** (0.12)	0.47
International conflict environment				
Introduction of a peacekeeping	1.13*** (0.3)	0.55	0.98*** (0.29)	0.47
International system structure	0.34 (0.29)	0.17	0.82*** (0.28)	0.4
Cut 1	−3.11 (1.82)		−3.74 (1.79)	
Cut 2	−2.79 (1.82)		−3.23 (1.78)	
Cut 3	−2.23 (1.81)		−2.56 (1.78)	
Cut 4	−1.43 (1.82)		−1.75 (1.78)	
N	106		106	
Log likelihood	−94.36		−101.33	
Prob > chi^2	0.0000		0.0000	
Pseudo R^2	0.2		0.24	

Values in parentheses are standard errors. All tests are two-tailed.
***p < 0.01
**p < 0.05
*p < 0.1

a new variable, they largely mirror those first reported in the chapter. The sole inconsistency is that the measure of conflict intensity fails to achieve statistical significance (although it remains in the expected direction) for both tests. Further, it is striking that the variable reflecting the size of the government army is statistically significant but signed in a direction that eludes meaningful interpretation. That the variable is positively signed suggests that the odds of power sharing appearing in a settlement are greater when government armies are large relative to their population. We view it as counterintuitive that governments with larger armies would prove more amenable to compromise by creating power-sharing and power-dividing institutions. Governments with this advantage should prefer military victory over negotiation given their advantage. That these results suggest otherwise calls their validity into question.

Predicting individual dimensions of power sharing: How does our statistical model perform when focused on a particular type of power-sharing or power-dividing institution rather than considering the aggregate number of types of arrangements specified in an agreement? We report such tests with the dependent variable taking the form of a dichotomous indicator reflecting the presence or absence of agreement in both negotiated settlements and truces to one of the four categories of power-sharing institutions—the political, military, territorial, and economic bases of state strength. We use a logistic regression model because our dependent variable is a dichotomous indicator.

In the findings below we report odds ratios as these are the most straightforward for interpretation using this statistical model. Odds ratios may be understood in terms of their deviation from the value of "1." Those indicators with a value less than "1" decrease the odds that a particular power-sharing or power-dividing provision will appear in a settlement; those indicators with a value greater than "1" increase the odds that a particular power-sharing or power-dividing provision will appear in a settlement.

We include these test results here for interested readers but emphasize that we consider this specification of the model as inconsistent with our theoretical expectations. Specifically, the tests reported below assume that each individual power-sharing dimension is agreed to in isolation from one another; conversely, the tests we present in the chapter's text are based on the more realistic assumption that the array of power-sharing and power-dividing mechanisms is considered as a set of institutions from which negotiators may add or subtract.

Table 12 presents the results of this test. In reviewing these results, it is

Table 12 Predicting individual dimensions of power-sharing and power-dividing institutions for settlements and truces

Logistic regression model

Variable	Political power-sharing odds ratio	Military power-sharing odds ratio	Territorial power-sharing odds ratio	Economic power-sharing odds ratio
Nature of the conflict				
Stakes of the conflict	0.63 (0.34)	0.77 (0.47)	5.1** (3.98)	0.86 (0.51)
Conflict duration (logged)	1.41** (0.24)	1.85*** (0.42)	2.2*** (0.63)	2.08*** (0.52)
Conflict intensity (logged)	0.84 (0.13)	0.66** (0.13)	0.99 (0.2)	0.7* (0.14)
Domestic conflict environment				
Previous level of democracy	1.06 (0.05)	1.01 (0.06)	1.11* (0.07)	1.03 (0.06)
Level of development	0.1 (0.02)	0.99 (0.02)	1.04 (0.03)	1.03 (0.03)
International conflict environment				
Introduction of a peacekeeping operation	5.71*** (3.12)	6.12*** (3.79)	2.03 (1.43)	0.99 (0.61)
International system structure	3.08** (1.61)	4.91*** (2.91)	3.39* (2.38)	0.81 (0.5)
N	106	106	106	106
Log likelihood	−49.88	−40.37	−33.13	−42.47
Prob > chi²	0.0000	0.0000	0.0000	0.04
Pseudo R²	0.26	0.34	0.39	0.15

Values in parentheses are standard errors. All tests are two-tailed.
***$p < 0.01$
**$p < 0.05$
*$p < 0.1$

notable that two of the variables identified as statistically significant in our original test retain this influence with the revised specification of the dependent variable. The measure reflecting the duration of the conflict proves statistically significant and in the expected direction in all four tests; similarly, the variable reflecting the structure of the international system proves statistically significant—although it only proves to be weakly influential (at the 0.10 level) in one case.

These tests also tell us a few things about the conditions that might predict the adoption of particular power-sharing or power-dividing institutions. First, territorial power sharing appears to have a stronger likelihood of being employed in identity-based civil wars. This makes intuitive sense given that identity conflicts often involve discord between the state and a regionally concentrated ethnic group. The provision of territorial autonomy provides an obvious means of addressing the concerns of a group dominant in a single region.

Second, while wars of greater intensity are consistently associated with a reduced willingness to cooperate with adversaries by creating power-sharing and power-dividing institutions, this variable is only statistically significant (and has its greatest negative impact) on shaping the potential for establishing a level of military cooperation. Again, this makes intuitive sense as wars yielding high numbers of casualties should make groups increasingly unwilling to compromise the means of providing for their own defense.

Finally, the promised introduction of peacekeepers appears to create an environment in which antagonists are most comfortable with sharing or dividing both political and military power. Settlement architects' willingness to share military power in the presence of peacekeepers seems logical enough; adversaries are willing to make compromises regarding the most immediate means they have at hand to defend their collectivities if third parties promise to provide for their safety should the actions of others make that necessary. Somewhat less clear is the reason those constructing negotiated agreements show an increased willingness in the presence of peacekeepers to agree to share or divide political power. Since the architects of civil war settlements are likely to understand that peacekeepers are not generally called upon to enforce promises by former belligerents to share political power, why the presence of those forces would encourage former adversaries to design political power-sharing measures is unclear.

Chapter 3

In this section of the Appendix we present more detail on the data set we use and the statistical methodology we use in Chapter 3. We also present an alternate specification of the model tested in Chapter 3, focusing on the effects that individual power-sharing dimensions may produce on the duration of peace.

VARIABLE CODING AND SOURCES

We refer the reader to the discussion above of the data set we use in Chapter 2 for an overview of the independent variables we use to test the hypotheses in Chapter 3. We code the dependent variable, duration of peace, which we test in Chapter 3, as follows:

Duration of peace: We operationalize our dependent variable as the number of months that peace endured after the signing of a settlement through December 31, 1999. A settlement is considered to have failed if civil war reemerges in the state.

METHODOLOGY

To test the effect of settlement institutionalization on the duration of peace, we use event history analysis. The particular model we use is a Cox proportional hazards model. This model does not assume a particular shape for the baseline hazard, that is, whether the risk of another war rises or declines, the longer peace lasts. The models we test estimate the effects of independent variables on the risk of peace failing in a particular time period given that peace has lasted up to that period of time. The tests can thus tell us whether the risk of war is lower when settlements are highly institutionalized or higher when, for example, the conflicts have been highly intense.

The hazard-rate statistic for the Cox proportional hazards model provides an easily interpretable measure of a variable's influence on the event of interest. The hazard rate is defined as the exponent of the coefficient. Its deviation from the value of "1" indicates the percentage increase or decrease on the likelihood of the incident occurring.[2] Variables with hazard rates below the baseline value of "1" and with negative coefficients decrease the potential of the event (in this case the renewed outbreak of another war) occurring; variables with hazard rates higher than "1" and with positive coefficients increase the risk of the event taking place.

ALTERNATIVE SPECIFICATIONS OF THE MODEL EMPLOYED IN CHAPTER 3

Following, we present alternative specifications of the model tested in Chapter 3. Using both the thirty-eight cases of fully negotiated settlements and the forty-nine cases of negotiated agreements, we examine the impact of this model on the duration of postwar peace.

The model we test examines the effect that the individual power-sharing dimensions have on the longevity of peace. This model duplicates the tests whose results appear in tables 7 and 8 in that it focuses on the same three

2. Bueno De Mesquita and Siverson 1995, 851.

explanations for the duration of peace. The one change we have made to this specification of the model is to replace the variable *settlement institutionalization* with four separate variables—*political power sharing, territorial power sharing, military power sharing,* and *economic power sharing.*[3] Each of these variables was coded "1" when a settlement called for that type of institution to be designed and "0" when it did not.

We do not specify any hypotheses regarding the presumed impact that each of the four different types of power-sharing or power-dividing institutions might have on the duration of peace. Our theoretical position is that extensively institutionalized agreements are most likely to produce an enduring peace. We have no expectation that any one of these institutions is generally more valuable or useful than others insofar as helping to foster an enduring peace is concerned. The effect any single type of power sharing or power dividing has on security concerns and thus on the duration of peace following a civil war settlement may well be conditioned on factors for which we cannot control in our models such as the history of intergroup relations (e.g., has some group historically been excluded from receiving economic benefits from the state to an extent that its security and other interests have suffered over time?) and group abilities to mobilize certain kinds of power. In other words, under certain sets of circumstances that are difficult theoretically to define, some types of power-sharing institutions may more accurately target the security concerns of particular groups than do others. Nevertheless, even if adversaries are somehow able to determine which particular power-sharing or power-dividing institution might by itself best help them structure an enduring peace, at least two important reasons exist to believe that extensively institutionalized settlements will prove most reassuring to groups emerging from war. First, because adversaries are aware that state power is multidimensional and that groups can use different dimensions of state power to increase their coercive capacity, former foes will want to design a number of different types of measures to prevent groups from controlling state power in any single area. Second, groups will hesitate to rely solely on one type of institutional measure to secure their interests in case the measure should fail to be implemented.

The results of our test of the impact that the individual power-sharing dimensions have on the duration of peace are presented in tables 13 and 14. Focusing only on the effect of this new variable, we find that only one of the

---

3. Each of these should be understood to refer to power-sharing and/or power-dividing institutions. In what follows we have used the term *power sharing* as a shorthand reference.

four power-sharing or power-dividing institutions—*territorial power sharing*—proves to be statistically significant. Designing a negotiated settlement or negotiated agreement to include this institution lowers the risk of a return to war. The modal value of this variable is "0," indicating that the majority of negotiated settlements and agreements do not include an institution of this nature as part of the settlement's terms. Changing the modal value of this variable to "1" gives us a sense of its impact on the duration of peace. Focusing first on the negotiated settlements in table 13, making this change lowers the risk of a return to war by 65 percent. In the case of the negotiated agreements in table 14, a change of this nature reduces the risk of war recurring by 90 percent.

We caution against drawing conclusions on the basis of the results that appear in the models in tables 13 and 14. Our reasoning for arriving at this conclusion is twofold. First, we do not have a sound theoretical reason for breaking down the *settlement institutionalization* variable into its component parts. We have done so in this context as a means of addressing any questions that may exist regarding these institutions' effects in isolation. Because theory did guide our specification of the model in tables 7 and 8, we place greater trust in the results of the model that includes the *settlement institutionalization* variable as part of the terms of settlement explanation for peace.

Second, we also caution against making too much of the alternatively specified model in policy-making terms. Noting that among the four power-sharing or power-dividing institutions only territorial power sharing emerges as statistically significant, some might be tempted to conclude that all negotiated settlements or negotiated agreements should include such a measure or even that negotiated conclusions to civil wars need include *only* this measure in order to prove stable. Such an inference could well prove problematic given that not all conflicts will necessarily lend themselves to the design of this type of institution. If the groups that are in conflict with one another are not associated with particular pieces of territory, constructing an institution of this nature would prove to be an enormous logistical challenge.

Chapter 4

This part of the Appendix contains a brief summary of the military power-sharing or power-dividing measure called for in each of the eighteen cases

Table 13 Hazard analysis of determinants of peace duration for negotiated settlements of civil war, 1945–1999, focusing on individual power-sharing and power-dividing dimensions

Variable	Coefficient	Hazard ratio	Change	Revised hazard rate/base hazard rate
Nature of the conflict				
Stakes of the conflict	2.63*	13.80	1 to 0	0.73
	(1.56)	(21.53)		
Conflict duration	−0.46	0.63	to Min	0.00
(logged)	(0.34)	(0.21)	to Max	0.37
Conflict intensity	0.24	1.27	to Min	0.45
(logged)	(0.17)	(0.21)	to Max	0.00
Conflict environment				
Previous level of	−0.29	0.75	to Min	0.00
democracy	(0.29)	(0.22)	to Max	0.20
Economic development	−0.17*	0.85	to Min	0.00
	(0.07)	(0.06)	to Max	0.38
International system	−0.52	0.59	1 to 0	0.00
structure	(1.14)	(0.67)		
Terms of settlement				
Political power sharing	0.12	1.13	1 to 0	0.89
	(1.94)	(2.19)		
Territorial power sharing	−5.62**	0.00	0 to 1	0.36
	(2.71)	(0.00)		
Military power sharing	−1.08	0.34	1 to 0	0.00
	(1.41)	(0.48)		
Economic power sharing	2.34	10.37	0 to 1	0.00
	(2.4)	(24.94)		
Peacekeeping operation	−2.71	0.07	1 to 0	0.00
	(2.12)	(0.14)		
Subjects	38			
Failures	13			
Time at risk	4355			
Log likelihood	−20.88			
Wald chi^2(8)	39.56			
Prob>chi^2	0.0000			

Values in parentheses are robust standard errors. All significance tests are two-tailed.
**p < 0.05
*p < 0.1

Table 14   Hazard analysis of determinants of peace duration after negotiated agreements to end civil war, 1945–1999, focusing on individual power-sharing and power-dividing dimensions

Variable	Coefficient	Hazard ratio	Change	Revised hazard rate/base hazard rate
Nature of the conflict				
Stakes of the conflict	1.30**	3.67	1 to 0	0.27
Conflict duration	−0.27	0.76	to Min	2.55
(logged)	(0.25)	(0.19)	to Max	0.53
Conflict intensity	0.21	1.24	to Min	0.53
(logged)	(0.18)	(0.23)	to Max	2.20
Conflict environment				
Previous level of democracy	−0.12*	0.88	to Min	2.10
	(0.07)	(0.07)	to Max	0.18
Economic development	−0.06	0.95	to Min	2.80
	(0.04)	(0.03)	to Max	0.37
International system structure	0.86	2.37	1 to 0	0.42
	(0.76)	(1.8)		
Terms of settlement				
Political power sharing	−0.59	0.55	1 to 0	1.81
	(0.54)	(0.30)		
Territorial power sharing	−2.26**	0.10	0 to 1	0.10
	(0.93)	(0.10)		
Military power sharing	−0.50	0.61	1 to 0	1.65
	(0.60)	(0.37)		
Economic power sharing	1.01	2.73	0 to 1	2.73
	(0.82)	(2.25)		
Peacekeeping operation	−1.01	0.36	1 to 0	2.77
	(0.67)	(0.24)		
Subjects	49			
Failures	18			
Time at risk	4831			
Log likelihood	−45.11			
Wald chi^2(8)	28.24			
Prob>chi^2	0.003			

Values in parentheses are robust standard errors. All significance tests are two-tailed.

**p < 0.05

*p < 0.1

we analyze in Chapter 4 as well as a synopsis of the progress that was made in implementing the measure during the five years following agreement on it.

Coding for the level of commitment necessary to fulfill the military power-sharing provisions and the degree of success in implementing the military power-sharing provisions is based on materials in *The Military Balance* and *Strategic Survey* from the International Institute for Strategic Studies. When necessary, these sources were supplemented by case study materials.

Three terms appear at the conclusion of each case in order to summarize its coding:

I. High/Low: Assesses the level of commitment necessary among former adversaries to fulfill the military power-sharing provisions of the settlement. Provisions that require adversaries to give up the ability independently to defend themselves and take considerable effort to implement are scored as involving a high level of commitment; settlements that call for power-sharing arrangements that require little action on the part of former combatants or even permit them to continue providing for their own defense are scored as calling for a low level of commitment.

II. Complete/Partial/Failed: Assesses the degree of success in implementing the military power-sharing provisions of the agreement. If all groups who agreed to the provisions make some effort to carry them out but fall short of fulfilling all obligations, implementation is deemed to have been partial. If one or more of the groups who agreed to implement the provisions fail to make any effort to do so, implementation is coded as having failed.

III. Peace/War: Assesses whether settlement implementation was associated with a durable peace or a return to war.

Angola: The Bicesse Accords signed in May 1991 called for the creation of a single national military in which the army was to be evenly divided between government (Popular Movement for the Liberation of Angola—MPLA) and National Union for the Total Independence of Angola (UNITA) troops. Although government troops and UNITA rebels began to gather at their respective assembly points and divest themselves of their arms, neither set of armed forces fully followed through on their commitments to demobilize and disarm. As a result, the merger of the two armed forces was not complete prior to the national elections held at the end of September 1992. At the time the elections were held, only 45 percent of MPLA troops had been demobilized and 24 percent of the forces assembled by UNITA had surrendered their weapons. UNITA withdrew from the integrated army in October. [*High* commitment; *partial* implementation; return to *war.*]

Angola: The Lusaka Protocol signed in November 1994 provided for the demobilization of troops and the creation of a unified national army. The integrated army was to consist of approximately 90,000 troops, with about 18,500 being UNITA soldiers. By early May 1998, 34,000 UNITA troops had been demobilized and 11,000 UNITA soldiers had been integrated into the army. Although the integration process was deemed concluded at this point and UNITA claimed to have completed the demobilization process, UNITA was reported to have nearly 25,000 fully equipped troops and support militia in reserve. [*High* commitment; *partial* implementation; return to *war.*]

Azerbaijan: The cease-fire accord agreed to in May 1994 called for the establishment of observer posts to be manned jointly by Armenian, Azerbaijani, and Russian troops. A provisional plan required establishing a minimum force of three battalions and three independent companies along the current line of contact between opposing forces, including the Lachin Corridor. The plan also called for supervising the withdrawal of troops to the agreed boundaries. The delay in implementing the plan resulted from a lack of consensus by Armenia and Azerbaijan regarding the future status of Nagorno-Karabakh. Although sporadic fighting still occurs, there has not been a return to civil war. [*Low* commitment; *failed* implementation; maintenance of *peace.*]

Bosnia: The Dayton Peace Accords, agreed to in November 1995, allowed the two entities that make up the state of Bosnia and Herzegovina, the Bosniak-Croat Federation and Republika Srpska, to maintain their own separate armies. The Bosnian and Croat armed forces completed a merger in 1997, forming a federation army. The merger was designed to place the federation's army on equal military footing with that of the Serb Republic. [*Low* commitment; *complete* implementation; maintenance of *peace.*]

Cambodia: Signed in October 1991, the Paris Agreement called for the regrouping, cantonment, and disarmament of at least 70 percent of the forces of the four warring Cambodian factions—the communist Cambodian government, the Khmer Rouge, Son Sann's forces, and Sihanouk's forces—to begin in June 1992. Once these forces had been demobilized, the remaining 30 percent of the factions' forces were to be incorporated into a new national army. Although the Phnom Penh government and the two noncommunist factions did cooperate to some extent in demobilizing their troops, the Khmer Rouge refused to regroup and disarm its forces. [*High* commitment; *failed* implementation; maintenance of *peace.*]

Chad: Signed in March 1996, the Franceville Agreement, as well as subsequent agreements signed by the government and additional armed dissident groups, called for the integration of rebel forces into the Chadian army. Integration of rebel forces into the national army proceeded slowly, fitfully, and incompletely, with some former rebel groups accusing the government of reneging on commitments to integrate their soldiers into the regular armed forces. The government responded to these accusations with efforts to expedite the reintegration of rebel forces into the army. [*High* commitment; *partial* implementation; maintenance of *peace.*]

Chechnya: The settlement signed in August 1996 called for military power-sharing measures designed to foster a mutual sense of security while Russian troops withdrew from the region by the end of the year. Checkpoints manned by both Chechen and Russian soldiers were to be established throughout the region. Six hundred fighters were designated to serve on joint Russian-Chechen patrols. Finally, joint offices, with about 2,000 people assigned to them, were to be established to police the agreement. The settlement's measures were implemented, with the last Russian soldiers leaving the republic of Chechnya on January 5, 1997. [*Low* commitment; *complete* implementation; return to *war.*]

Djibouti: The December 1994 peace agreement called for the integration of 500 FRUD (Front for the Restoration of Unity and Democracy) rebel combatants into Djibouti's regular army. A ceremony held in November 1994 marked the integration of the FRUD troops into the Djibouti army, with several dozen men promoted to officer and NCO (noncommissioned officer) ranks. The integration of FRUD troops into the army was followed by the initiation of a demobilization program designed to reduce the size of the military from its wartime footing. [*High* commitment; *complete* implementation; maintenance of *peace.*]

El Salvador: The Chapultepec Agreement signed in January 1992 called for the dismantling of several elements of the state security forces to which the Farabundo Martí National Liberation Front (FMLN) objected, among them the military-controlled police forces that had been used to target the FMLN. The agreement mandated that these security forces be replaced by a newly created national civilian police force into which former rebels and soldiers were to be integrated. These measures were fully implemented by the end of 1994. [*High* commitment; *complete* implementation; maintenance of *peace.*]

Georgia, South Ossetia: Under the Russia-Georgia Dagomys Accord and Sochi Cease-Fire Agreement concluded in June/July 1992, a mixed peacekeeping force consisting of a Russian regiment of the airborne division and Georgian and South Ossetian units was inserted into the contested zone. The mandate of the joint peacekeeping force extends to policing cease-fires, serving on checkpoints, and controlling the situation on the ground through regular military patrols. Although the agreement called for an equal proportion of 500 troops each, Russia took the lead role in the joint peacekeeping force because of Georgian and South Ossetian peacekeepers' poor equipment and lack of volunteers. [*Low* commitment; *complete* implementation; maintenance of *peace.*]

Lebanon: The Taif Accord signed in October 1989 called for Lebanese militias to transfer their weapons to the Lebanese government, disband as militias, and re-form as part of internal security forces. An exception was made for Hezbollah, which was allowed to retain its military wing in order to fight against the Israeli security presence in Lebanon. Many militias did disband, or were at least contained to their local territory, and most are largely disarmed. Some of the militias have been integrated into the national army. [*High* commitment; *partial* implementation; maintenance of *peace.*]

Mali: In a May 1994 accord, one of a series of pacts leading to the final peace settlement reached in 1995, the Malian government and the MFUA (Unified Movements and Fronts of Azawad) agreed to integrate 1,500 former rebels into the national army, 150 into the police, 120 into the civil service, 100 into the customs services, and 50 into the water and forestry administration. The demobilization of the rebels proceeded apace with the numbers of fighters integrated into the army exceeding the number originally called for in the 1994 agreement. On January 10, 1996, military officials reported that 2,705 rebels had been integrated into the national army and on February 9, 1996, army officials deemed the demobilization of the rebels completed. [*High* commitment; *complete* implementation; maintenance of *peace.*]

Mozambique: Signed in October 1992, Mozambique's peace agreement called for the government and its opponent, RENAMO, to merge their armed forces on the basis of equal numbers to form a new 30,000-troop national army. The high command of the new combined force was to consist of joint commanders from the government and RENAMO. Although confining and demobilizing government and RENAMO troops proceeded slowly, the agreement's military power-sharing measures were fully implemented in fewer than five years. [*High* commitment; *complete* implementation; maintenance of *peace.*]

Nicaragua: A series of accords negotiated among the government-elect of Violeta Chamorro, the outgoing Sandinista government, and the Nicaraguan Resistance (the contras) during the two months following Chamorro's election in February 1990 provided for a number of military power-sharing measures. These include allowing contra forces to have their own security forces in their "development poles" (settlement areas to be set aside for former contra forces); promising to protect the existing privileges and rank of Sandinista officers serving in the national army; promising not to replace these officers with ex-members of the national guard or the contras; and retaining Sandinista General Humberto Ortega as head of the armed forces. These measures were implemented, but resource scarcity meant few funds were available for the development poles, and Ortega supervised a large reduction of the armed forces. [*High* commitment; *complete* implementation; maintenance of *peace*.]

Philippines: The settlement signed in September 1996 called for integrating approximately 7,500 members of the Moro National Liberation Front (MNLF) rebels' military wing into the national army and security forces and establishing a regional security force in Mindanao. Implementing the measures proceeded apace, with at least 6,750 MNLF members integrated into special and auxiliary units of the Philippines' armed forces and the Philippine National Police four years after the settlement was signed. [*High* commitment; *complete* implementation; maintenance of *peace*.]

Rwanda: The Arusha Peace Accord signed in August 1993 called for the integration of the armed forces and the gendarmes. Government forces were to make up 60 percent of the troops in the new army while rebel forces were to account for the remaining 40 percent. Command posts were to be evenly divided between the two sets of forces. The protocol calls for demobilizing, disengaging, and integrating the new army to be completed within seven to nine months. The process did not take place before war broke out again eight months after the accord was signed. [*High* commitment; *failed* implementation; return to *war*.]

Sierra Leone: The Abidjan Accord signed in November 1996 set out a process to encamp, disarm, demobilize, and reintegrate Revolutionary United Front (RUF) combatants. The Sierra Leone army was to be reduced in size and RUF members were to be allowed to enter the restructured unified armed forces. Although the RUF's Sankoh refused to allow the United Nations to deploy peacekeepers and monitors, a limited demobilization did get underway in the midst of a deteriorating security situation. President Kabbah's decision to disband the army and rely on Economic Community of West African States Monitoring Group (ECOMOG) forces and the Kamajors marginalized the country's discredited armed forces. The country returned to full civil war when the army, joined by the RUF, staged a coup on May 25, 1997. [*High* commitment; *failed* implementation; return to *war*.]

South Africa: A series of conferences and agreements beginning in December 1991 culminated in the interim constitution agreed to in November 1993. On the military front, it was agreed that an estimated 30,000 personnel from forces other than the country's defense force, namely the African National Congress (ANC) and Homelands (i.e., Inkatha Freedom Party forces), were to be absorbed into a new South African National Defence Force (SANDF). Although President Mandela summarily dismissed approximately 2,000 former guerrillas from the SANDF following a series of strikes and mutinies on their part, the integration of these so-called nonstatutory forces was completed in 1997. [*High* commitment; *complete* implementation; maintenance of *peace*.]

REFERENCES

Alden, Chris. 1995. "The UN and the Resolution of Conflict in Mozambique." *Journal of Modern African Studies* 33 (1): 103–28.

AllAfrica, Inc., Africa News. 2002. "Peace Process Begins Shakily with Fragmented UNITA." March 20.

Atlas, Pierre M., and Roy Licklider. 1999. "Conflict Among Allies After Civil War Settlement: Sudan, Zimbabwe, Chad, and Lebanon." *Journal of Peace Research* 36 (1): 35–54.

Ball, Nicole, and Tammy Halevy. 1996. *Making Peace Work: The Role of the International Development Community.* Washington, D.C.: Overseas Development Council.

Barry, Brian. 1975. "Review Article: Political Accommodation and Consociational Democracy." *British Journal of Political Science* 5 (4): 477–505.

Bayron, Heda G. 2003. "Moro Group in Transition." *Business World* (Philippines), August 15, 26.

Bertrand, Jacques. 2000. "Peace and Conflict in the Southern Philippines: Why the 1996 Peace Agreement Is Fragile." *Pacific Affairs* 73 (1): 37–54.

Bratton, Michael. 1989. "Beyond the State: Civil Society and Associational Life in Africa." *World Politics* 41 (3): 407–30.

Brecke, Peter, and William J. Long. 2003. *War and Reconciliation: Reason and Emotion in Conflict Resolution.* Cambridge: MIT Press.

Bueno De Mesquita, Bruce, and Randolph Siverson. 1995. "War and the Survival of Political Leaders: A Comparative Study of Regime Types and Political Accountability." *American Political Science Review* 89 (4): 841–55.

Business World (Philippines). 2000. "P68 Billion Spent Under Peace Pact with Moro Rebels." October 18.

Byman, Daniel. 2002. *Keeping the Peace: Lasting Solutions to Ethnic Conflict.* Baltimore: The Johns Hopkins University Press.

Byrne, Hugh. 1996. *El Salvador's Civil War: A Study of Revolution.* Boulder, Colo.: Lynne Rienner Publishers.

Byrnes, Rita M., ed. 1997. *South Africa: A Country Study.* 3rd ed. Washington, D.C.: Federal Research Division, Library of Congress.

Callahan, David. 1997. *Unwinnable Wars: American Power and Ethnic Conflict.* New York: Hill and Wang.

Chalk, Peter. 1997. "The Davao Consensus: A Panacea for the Muslim Insurgency in Mindanao?" *Terrorism and Political Violence* 9 (2): 79–98.

Child, Jack. 1992. *The Central American Peace Process, 1983–1991: Sheathing Swords, Building Confidence.* Boulder, Colo.: Lynne Rienner Publishers.

Coser, Lewis. 1956. *The Functions of Social Conflict.* Glencoe, Ill.: Free Press.

Crocker, Chester, and Fen Osler Hampson. 1996. *Nurturing Peace: Why Peace Settlements Succeed or Fail.* Washington, D.C.: United States Institute of Peace Press.

Davidow, Jeffrey. 1984. *A Peace in Southern Africa: The Lancaster House Conference on Rhodesia, 1979.* Boulder, Colo.: Westview Press.

Doyle, Michael. 1999. "War and Peace in Cambodia." In *Civil Wars, Insecurity, and Intervention,* ed. Barbara F. Walter and Jack Snyder. New York: Columbia University Press.

Doyle, Michael W., and Nicholas Sambanis. 2000. "International Peacebuilding: A Theoretical and Quantitative Analysis." *American Political Science Review* 94 (4): 779–801.

Dubey, Amitabh. 2002. "Domestic Institutions and the Duration of Civil War Settlements." Presented at the International Studies Association Annual Meeting, New Orleans.

Eckstein, Harry. 1975. "Case Study and Theory in Political Science." In *Handbook of Political Science, Volume One: Political Science: Scope and Theory,* ed. Fred I. Greenstein and Nelson W. Polsby. Reading, Mass.: Addison-Wesley.

The Economist. 1990. "The Road Back from Jamba." July 28.

Esman, Milton. 1994. *Ethnic Politics.* Ithaca: Cornell University Press.

Facts on File World News Digest. 1989a. "Angolan Government, Rebels Agree to Truce; dos Santos, Savimbi Meet in Zaire." June 30.

———. 1989b. "U.S. Presses Angolan Rebel Leader." October 13.

Fearon, James D. 1995. "Rationalist Explanations for War." *International Organization* 49 (3): 379–414.

———. 1997. "Signaling Foreign Policy Interests: Tying Hands Versus Sinking Costs." *Journal of Conflict Resolution* 41 (1): 68–90.

———. 1998. "Commitment Problems and the Spread of Ethnic Conflict." In *The International Spread of Ethnic Conflict,* ed. David A. Lake and Donald Rothchild. Princeton: Princeton University Press.

Fearon, James D., and David Laitin. 2003. "Ethnicity, Insurgency, and Civil War." *American Political Science Review* 97 (1): 75–90.

Fernandez, Edwin O., and Cynthia D. Balana. 2000. "Let Misuari Deal with MNLF Renegades." *Philippine Daily Inquirer,* March 14, 1.

Fortna, Virginia Page. 2004. "Does Peacekeeping Keep Peace? International Intervention and the Duration of Peace After Civil War." *International Studies Quarterly* 48 (2): 269–92.

Gee, John. 2002. "Is Misuari Finished? Former Muslim Rebel, Mindanao Governor Fails to Extend His Reign." *Washington Report on Middle East Affairs* 21 (1): 34–37.

Genicot, Garance, and Stergios Skaperdas. 2002. "Investing in Conflict Management." *Journal of Conflict Resolution* 46 (1): 154–70.

Ghobarah, Hazem Adam, Paul Huth, and Bruce Russett. 2003. "Civil Wars Kill and Maim People—Long After the Shooting Stops." *American Political Science Review* 97 (2): 189–202.

Gurr, Ted Robert. 1990. "Ethnic Warfare and the Changing Priorities of Global Security." *Mediterranean Quarterly* 1 (1): 82–98.

————. 1993. *Minorities at Risk: A Global View of Ethnopolitical Conflicts.* Washington, D.C.: United States Institute of Peace.

————. 1994. "Peoples Against States: Ethnopolitical Conflict and the Changing World System: 1994 Presidential Address." *International Studies Quarterly* 38 (3): 347–77.

Gutierrez, Eric. 1999. "The Politics of Transition." *Accord: An International Review of Peace Initiatives* 6, http://www.c-r.org/accord/.

Hampson, Fen Osler. 1990. "Building a Stable Peace: Opportunities and Limits to Security Cooperation in Third World Regional Conflicts." *International Journal* 45 (2): 454–89.

Hartzell, Caroline. 1999. "Explaining the Stability of Negotiated Settlements to Civil Wars." *Journal of Conflict Resolution* 43 (1): 3–22.

————. 2004. "Civil War Settlements and Enduring Peace: A Test of the Wagner and Licklider Hypotheses." Paper presented at the 2004 annual conference of the Midwest Political Science Association, Palmer House Hilton, Chicago, Illinois.

Hartzell, Caroline, and Matthew Hoddie. 2003. "Institutionalizing Peace: Power Sharing and Post–Civil War Conflict Management." *American Journal of Political Science* 47 (2): 318–32.

Hartzell, Caroline, Matthew Hoddie, and Donald Rothchild. 2001. "Stabilizing the Peace After Civil War: An Investigation of Some Key Variables." *International Organization* 55 (1): 183–208.

Healy, Tim, and Antonio Lopez. 1996. "The Anatomy of a Deal: How Ramos's Government and Muslim Rebels Made Peace in Mindanao." *Asiaweek,* September 13, http://www.asiaweek.com/asiaweek/.

Hegre, Håvard, Scott Gates, Nils Petter Gleditsch, and Tanja Ellingsen. 2001. "Toward a Democratic Civil Peace?" *American Political Science Review* 95 (1): 33–48.

Heintze, Hans-Joachim. 1997. "Autonomy and Protection of Minorities Under International Law." In *Federalism Against Ethnicity? Institutional, Legal, and Democratic Instruments to Prevent Violent Minority Conflicts,* ed. Gunther Bachler. Zurich: Verlag Ruegger.

Hoddie, Matthew, and Caroline Hartzell. 2003. "Civil War Settlements and the Implementation of Military Power-Sharing Arrangements." *Journal of Peace Research* 40 (3): 303–20.

Horowitz, Donald L. 1985. *Ethnic Groups in Conflict.* Berkeley and Los Angeles: University of California Press.

————1990a. "Ethnic Conflict Management for Policymakers." In *Conflict and Peacemaking in Multiethnic Societies,* ed. Joseph V. Montville. New York: Lexington Books.

————. 1990b. "Making Moderation Pay: The Politics of Ethnic Conflict Management." In *Conflict and Peacemaking in Multiethnic Societies,* ed. Joseph V. Montville. New York: Lexington Books.

Howe, Herbert. 1996. "Lessons of Liberia: ECOMOG and Regional Peacekeeping." *International Security* 21 (3): 145–76.

Human Rights Watch. 1999. "UN Role in Sierra Leone Peace Deal Condemned." *Human Rights News,* July 8, http://hrw.org/english/docs/1999/07/08/sierra964.htm.

Ikenberry, G. John. 2001. *After Victory: Institutions, Strategic Restraint, and the Rebuilding of Order After Major Wars.* Princeton: Princeton University Press.

Islam, Syed Serajul. 1998. "The Islamic Independence Movements in Patani of Thailand and Mindanao of the Philippines." *Asian Survey* 38 (5): 441–56.

Jackman, Robert W. 1985. "Cross-National Statistical Research and the Study of Comparative Politics." *American Journal of Political Science* 29 (1): 161–82.

Jones, Clayton. 1986. "The Philippines' Other Insurgency." *Christian Science Monitor*, International Section, July 24, 1.

Kambwa, Augusto Eduardo, et al. 1999. "Angola." In *Comprehending and Mastering African Conflicts: The Search for Sustainable Peace and Good Governance*, ed. Adebayo Adedeji. London: Zed Books.

Kaufmann, Chaim. 1996. "Possible and Impossible Solutions to Ethnic Civil Wars." *International Security* 20 (4): 136–75.

———. 1999. "When All Else Fails: Evaluating Population Transfers and Partition as Solutions to Ethnic Conflict." In *Civil Wars, Insecurity, and Intervention*, ed. Barbara F. Walter and Jack Snyder. New York: Columbia University Press.

Keesing's Contemporary Archives. Various years. London: Longman.

King, Gary, Robert O. Keohane, and Sidney Verba. 1994. *Designing Social Inquiry.* Princeton: Princeton University Press.

Krain, Matthew. 1998. "Contemporary Democracies Revisited: Democracy, Political Violence, and Event Count Models." *Comparative Political Studies* 31 (2): 139–64.

Krain, Matthew, and Marissa Myers. 1997. "Democracy and Civil War: A Note on the Democratic Peace Proposition." *International Interactions* 23 (1): 109–18.

Kroeger, Alix. 2002. "Bosnia Ethnic Rights Reforms Imposed." *BBC News*, April 19, http://news.bbc.co.uk/1/hi/world/europe/1940299.stm.

Kumar, Krishna, ed. 1997. *Rebuilding Societies After Civil War: Critical Roles for International Assistance.* Boulder, Colo.: Lynne Rienner Publishers.

Kumar, Radha. 1997. "The Troubled History of Partition." *Foreign Affairs* 76 (1): 22–34.

Lacey, Marc. 2004. "A Decade After Massacres, Rwanda Outlaws Ethnicity." *New York Times,* April 9, A3.

Lake, David. 2003. "International Relations Theory and Internal Conflict: Insights from the Interstices." *International Studies Review* 5 (4): 81–89.

Leeds, Brett Ashley. 1999. "Domestic Political Institutions, Credible Commitments, and International Cooperation." *American Journal of Political Science* 43 (4): 979–1002.

Licklider, Roy, ed. 1993. *Stopping the Killing: How Civil Wars End.* New York: New York University Press.

———. 1995. "The Consequences of Negotiated Settlements in Civil Wars, 1945–1993." *American Political Science Review* 89 (3): 681–90.

Lieberson, Stanley. 1991. "Small N's and Big Conclusions: An Examination of the Reasoning in Comparative Studies Based on a Small Number of Cases." *Social Forces* 70 (2): 307–20.

Lijphart, Arend. 1968. *The Politics of Accommodation: Pluralism and Democracy in the Netherlands.* Berkeley and Los Angeles: University of California Press.

———. 1971. "Comparative Politics and the Comparative Method." *American Political Science Review* 65 (3): 682–98.

———. 1975. "The Comparable-Cases Strategy in Comparative Research." *Comparative Political Studies* 8 (2): 158–77.

————. 1977. *Democracy in Plural Societies: A Comparative Exploration.* New Haven: Yale University Press.

————. 1996. "The Puzzle of Indian Democracy: A Consociational Interpretation." *American Political Science Review* 90 (2): 258–68.

————. 1999. *Patterns of Democracy: Government Forms and Performance in Thirty-Six Countries.* New Haven: Yale University Press.

Lustick, Ian. 1979. "Stability in Deeply Divided Societies: Consociationalism Versus Control." *World Politics* 31 (3): 325–44.

Luttwak, Edward. 1999. "Give War a Chance." *Foreign Affairs* 78 (4): 36–44.

MacIntyre, Andrew. 2003. *The Power of Institutions: Political Architecture and Governance.* Ithaca: Cornell University Press.

Marshall, Monty G., and Keith Jaggers. 2002. *Polity IV Project.* College Park: Integrated Network for Societal Conflict Research (INSCR) Program, Center for International Development and Conflict Management (CIDCM), University of Maryland. [Data set available at http://www.bsos.umd.edu/cidcm/inscr/polity.]

Mason, T. David, and Patrick J. Fett. 1996. "How Civil Wars End: A Rational Choice Approach." *Journal of Conflict Resolution* 40 (4): 546–68.

Mason, T. David, Joseph P. Weingarten Jr., and Patrick J. Fett. 1999. "Win, Lose, or Draw: Predicting the Outcome of Civil Wars." *Political Research Quarterly* 52 (2): 239–68.

May, Ronald J. 1997. "Ethnicity and Public Policy in the Philippines." In *Government Policies and Ethnic Relations in Asia and the Pacific,* ed. Michael E. Brown and Šumit Ganguly. Cambridge: MIT Press.

McKenna, Thomas. 2004. "Muslim Separatism in the Philippines: Meaningful Autonomy or Endless War?" *Asia Source: A Resource of the Asia Society,* http://www.asiasource.org/asip/mckenna.cfm.

The Military Balance. Various years. London: International Institute for Strategic Studies.

Milne, R. S. 1967. *Government and Politics in Malaysia.* Boston: Houghton Mifflin.

Msabaha, Ibrahim. 1995. "Negotiating an End to Mozambique's Murderous Rebellion." In *Elusive Peace: Negotiating an End to Civil War,* ed. I. William Zartman. Washington, D.C.: Brookings Institution.

Mwiinga, Jowie. 1994. "Angola—Politics: Talks Drag On." *IPS—Inter Press Service/ Global Information Network,* September 19.

Noble, Lela G. 1981. "Muslim Separatism in the Philippines, 1972–1981: The Making of a Stalemate." *Asian Survey* 21 (11): 1097–114.

Nordlinger, Eric. 1972. *Conflict Regulation in Divided Societies.* Cambridge: Center for International Affairs, Harvard University.

North, Douglass. 1990. *Institutions, Institutional Change, and Economic Performance.* Cambridge: Cambridge University Press.

Paris, Roland. 1997. "Peacebuilding and the Limits of Liberal Internationalism." *International Security* 22 (2): 54–89.

————. 2004. *At War's End: Building Peace After Civil Conflict.* Cambridge: Cambridge University Press.

Posen, Barry. 1993. "The Security Dilemma and Ethnic Conflict." In *Ethnic Conflict and International Security,* ed. Michael Brown. Princeton: Princeton University Press.

————. 1996. "Military Responses to Refugee Disasters." *International Security* 21 (1): 72–111.

Power, Samantha. 2002. *A Problem from Hell: America and the Age of Genocide.* New York: Basic Books.

Przeworski, Adam. 1991. *Democracy and the Market: Political and Economic Reforms in Eastern Europe and Latin America.* Cambridge: Cambridge University Press.

Quimpo, Nathan Gilbert. 2001. "Options in Pursuit of a Just, Comprehensive, and Stable Peace in the Southern Philippines." *Asian Survey* 41 (2): 271–90.

Reed, Jack. 1989a. "Angolan Cease-Fire Takes Effect at Midnight." *United Press International,* June 23.

————. 1989b. "Savimbi Denies Exile Agreement." *United Press International,* June 26.

Regional Surveys of the World: The Far East and Australasia. 2002. London: Europa Publications.

Reiter, Dan. 2003. "Exploring the Bargaining Model of War." *Perspectives on Politics* 1 (1): 27–43.

Roeder, Philip. 2005. "Power Dividing as an Alternative to Ethnic Power Sharing." In *Sustainable Peace,* ed. Philip Roeder and Donald Rothchild. Ithaca: Cornell University Press.

Rothchild, Donald. 1997. *Managing Ethnic Conflict in Africa: Pressures and Incentives for Cooperation.* Washington, D.C.: Brookings Institution.

Rothchild, Donald, and Caroline Hartzell. 1992. "The Case of Angola: Four Power Intervention and Disengagement." In *Foreign Military Intervention: The Dynamics of Protracted Conflict,* ed. Ariel E. Levite, Bruce W. Jentleson, and Larry Berman. New York: Columbia University Press.

Sambanis, Nicholas. 2000. "Partition as a Solution to Ethnic War: An Empirical Critique of the Theoretical Literature." *World Politics* 52 (4): 437–83.

Sisk, Timothy D. 1996. *Power Sharing and International Mediation in Ethnic Conflicts.* Washington, D.C.: United States Institute of Peace.

Sisk, Timothy D., and Christoph Stefes. 2005. "Power Sharing as an Interim Step in Peace Building: Lessons from South Africa." In *Sustainable Peace: Power and Democracy After Civil Wars,* ed. Philip G. Roeder and Donald Rothchild. Ithaca: Cornell University Press.

Sivard, Ruth Leger. Various years. *World Military and Social Expenditures.* Leesburg, Va.: WMSZ Publications.

Smelser, Neil. 1973. "The Methodology of Comparative Analysis." In *Comparative Research Methods,* ed. Donald Warwich and Samuel Osherson. Englewood Cliffs, N.J.: Prentice Hall.

Snyder, Jack, and Robert Jervis. 1999. "Civil War and the Security Dilemma." In *Civil Wars, Insecurity, and Intervention,* ed. Barbara Walter and Jack Snyder. New York: Columbia University Press.

de Soto, Alvaro, and Graciana del Castillo. 1994. "Obstacles to Peacebuilding." *Foreign Policy* 94 (Spring): 69–74.

Spear, Joanna. 1996. "Arms Limitations, Confidence-Building Measures, and Internal Conflict." In *The International Dimensions of Internal Conflict,* ed. Michael E. Brown. Cambridge: MIT Press.

Stedman, Stephen John. 1991. *Peacemaking in Civil War: International Mediation in Zimbabwe, 1974–1980.* Boulder, Colo.: Lynne Rienner Publishers.

———. 1993. "The End of the American Civil War." In *Stopping the Killing: How Civil Wars End,* ed. Roy Licklider. New York: New York University Press.

———. 1996. "Negotiation and Mediation in Internal Conflicts." In *The International Dimensions of Internal Conflict,* ed. Michael Brown. Cambridge, Mass.: MIT Press.

———. 1997. "Spoiler Problems in Peace Processes." *International Security* 22 (Autumn): 5–53.

Stedman, Stephen John, and Donald Rothchild. 1996. "Peace Operations: From Short-Term to Long-Term Commitment." *International Peacekeeping* 3 (2): 17–35.

Stedman, Stephen John, Donald Rothchild, and Elizabeth M. Cousens, eds. 2002. *Ending Civil Wars: The Implementation of Peace Agreements.* London: Lynne Rienner Publishers.

Stockholm International Peace Research Institute. Various years. SIPRI *Yearbook: Armaments, Disarmament, and International Security.* Stockholm: Almquist and Wiksell.

Strategic Survey. Various years. London: International Institute for Strategic Studies.

Tan, Abby. 1996. "Philippines' Christians Rebel over Peace Pact with Muslim Minority." *Christian Science Monitor,* July 8, 7.

Tan, Andrew. 2000. "Armed Muslim Separatist Rebellion in Southeast Asia: Persistence, Prospects, and Implications." *Studies in Conflict and Terrorism* 23 (4): 267–88.

Tilly, Charles, ed. 1975. *The Formation of National States in Western Europe.* Princeton: Princeton University Press.

Toft, Monica Duffy. 2003. *The Geography of Ethnic Violence: Identity, Interests, and the Indivisibility of Territory.* Princeton: Princeton University Press.

Touval, Saadia. 1982. *The Peace Brokers: Mediators in the Arab-Israeli Conflict.* Princeton: Princeton University Press.

Vance, Cyrus. 1983. *Hard Choices: Critical Years in America's Foreign Policy.* New York: Simon and Schuster.

Van Evera, Stephen. 1997. *Guide to Methods for Students of Political Science.* Ithaca: Cornell University Press.

Wagner, Robert Harrison. 1993. "The Causes of Peace." In *Stopping the Killing: How Civil Wars End,* ed. Roy Licklider. New York: New York University Press.

Wallensteen, Peter, and Margareta Sollenberg. 1997. "Armed Conflicts, Conflict Termination, and Peace Agreements, 1989–96." *Journal of Peace Research* 34 (3): 339–58.

Walter, Barbara. 1997. "The Critical Barrier to Civil War Settlement." *International Organization* 51 (3): 335–64.

———. 1999. "Designing Transitions from Civil War." In *Civil Wars, Insecurity, and Intervention,* ed. Barbara Walter and Jack Snyder. New York: Columbia University Press.

———. 2002. *Committing to Peace: The Successful Settlement of Civil Wars.* Princeton: Princeton University Press.

Waterman, Harvey. 1993. "Political Order and the 'Settlement' of Civil Wars." In *Stopping the Killing: How Civil Wars End,* ed. Roy Licklider. New York: New York University Press.

Weiner, Myron. 1983. "The Political Consequences of Preferential Politics: A Comparative Perspective." *Comparative Politics* 16 (1): 35–52.

Wenner, Manfred. 1993. "The Civil War in Yemen, 1962–70." In *Stopping the Killing: How Civil Wars End,* ed. Roy Licklider. New York: New York University Press.

Werner, Suzanne. 1999. "The Precarious Nature of Peace: Resolving the Issues, Enforcing the Settlement, and Renegotiating the Terms." *American Journal of Political Science* 43 (3): 912–34.

Wines, Michael. 2004. "South Africa Dissolves Party That Was Architect of Apartheid." *New York Times,* August 9, A4.

Woodward, Susan L. 1999. "Bosnia and Herzegovina: How Not to End a Civil War." In *Civil Wars, Insecurity, and Intervention,* ed. Barbara F. Walter and Jack Snyder. New York: Columbia University Press.

Zartman, I. William. 1989. *Ripe for Resolution: Conflict and Intervention in Africa.* Updated ed. New York: Oxford University Press.

———, ed. 1993. *Europe and Africa: The New Phase.* London: Lynne Rienner Publishers.

INDEX

Abu Sayyaf group, 14 n. 19
accommodation: conflict management and, 65; end of cold war and improved climate for, 54–55
administrative proportional representation, 30
Afghanistan: civil war in, 5 n. 7, 11; peace settlement in, 21; postconflict environment in, 84 n. 26; power-sharing institutions in, 39, 150 n. 19
African National Congress (ANC), 140, 177; naming of, 1; territorial autonomy issues and, 35
Agreement on Provisional Arrangements in Afghanistan Pending the Reestablishment of Permanent Government Institutions, 39
al-Nimeiry, Gaafar, 69
alternative model specification, negative binomial regression, 62 n. 22, 167–69
Alvor Accord (Angola), 111–13
Angola: Alvor Accord in, 111–13; Bicesse Accords, 14, 115–19, 172–73; civil war in, 11; continuity of civil war in, 122 n. 28; economic issues in civil war of, 35–36; Gbadolite Accord in, 21–22, 43, 113–15, 155; Lusaka Protocol, 119–25, 173; military power-sharing in, 100, 172–73; negotiated settlement in, 19–20, 109–25, 138–39; settlement institutionalization in, 124–25; third-party mediation in, 123–25
Anstee, Margaret, 118–19
Aquino, Corazon, 129–30
Argentina, civil war in, 5
army size, military power-sharing/power-dividing institutions, 98, 162–64
Arusha Peace Accord, 176
Atlas, Pierrre, 94
authoritarian inastitutions, 25–26
Autonomous Region for Muslim Mindanao (ARMM), 130, 137–38

Azerbaijan: military power-sharing in, 173; negotiated settlement in, 98 n. 22

Baker, James, 115
balance of power: security concerns linked to, 27–28; territorial autonomy and, 34–35
Bangladesh, peacekeeping operations in, 91
bargained resolutions: democratic norms and, 52; economic development and creation of, 106–7; effectiveness of conflict resolution in, 10–11; impact on negotiated settlement of, 44–45; Philippines case study, 125–38
bargaining failure, civil war as product of, 16–18
behavior: costly signaling and modification of, 96–97; institutional regulation of, 26–28, 41–42
Bicesse Accords (Angola), 14, 138–39; Lusaka Protocol compared with, 120–25; military power-sharing in, 100, 115–19, 172–73; settlement institutionalization in, 124–25
bipolar confrontations, post-cold war, 74 n. 15
Blondin Beye, Alioune, 120
Bosnia: Dayton Accords and, 33; incentives for moderation in, 148–50; life expectancy as indicator of civil war, 73, 81; military power-sharing in, 173; power-sharing inefficiencies in, 151
Bosniak-Croat Federation, 33, 176
Boutros Boutros-Ghali, 119
Burundi, 57
Bush, George W., 90

Cambinda oil enclave, 35
Cambodia: failure of military power-sharing in, 100–101, 173; international proxies in civil war in, 54–55; negotiated settlement of conflict in, 3; third-party mediation in conflict in, 88

identity issues, in conflicts, 50–51, 69–70
ideology, conflicts based on, 50–51, 69–70
implementation process for civil war settlements: Angolan case study, 117–19; early research on, 87–88; power-sharing/power-dividing institutions and, 144–45
incentives for moderation, civil war conflict resolution and, 148–50
income, distribution policies, 35–36
individual dimensions of power sharing, prediction of, 164–66
inducement strategy, third-party mediation and, 105–6
inefficient governance, power-sharing and, 151–54
inflexibility, of power-sharing, 152
Inkatha Freedom Party, 177
institutionalization of peace: Angolan case study, 124–25; guidelines for, 64–85; policy implications of, 155–57; power-sharing/power-dividing institutions and, 143–44
institution-building process: Angolan Gbadolite Accords and, 114–15; Bicesse Accords (Angola) and, 116–19; costs of, 41–42; principles of, 13–15; Tripoli Agreement in Philippines and, 128–29
institutions: choice of, in negotiated settlements, 26–28; construction of order through, 11–12; determinants of choice in, 12–13; durability of peace linked to, 15–16; negotiated settlements and role of, 2–5, 21–23; proportional strategies in, 30–31; social conflict and role of, 1
intensity of conflict: duration of negotiated settlements and, 80–84, 104 n. 30; impact on power sharing of, 164–66; influence on negotiated settlements, 51, 60–63, 70–71
International Monetary Fund (IMF), 67
international systems: Bicesse Accords and, 115–19; durability of peace agreements and, 81–84; influence on negotiated settlement of, 53–55, 59–63, 73–74; Lusaka Protocol (Angola) and, 120–25; truth commissions and, 80 n. 19; variable coding and sources for, 162
interstate conflicts: bargaining model of, 17–18; factors in resumption of, 65 n. 2
intrastate conflicts, frequency of, 2
Iraq: power-sharing institutions in, 150 n. 19; U.S. intervention in, 91
Islamic Council of Foreign Ministers(ICFM), 127–29

issue indivisibility, in negotiated settlements, 17 n. 23, 18 n. 26
Italy, Mozambique Peace Agreement and, 53

Janatha Vimukthi Peramuna (JVP), 8 n. 8
Jayewardene, J. R., 8
Joint Commission for the Constitution of Armed Forces (CCFA) (Angola), 117–19
joint observer commissions, as peacekeeping tool, 96–98

Kabbah, Alhaji Ahmad Tejan, 13–14, 176–77
Kaufmann, Chaim, 50, 147
Keesing's Contemporary Archives, 159–62
Khmer Rouge, 101, 173
Kosovo: civil war in, 10, 77; peacekeeping operations in, 84 n. 25

Lagu, Joseph, 32
Laitin, David, 71 n. 8
leadership costs: in negotiated settlements, 67–68; Philippines negotiated settlement and role of, 133–37
Lebanon, military power-sharing in, 152, 175
Lebanon National Pact of 1943, 152
legitimacy concerns, in negotiated settlements, 13–15
Liberal Party (Colombia), 3, 24
Liberian civil war, peacekeepers' involvement in, 89–92
Licklider, Roy, 94
life expectancy, economic development linked to, 53, 73
Lijphart, Arend, 38–39, 102, 148–49
Lomé Peace Accord, 13–14
Lusaka Protocol (Angola), 100, 119–25, 173

majoritarian strategies, power sharing through, 29–31
Malaysia: negotiated settlement of civil war in, 4; territorial autonomy in, 34–35, 66
Mali, military power sharing in, 175
Managua Protocol on Disarmament, 32–33, 36
Mandela, Nelson, 57
Marcos, Ferdinand, 126–29, 136
market competition, economic power-sharing/power-dividing institutions and, 35–36
Military Balance, The, 172
military power-sharing/power-dividing institutions, 31–33; Angola case study, 111–25, 172–73; armed forces size as factor in, 98, 162–64; in Azerbaijan, 98, 173; in Bosnia, 151, 173; in Chad, 32, 174; Davao Consensus in

"This engaging and rigorous research addresses one of the most vexing issues in achieving postwar peace: forging and maintaining power-sharing among the protagonists in conflict. They argue, quite convincingly and with a diverse research design—and against conventional wisdom—that more power-sharing is better to achieve durable peace in war-torn societies. Scholars and practitioners working to negotiate and implement settlements in civil wars will want to read this volume and reconsider some of the skepticism that swirls around power-sharing today."

—TIMOTHY SISK, UNIVERSITY OF DENVER

"This landmark study is the best book available on the relatively recent experiment of ending civil wars by constructing power-sharing governments from former adversaries. The identification of four dimensions of power-sharing is a major theoretical development. The original dataset is subjected to sophisticated quantitative analysis and is buttressed by impressive in-depth case studies. The conclusions are important for both theoretical and policy reasons. Every future researcher will have to take this analysis into consideration."   —ROY LICKLIDER, RUTGERS UNIVERSITY

The recent efforts to reach a settlement of the enduring and tragic conflict in Darfur demonstrate how important it is to understand what factors contribute most to the success of such efforts. In this book, Caroline Hartzell and Matthew Hoddie review data from all negotiated civil war settlements between 1945 and 1999 in order to identify these factors.

What they find is that settlements are more likely to produce an enduring peace if they involve construction of a diversity of power-sharing and power-dividing arrangements between former adversaries. The strongest negotiated settlements prove to be those in which former rivals agree to share or divide state power across its economic, military, political, and territorial dimensions.

CAROLINE A. HARTZELL is Associate Professor of Political Science at Gettysburg College.

MATTHEW HODDIE is Assistant Professor of Political Science at Towson University.

THE PENNSYLVANIA STATE UNIVERSITY PRESS

UNIVERSITY PARK, PENNSYLVANIA

WWW.PSUPRESS.ORG

ISBN: 978-0-271-03208-5